Oxford Studies in European Law
Series Editors: Paul Craig and Gráinne de Búrca

AN EVER MORE POWERFUL COURT?

OXFORD STUDIES IN EUROPEAN LAW

Series Editors: Paul Craig, Professor of English Law at St John's College, Oxford and Gráinne de Búrca, Professor of Law at New York University School of Law

The aim of this series is to publish important and original research on EU law. The focus is on scholarly monographs, with a particular emphasis on those which are interdisciplinary in nature. Edited collections of essays will also be included where they are appropriate. The series is wide in scope and aims to cover studies of particular areas of substantive and of institutional law, historical works, theoretical studies, and analyses of current debates, as well as questions of perennial interest such as the relationship between national and EU law and the novel forms of governance emerging in and beyond Europe. The fact that many of the works are interdisciplinary will make the series of interest to all those concerned with the governance and operation of the EU.

OTHER TITLES IN THIS SERIES

The Human Rights of Migrants and Refugees in European Law
Cathryn Costello

The Concept of State Aid under EU Law
From internal market to competition and beyond
Juan Jorge Piernas López

Justice in the EU
The Emergence of Transnational Solidarity
Floris de Witte

The Euro Area Crisis in Constitutional Perspective
Alicia Hinarejos

The European Fundamental Freedoms
A Contextual Approach
Pedro Caro de Sousa

National Identity in EU Law
Elke Cloots

The Constitutional Foundations of European Contract Law
A Comparative Analysis
Kathleen Gutman

The Criminalization of European Cartel Enforcement
Theoretical, Legal, and Practical Challenges
Peter Whelan

Fundamental Rights in Europe
Challenges and Transformations in Comparative Perspective
Federico Fabbrini

The Principle of Loyalty in EU Law
Marcus Klamert

Constitutional Pluralism in the EU
Klemen Jaklic

EU Consumer Law and Human Rights
Iris Benöhr

The Principle of Mutual Recognition in EU Law
Christine Janssens

The Coherence of EU Free Movement Law
Constitutional Responsibility and the Court of Justice
Niamh Nic Shuibhne

European Law and New Health Technologies
Edited by Mark Flear, Anne-Maree Farrell, Tamara Hervey, and Thérèse Murphy

European Agencies
Law and Practices of Accountability
Madalina Busuioc

An Ever More Powerful Court?

The Political Constraints of Legal Integration in the European Union

DORTE SINDBJERG MARTINSEN
Department of Political Science, University of Copenhagen

OXFORD
UNIVERSITY PRESS

OXFORD
UNIVERSITY PRESS

Great Clarendon Street, Oxford, OX2 6DP,
United Kingdom

Oxford University Press is a department of the University of Oxford.
It furthers the University's objective of excellence in research, scholarship,
and education by publishing worldwide. Oxford is a registered trade mark of
Oxford University Press in the UK and in certain other countries

First Edition published in 2015

Published in the United States of America by Oxford University Press
198 Madison Avenue, New York, NY 10016, United States of America

British Library Cataloguing in Publication Data
Data available

Library of Congress Control Number: 2015945727

ISBN 978–0–19–875339–1

SERIES EDITORS' PREFACE

This book examines the extent to which the judgments of the Court of Justice of the European Union influence the political and legislative branches of the EU. Focusing in particular on the area of European social policy, it revisits the question of the 'political power' of the European Court by examining more closely the circumstances under which the rulings of the Court are translated into legislative form and are made generally binding on all states, and when they are altered, ignored, or reversed by the political branches.

Adopting a broad time-span by looking at the course of European integration over six decades, albeit through the more focused lens of a series of specific case studies, the author suggests that the question of the influence and impact of the European Court on the political and legislative process is more complex and nuanced than has often been assumed by existing scholarship. Much of the relevant literature on the political influence and impact of the rulings of the European Court has tended to focus on the possibility of constitutional override, including treaty override, of Court judgments, and has assumed that there will be little likelihood of political or legislative pushback. Martinsen's book, however, hones in on this less-closely studied arena of EU legislative and executive responses to European Court rulings.

Her inquiry is, thus, as much into the question of how political action can curtail judicial impact as into how judicial decisions may influence or constrain political action, particularly in the contested area of European social policy. Drawing on earlier work by political scientists such as Karen Alter and Lisa Conant, she argues that the capacity of judicial rulings to really influence EU integration and policies depends on whether CJEU rulings in specific cases are translated into more widely applicable policy prescriptions through being generalized and applied authoritatively to all Member States.

This book is clearly and authoritatively written, carefully researched, and impressively convincing in its argumentation. It presents a set of interesting and important new empirical studies of the impact of the Court's rulings across a range of salient and sometimes controversial areas of social policy, including cross-border health care, the regulation of working time, and the posting of workers. The author carefully parses the concept of 'influence' and provides a helpful typology of the possible legislative responses to judicial decision making. These she divides into four main groups on a sliding scale of influence from strongest to weakest: codification, modification, non-adoption, and override. Interestingly, the book finds little evidence of either the strongest or the weakest response (codification or override) in the areas she studies, but more evidence of the two intermediate legislative responses, namely modification and non-adoption. The author also makes the interesting observation that legislative non-adoption—an outcome which sometimes results from inter-institutional differences and struggles—does not mean that the judgment remains in place as authoritative law, but rather creates what she calls a form of 'regulatory limbo which is harmful to both the legitimacy of the court and to the effectiveness of EU regulation'.

Further, Martinsen argues that while political responses to judicial decisions may be slow and take years to unfold, this does not mean that there is no response. On the contrary, rather than the EU legislative and policy process being too fragmented and complex to be capable of responding to Court of Justice rulings, as previous literature has suggested, her study finds that that process operates over a lengthy time horizon and is more continuous and persistent than often assumed. The role of the Commission as first-mover and as a strategic respondent to the Court's rulings—although often an internally divided one—also proves to be of significance in explaining the nature and variety of policy responses to judicial decisions.

The analysis provided in this book thus reveals a story neither of EU juristocracy and overreach nor of EU political and legislative supremacy. Instead, drawing on an illuminating set of case studies, it provides a nuanced identification of the kinds of factors that seem to condition the capacity and power of courts to influence political change and the capacity and power of legislatures and politicians to limit the influence of judicial decision making.

In sum, this book makes an important contribution to a range of salient contemporary scholarly and policy debates: on the future of 'social Europe', on the role and power of the Court of Justice, and on the relationship between law and politics in the process of European integration. The book will be of great interest to scholars and students of EU law and EU politics alike, as well as to political and legal actors working in the field of European social policy and European integration more generally.

Paul Craig and Gráinne de Búrca

ACKNOWLEDGEMENTS

The role of the Court of Justice of the European Union (CJEU) in welfare policy making has been the central interest in my research since my PhD years at the European University Institute in Florence. For years, I studied how the Court pushed ahead EU competences in the healthcare arena with its dynamic interpretations, able to do so in the absence of political voice. The project of this book was designed in line with my previous inquiries, but now turned to study the influence of the CJEU on subsequent legislative processes and outputs. From the outset I expected to confirm the authority of the Court, assuming that when Court rulings were brought into legislative processes to justify change, politicians would gradually accommodate their positions in line with legal integration. In particular, I expected the European Commission and the Court to constitute a powerful tandem in this regard, able to push integration forward and make politics accept the premises of the voice of law. Formed by these assumptions, I began my empirical work. But the actors within decision making whom I interviewed, as well as the official and unofficial documents that I gathered, told me a different story. The findings pointed to a much more mixed kind of judicial influence on policies, varying over time and in terms of where EU legislative politics had the capacity to condition the impact of legal integration. So I had to start all over again, and the writing of this book took much longer than first planned.

The completion of this longer journey was made possible only by all the support and constructive feedback I got from many colleagues and friends. Many commented on draft chapters of this book as well as the journal article that draws on the same empirics. The latter should soon appear in *Comparative Political Studies* with the title 'Judicial Influence on Policy Outputs? The Political Constraints of Legal Integration in the European Union'. First of all, I would like to thank my colleagues at the Centre for European Politics and at the Department of Political Science, University of Copenhagen. They have given me the environment, critique, and support I needed to continue and finish this: Rebecca Adler-Nissen, Gunnar Gjelstrup, Caroline Grøn, Hanne Foss Hansen, Lene Hansen, Henrik Hermansson, Hanne Nexø Jensen, Mads Dagnis Jensen, Lars Bo Kaspersen, Jette Steen Knudsen, Peter Dahler Larsen, Ian Manners, Lars Mäder, Jens Ladefoged Mortensen, Peter Nedergaard, Anne Rasmussen, Ben Rosamond, Ayca Uygur Wessel, and Marlene Wind.

I am also much indebted to many colleagues outside my department who took the time to comment on my work at conferences and other events: Hartmut Aden, Karen J. Alter, Derek Beach, Michael Blauberger, Lisa Conant, Gareth Davies, Erik Oddvar Eriksen, Gerda Falkner, John Erik Fossum, Miriam Hartlapp, Tamara Hervey, Martin Höpner, Deborah Mabbett, Ellen Mastenbroek, Juan Mayoral, Wolfgang Mazal, Renate Mayntz, Johan P. Olsen, Mark A. Pollack, Caroline de la Porte, Morten Rasmussen, Britta Rehder, Christilla Roederer-Rynning, Ingrid Schneider, Waltraud Schelkle, Susanne K. Schmidt, Guido Schwellnus, Daniel Seikel, Dimiter Toshkov, Maarten Vink, and Anne van Wageningen. In particular, I would like to thank Fritz W. Scharpf for commenting on this work on several occasions. Your feedback and constructive critique has been highly stimulating to me.

This project was supported by the Danish Research Council and is part of the 'Healthcare and Social Policy Regulation in the European Union' project (no. 10-079675/FSE). The financial support from the Research Council is gratefully acknowledged. The project has run since 2011 and I would like to thank in particular my great colleague from Leiden University, Hans Vollaard, for his most valuable support and engagement, as well as Karsten Vrangbæk and Nikolay Vasev from the University of Copenhagen. Thanks also go to the research assistance I got from, first, Ida Bæk Hjermitslev, then Jessica Sampson Thierry, and, later, Sofie Hvid-Jørgensen and Jens Bang Larsen. It would not have been possible without you.

I am ever so grateful to all the seventy-eight actors within EU decision-making that I interviewed for this book. Only their willingness to share time, knowledge, and experience on the daily decision-making processes of the EU made it possible to gather new insights into the complex interplay of law and politics.

I also wish to thank Oxford University Press, especially Gráinne de Búrca and the two anonymous reviewers, for constructive comments and for granting me the opportunity to turn the project into this book. Also many thanks to Elinor Shields for processing this so smoothly.

Finally, there is all the gratitude impossible to express fully to my family with whom I share the daily life and joys of European citizenship. My deepest thanks go to my husband Biel and our three children, Otto, Elia, and Josep, to whom this book is dedicated.

Dorte Sindbjerg Martinsen
Copenhagen, Denmark

CONTENTS

1

Introduction

The ability of courts to generate political change has long been debated in studies of national, comparative, and international politics (Epp [1998]; McCann [1994]; Rosenberg [2008]; Stone Sweet [2000]). While observers agree that courts are powerful authorities in third-party dispute resolution, the broader impact of this resolution is disputed. Are courts powerful generators of change? Do court-generated principles, norms, and rights lead to changes in public policies, thus becoming generally applicable? Or do court-interpreted rules and norms merely apply to the case at hand? What are the implications for democratic politics if legislative politics is subordinated to judicial power? What factors may condition the power of courts to produce broader political change? Courts as generators of political change have been examined and questioned in studies of American, international, and European Union (EU) politics, and a debate has developed between 'dynamic' and 'constrained' views of the judiciary.[1]

A growing body of literature argues along the line of the 'dynamic view'. According to this view, a judicialization of politics has occurred in which courts have become increasingly powerful, political actors in many contemporary democracies (Cichowski [2007]; Kelemen [2008, 2013]; Stone Sweet [2000, 2004]). Judicialization of politics marks 'a process that involves greater reliance on courts and judicial procedures to address major public policy issues and political disputes' (Kelemen [2013: 295]). In this view, courts can be key drivers of social and political change, and political autonomy becomes limited by jurisprudence. The traditional notion of parliamentary sovereignty is replaced by models of democracy in which constitutional courts have the

[1] To borrow the distinction from Rosenberg's seminal work *The Hollow Hope. Can Courts bring about Social Change?* (Rosenberg [2008: 9ff.]).

power of judicial review, thereby limiting the room for politics (Kelemen [2013: 295]). Conversely, another group of scholars presents a 'constrained view', questioning courts' broader societal impact and arguing that it is conditioned by a large set of institutional, political, and cultural factors (Bailey and Maltzman [2011]; Carrubba and Gabel [2015]; Conant [2002]; Epp [1998]; Hirschl [2009]; Kagan [2008]; Rosenberg [2008]; Vanberg [2005]; Wind [2010]). In this view, courts are not able to act as independent movers in fostering change, despite their power of judicial review, but depend on the countervailing political, administrative, and normative powers. Politics has the means to quell unwelcome jurisprudence (Fisher [1988]; Hirschl [2009]; Miller [2009]).

One court that has become famed—sometimes shamed—for its political power is the Court of Justice of the European Union (CJEU). In the scholarly literature, this supranational court has been regarded as a 'master of integration' for its capacity to strengthen integration sometimes against the will of member states (Alter [1998, 2001, 2009]; Burley and Mattli [1993]; Höpner and Schäfer [2012]; Pollack [2003]; Stone Sweet and Brunell [2012]; Weiler [1991]). In the public debate, the CJEU has been severely criticized for extending Union competences at the expense of the member states. From time to time fierce statements against the Court have been loudly expressed, as here from former German president and former president of the German Constitutional Court Roman Herzog, under the heading 'Stop the European Court of Justice':

> Judicial decision-making in Europe is in deep trouble. The reason is to be found in the European Court of Justice (ECJ), whose justifications for depriving member states of their very own fundamental competences and interfering heavily in their legal systems are becoming increasingly astonishing. In so doing, it has squandered a great deal of the trust it used to enjoy. (Herzog and Gerken [2008: 1])

The dominant narrative about the European Court is one of an unusually powerful constitutional court, able to progress European integration over time and into new policy sectors. This narrative, however, has not gone unchallenged. Scholars have noted that, owing to our scholarly reliance on this progressive narrative, we have tended to disregard all those instances in which the Court was ignored or constrained by political, administrative, and constitutional counteractions (Carrubba and Gabel [2015]; Conant [2002, 2006]; Larsson and Naurin [2016]; Nowak [2010]; Rasmussen [2013]). It has been argued that, in our reliance on the constitutional transformation of the Community legal order, we have tended to treat law and the role of the CJEU uncritically as instruments of integration, disregarding the more complex interplay of law and politics (Armstrong [1998]). The jury is still out, and the stark disagreement on judicial power in EU politics has recently been reinvigorated (Carrubba et al. [2012]; Stone Sweet and Brunell [2012]). In that revisited confrontation, however, the dynamic court view has not hesitated to declare itself as 'win[ning] by a landslide' (Stone Sweet and Brunell [2012: 204]).

Where is politics in all this? I argue that, in our preoccupation with judicial power, we have neglected to study the various ways in which legislative politics may respond to law. Political responses have mainly been examined as the ability of politics to overturn unwanted jurisprudence, and we have come to conclude that politics is unable to provide meaningful responses to what comes out of the court-room. Thus it is hardly surprising that we tend to focus on court actions in their own right and that 'scholars who focus on courts and make them the centre of attention tend to conclude that courts and judicial initiative matter' (McCann [2009: 838]). This book aims to uncover what becomes of law after it leaves the hands of the judiciary and enters legislative politics with its battles, dialogues, and compromises—i.e. the *ex post* legislative responses after judicial decisions have been rendered (Ginsburg [2014: 490–4]). Again, the legislative impact of jurisprudence is highly important for the extent to which court conclusions matter for the regulated, the citizens and firms, onto whom European law is applied. What became the legislative effect of all the judicial review that extended EU competences to define working time, export social assistance benefits across borders, and seek healthcare in another member state, or that limited workers' rights to take collective action, i.e. to strike against what was regarded as social dumping? These questions are of empirical as much as theoretical relevance for the study of law and politics and are where this book begins.

Judicial Influence on EU Social Policy Output

This book examines the ability of the CJEU to foster political change for an EU social policy, including healthcare. In doing so, it aims to examine the link between legal and political integration. The conventional assumption is that this causal link exists, i.e. that the rulings of the Court progress European integration. However, our understanding of when and under which conditions judicial decisions influence EU policy outputs and when they do not remains limited. The book explores the interactions between law and politics, i.e. how judicial–legislative interactions determine the scope and limits of European integration in the daily decision-making processes of an EU social policy. In addition to investigating the dynamics of law and politics, the book examines the historical and current states of an EU social policy—a policy field marked by inherent tensions between social considerations and internal market dynamics and where the legal-political game of daily decision making determines the scope of Union policies. The book studies social policy developments over time in the large historical view from 1957 to 2014. Additionally, three detailed case studies are conducted: EU regulation of working time, patients' rights in cross-border healthcare, and EU posting of worker regulations. For the reader uninterested in judicial influence, this book can be read as a policy process study within the social realm, examining both historical and current dynamics and content of the policy area and the inter-institutional dynamics developing this.

The effect of CJEU decisions has mainly been examined as the impact at the national level, i.e. on national court decisions or national politics. Scholarly work has advanced our knowledge considerably about the national consequences of EU litigation and when and why judicial Europeanization may occur (Alter [2009]; Alter and Vargas [2000]; Blauberger [2012, 2014]; Blauberger and Krämer [2014]; Conant [2002]; Davies [2012a, 2012b]; Martinsen [2011]; Nowak [2010]; Panke [2007]; Schmidt [2014]; Seikel [2014, 2015]; Slepcevic [2009]). Impact at the national level has been observed to vary considerably, and national compliance with judicial decisions has been identified as contained (Blauberger and Krämer [2014]; Conant [2002]; Davies [2012a]; Hatzopoulos and Hervey [2013]). Although the field of judicial Europeanization is still developing, it has made great advances over the last decade.

In contrast, our knowledge about how jurisprudence influences EU policies is vague. The causal link between judicial decisions and political integration essentially remains an unproven assumption. Although it is some years since political science discovered the role of the Court in integration—while lawyers warned that it should not be overestimated (Armstrong [1998]; De Búrca [2005]; Wincott [2001])—we lack systematic examination of the dynamics through which law may affect policies. So far, the interaction between CJEU jurisprudence and EU political decision-making has mainly been researched as the ability of EU politics to override unwanted jurisprudence,[2] i.e. where the

[2] The works of Alter and Meunier-Aitsahalia, Conant, and Nowak are seminal exceptions here, examining the political processes and outputs that followed innovative judicial decisions. Alter

legislature adopts legislation undoing the effect of the Court's judgment (Davies [2014: 1579]). Accordingly, the focus here is on legislative control of legal integration. On this point, the dynamic court view concludes that there exist no important examples of successful legislative override of legal integration (Stone Sweet and Brunell [2012: 205]). This non-finding thus proves: (1) the power of the Court, and, as the other side of the coin, (2) political disempowerment, i.e. the inability of EU legislative politics to reassert control and respond to jurisprudence in meaningful ways. Furthermore, lawyers emphasize that, because the EU is so highly constitutionalized, overriding politically unwelcome judicial decisions would usually require a Treaty amendment, making it impossible in practice (Davies [2014]). The constrained court view, in contrast, has argued that threats of non-compliance and legislative override *do* influence Court behaviour, by the judiciary exercising more self-restraint and taking political preferences into account (Carrubba and Gabel [2015]; Carrubba et al. [2008, 2012]; Garrett et al. [1998]; Larsson and Naurin [2016]). The preferences of the member states' governments affect the CJEU case law and limit the independence of the Court.

Thus, the investigation of political responses to legal integration has so far focused on legislative override—whether it occurs and whether it constitutes a credible threat that affects judicial behaviour. However, override is only one form of political reaction to CJEU jurisprudence. Other types of political response to legal integration, ranging from override to approval, may condition judicial influence on policies. In sum, our conceptual, theoretical, and empirical understanding of judicial influence on political integration remains limited. I argue that the call for advancing our understanding of judicial influence is strong because it goes to the heart of the balance of power between legislators and courts, between majoritarian and non-majoritarian institutions' capacity to steer integration. It concerns separation of power. Judicial influence on EU policies cannot be explored only by examining the possibility of override but must develop a more nuanced understanding of political reactions to unwanted and wanted CJEU judgments. Further research is needed into law as an enabling and constraining force on politics (De Búrca [2005]); however, if we are to capture the causal dynamics between legal and

and Meunier-Aitsahalia have done this for mutual recognition and the development of the Single European Act, as has Nowak (Alter and Meunier-Aitsahalia [1994]; Nowak [2010]). Conant's work *Justice Contained* analysed four cases of law—politics interaction involving liberalization of telecommunications, electricity, and social security policy, investigating legislative responses to judicial decisions (Conant [2002]).

political integration, we must also investigate how politics responds to and eventually constrains judicial impact.

The research puzzle of this book brings both judicial influence and political responses into question, examining *to what extent and under which conditions CJEU decisions influence EU social policy outputs, i.e. EU secondary legislation.* 'Policy outputs' are defined here as EU secondary legislation as proposed by the European Commission and adopted by the European Parliament (EP) and the Council of the European Union.[3] I argue that we must study the interaction between law and politics beyond or below the constitutional framework and expand our research to also cover how jurisprudence affects secondary legislation. By focusing only on constitutional responses to legal integration we miss the greater part of judicial–legislative interactions. In fact, the ordinary decision-making processes of the EU contain important attempts to codify—or correct—jurisprudence from individual decisions into general legislation. There are intense daily struggles and dialogues on what is the meaning of a Court decision, what legislative actions it permits, how can it be quelled and how future effects can be avoided. These day-to-day interactions with Court decisions take place beyond or below the high politics of constitutional reforms,[4] but are decisive to impact and essential to the authority of the Court. In essence, these negotiations over legislative acts are federal battles, setting the scope and limits of Union competences *versus* national ones, but are also ideological battles with political positions split along key conflict lines.

We must uncover the dynamics between legal and political integration in the ordinary, daily, decision-making processes for two reasons. Doing so is necessary because, first, as set out above, they mirror the ability of law (as opposed to that of politics) to set the course of integration. If political integration occurs through law, the legislators have lost decision-making power to the judiciary. Second, the eventual political adoption of CJEU interpretations of the 'law of the land' implies that these will become more generally applicable. EU legislative politics constitutes an important threshold of

[3] In the Lisbon Treaty, which became effective on 1 December 2009, the Council of Ministers was renamed the Council of the European Union. In this book, the Council of the European Union will generally be referred to as 'the Council'.

[4] The early work of Miller has a similar argument regarding the interactions between US federal courts and Congress, arguing that the normal day-to-day interactions in Congressional committees condition judicial influence (Miller [1992]).

what should be the broader impact of Court-generated principles and interpretations. A causal link between legal and political integration is the most important test of judicial influence because a legal decision that is codified by legislation expands from singularity to general enforceability, i.e. from specific application to the individual case at hand to application 'across the board' (Wasserfallen [2010]). When the interpretations and doctrines of the Court are incorporated into EU policy outputs, member states become generally bound by them and cannot shield themselves with the argument that the reasoning of the Court does not apply to their particular systems, rules, or practices. Judicial interpretations of the 'law of the land' come to bind all member states across European societies in general, whereas national implementation of case law remains more uncertain and variable (Wasserfallen [2010: 1129 and 1133]). Therefore, it is crucial to advance our knowledge of the extent to which—and how—legal integration may lead to political integration.

Defining Judicial Influence

The study of power and influence forms a core part of political science and explains in part why political scientists have taken a great interest in the CJEU. Existing studies of the role of the Court in European integration tend to examine the 'power' of the Court. Power either is not defined or refers to Dahl's classic pluralist definition, that being when A, the Court, has power over B, the government and its parliamentary majority, to the extent that A can induce B to take some action that B would not otherwise take (Stone Sweet [1995: 301; 2000: 75]).

The present study examines the Court's *influence* on EU policy outputs. It focuses on the extent to which and the conditions under which Court-generated principles, reasoning, and interpretations impact on policy outputs. As March noted in 1955, influence is key to the study of decision making;

> The interest in influence stems, in turn, from its conception as a fundamental intervening variable for the analysis of decision-making. Influence is to the study of decision-making what force is to the study of motion—a generic explanation for the basic observable phenomena. (March [1955: 432])

Influence involves causality and is generally understood as:

an actor's ability to shape a decision in line with her preferences, or, in other words, 'a causal relation between the preferences of an actor regarding an outcome and the outcome itself'. (Dür [2008: 561])

As noted in discussions of the concept of power, the study of influence should go beyond a classic, pluralist conception of influence as exercised in decision making and examine influence as the ability to shape the *context* and the *conduct* of actors (Hay [1997]). It should attempt to move beyond simplistic causal assumptions (Weiler [1991: 2426]). *Context-shaping influence* denotes the ability to redefine or limit the range of policy options or 'what is socially, politically and economically possible for others' (Hay [1997: 50]). In relation to the Court, this would mean that context-shaping influence forecloses a range of policy options that are not compatible with the constitutional principles of the EU, such as the free movement principles. It would thereby exert influence through shaping the context in which decisions are made, i.e. the range of options. *Conduct-shaping influence* occurs when actors shape their conduct, strategies, and behaviour to fit what the Court has already ruled or is likely to articulate in the future. According to Stone Sweet, conduct-shaping influence constitutes 'judicialisation of politics', i.e. when legislators:

routinely take decisions that they would not have taken in the absence of review, and governing majorities anticipate likely decisions of the court and constrain their behaviour accordingly. (Stone Sweet [2000: 202])

In the present study, judicial influence on policy outputs can be identified from both a more abstract perspective and a concrete, operationalized sense. In an overall, abstract view, judicial influence on EU policy outputs takes place when the established regulatory status quo (SQ_{reg}^{1}) is challenged by a new court-generated status quo (SQ_{Court}), which is then codified into or altered by EU legislation (SQ_{reg}^{2}). SQ_{reg}^{1} can be confined to a simple statute or the Treaty. Judicial review is exercised, and its substance or scope is disturbed by SQ_{Court}. EU legislative politics is called upon to address the discrepancy between SQ_{reg}^{1} and SQ_{Court} and can undo or approve SQ_{Court} by means of SQ_{reg}^{2}. When SQ_{Court} equals SQ_{reg}^{2}, full codification and, hence, maximum judicial influence has occurred. When SQ_{Court} is rolled back to the conditions of SQ_{reg}^{1}, a legislative override has taken place.

In the concrete, operationalized sense, judicial influence on EU policy outputs takes place when Court-generated principles and interpretations are attained in the final policy outputs.

Operationalizing Judicial Influence

The case law of the Court may impact on different sequences of policy making; agenda setting, preference shaping, and decision making. It may influence concrete decisions and shape conduct and context. Studying judicial influence resembles the study of ideas' impact on policies, enquiring into which ideas, norms, principles, or rule interpretations come to produce change, and how and why they do while others do not (Campbell [2002]). As known from the study of ideas, it involves considerable analytical challenges to link those transformative processes from idea through polity onto policy outputs. However, this effort is necessary when we enquire into the transformative impact of jurisprudence.

To meet this challenge, I have developed a 'law attainment' approach as a first step to analysing judicial influence on EU policy outputs. The 'law attainment' approach draws on the 'preference attainment' approach developed for the study of interest organizations' influence on policy outputs (Dür [2008]; Klüver [2011]). However, the purpose is not to research whether the preferences of the Court are attained but rather whether the rules, principles, and interpretations generated by the Court are attained in legislative acts, i.e. cause political integration—or whether they are overridden. I compare the interpretation of rules and principles as established by judicial decisions and as proposed by the Commission with the final policy outputs adopted by the EU legislators. If judicial interpretations of rules and norms are attained in the final policy outputs, then judicial influence has been exercised.

However, as noted by Klüver, studying the attainment of preferences, or, as here, judicial interpretations, has an important shortcoming: it is unable to open the black box 'of processes through which influence is exercised' (Klüver [2011: 490]). Thus the law attainment approach cannot investigate the dynamics of politics and law in this area, which is likely to affect which judicial interpretations do and do not endure. This approach is unable to map out the importance of different political positions, how and why they might change, how and why jurisprudence shapes context and conduct, and so forth.

Therefore, three case studies have been added to research this process and thus under which conditions CJEU decisions can come to influence policy outputs. The case studies intend to capture how political positions may be formed for or against the case law of the Court, how political conduct may be shaped by jurisprudence, and how context, i.e. policy options, may change owing to judicial decisions.

On Methods, Case Selection, and Data

The case study is found to be the appropriate method for this book's type of social enquiry because it allows us to examine the details of the dynamics and the factors of judicial influence that condition policy outputs (Gerring [2004: 348–9]). The case study method is employed to uncover new areas in the complex and dynamic relationship between law and politics, which large-n quantitative studies may overlook. As a method, the 'law attainment' approach has been combined with process tracing to 'open the black box' between judicial decisions and policy outputs (Klüver [2011: 490]). Process tracing allows us to try to establish causality between different judicial decisions, legislative proposals, political positions, interactions, and policy outputs (Beach and Pedersen [2013]; George and Bennett [2005]). It allows us to link these incidents between different points in time, T_1 and T_2, and establish why judicial influence may occur as a result of one political decision-making process but not another. Process tracing enables us to systematically connect the dots from initial legislation, to jurisprudence, to member state reactions, to legislative reactions and interaction, to final outputs. Process tracing is thus a meaningful tool to analytically revisit expectations as to when and why judicial influence on policy outputs occurs.

EU social policy, including healthcare, has been selected as the case.[5] I argue that EU social policy constitutes a strong test case (George and Bennett [2005: 120–3]) for uncovering a potential causal link and mechanisms between legal and political integration because the policy area fulfils two criteria: first, legal integration has occurred to a relatively large extent in the policy area; second, when legal integration occurs, we should assume that politicians will engage.

[5] Social policy is defined across the broad spectrum of welfare policies, including the labour market, healthcare, gender equality, and welfare-redistributive policies, but not education policies.

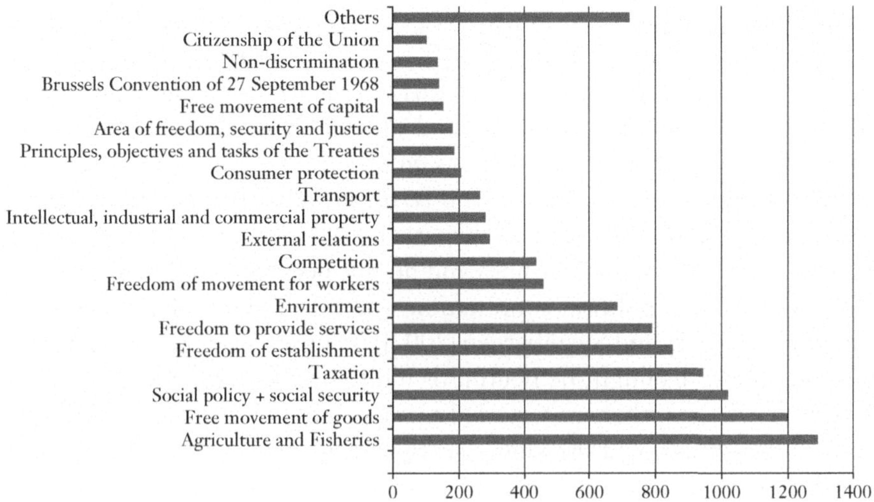

Fig. 1.1 Preliminary References and Infringement Procedures in Total 1961–2014

As to the first criterion, the CJEU issued rulings in 1,025 EU social policy cases between 1961 and 2014, out of a total of 7,547 cases, making social policy the policy area with the third most Court cases within EU jurisdiction.[6] The rulings have been sorted according to the CJEU's categories of substantive matters. The category 'Approximation of laws' is not included in figure 1.1 because it does not represent a policy area as such. The categories 'Social provisions' and 'Social security' have been merged in the figure. Only agriculture and fisheries and the free movement of goods have been the subjects of more cases before the CJEU than social provisions and social security.

We thus have reason to assume that legal integration propels political integration in the social policy area, calling for politicians to respond and change the established regulatory status quo. Concerning the second criterion, we assume that judicial interpretations of social legislation matter to politicians. EU social policy constitutes a policy field where much is at stake and politicians disagree on the way forward (Ferrera [2005]). It is a policy area likely to

[6] The data on CJEU case law have been compiled by means of the Court of Justice of the European Union's database, http://curia.europa.eu. All judicial decisions between 1 January1958 and 1 July 2014 have been compiled for cases ruled under articles 258 and 267 in the Treaty on the Functioning of the European Union (TFEU). The data-set is accessible at the author's webpage at www.politicalscience.ku.dk. Article TFEU 258 specifies the infringement procedure according to which the European Commission can take a member state to the CJEU for non-compliance with EU law. Article 267 specifies the preliminary reference procedure by which national courts

create divergent political positions owing to ideological controversies and the increased socio-economic heterogeneity of an EU consisting of twenty-eight member states (Höpner and Schäfer [2012: 436–8]). EU social policy often intersects with the internal market and thus divides political actors along key conflict lines: market freedom *versus* social rights, deregulation *versus* social (re)-regulation, EU integration *versus* subsidiarity, open labour markets *versus* protection of national job markets, and so forth. Judicial decisions interpret along these conflict lines and do not occur in a political vacuum. We should assume political contestation when the Court rules along these dimensions (Marks and Steenbergen [2002]). In other instances of legal integration, politicians might be neutral or indifferent because the integration does not challenge what are regarded as important political ideas or institutions. However, as noted elsewhere, a certain degree of conflict or ideological controversy is required to fruitfully examine the relationship between law and politics.[7]

Judicial influence will be analysed over time for the social policy area, from when the first proposal was presented by the European Commission in 1958 to July 2014. Furthermore, three case studies will be conducted to examine and explain variation in judicial influence and political responses: EU regulation of working time, patients' rights in cross-border healthcare, and EU posting of workers' regulation. The studies were selected because they were main initiatives in EU social and health policies negotiated within the constitutional framework of the Lisbon Treaty. They were identified as main initiatives by key respondents during an explorative round of interviews conducted in the spring of 2009. Choosing these three as case studies has made it possible to trace the negotiation processes as they unfolded between and within the European Commission, the Council and the EP, and thus to collect empirical data on more recent political responses to CJEU jurisprudence, i.e. those that unfolded between 2009 and 2014. The three case studies provide insight into the current dynamics, scope, and limits on Social Europe of EU28.

So far, studies of the dynamics between law and politics have mainly investigated the period before the 2004 enlargement (see e.g. Carrubba and Gabel [2015]; Carrubba et al. [2008]; Stone Sweet and Brunell [2012]). This book takes a historical view but proceeds to the latest institutional and

can send preliminary references to the CJEU to obtain its interpretations of EU law (Stone Sweet and Brunell [2012: 206]).

[7] For similar arguments discussing where the relationship between law and politics can most fruitfully be examined, see Garrett et al. (1998: 151); Rosenberg (2008: 4). In many other areas

socio-economic setting of the EU, enabling us to revisit our empirical and theoretical knowledge based on evidence collected in the most recent context. The three cases are characterized by a high degree of legal certainty, with the Court having interpreted a number of cases over a considerable period, creating judicial precedent. In the case of patients' rights and in part in that of the posting of workers, judicial decisions were based on Treaty interpretations, while in that of working time and in part in that of the posting of workers legal interpretations were based on secondary legislation. The cases chosen thus imply different institutional thresholds for politics to respond to jurisprudence. As demonstrated below, political actors responded to jurisprudence both on an ideological left *versus* right conflict line and on a conflict line for or against further European integration (Marks and Steenbergen [2002]). Judicial decisions did not leave politics indifferent.

Data for this book have been collected from official and unofficial documents and through a large set of semi-structured interviews with key respondents involved in the decision-making processes. Seventy-eight interviews were conducted with key actors, including:

- Council representatives, who included:
  - civil servants from the national representations,
  - national experts negotiating in Council working groups and the Permanent Representatives Committee (Coreper), and
  - Presidency civil servants;
- Commission civil servants from the different Directorates General involved;
- national civil servants;
- Members of the European Parliament (MEP), including:
  - rapporteurs,
  - shadow rapporteurs,
  - ordinary members, and
  - EP policy advisors;
- representatives of national and European social partners; and
- representatives of national parliaments.

The interviews were conducted between February 2007 and April 2014 to identify policy processes as they unfolded. The interviews were carefully planned. An early interview was held in February 2007, at that time examining the law–politics dynamics within the field of social security for migrant workers, which generated the motivation and idea to examine these complex interactions for the entire EU social policy area, including healthcare. A new set of explorative and preparatory interviews was held in February 2009 to identify the main social policy initiatives under legislative consideration. Against this background, the key respondents were identified and the plans for additional interviews were made. At the end of each interview, the respondent was asked to identify other key respondents for the subject matter, which over time expanded the number of interviewees and made it possible to identify and gain access to the relevant actors. At the beginning of the interviews, the respondents were promised anonymity and informed how citations would be used with reference only to their institutions and the dates of the conducted interviews. All interviews but one were recorded.[8] Almost all the interviews were subsequently transcribed.[9]

To conduct the analysis of Court influence on EU social policy outputs over time, all the new regulations, directives, and subsequent major amendments adopted between 1 January 1958 and 1 July 2014 were compiled. Where possible to trace, rejected policy proposals were also included in the compilation. All the original Commission proposals were collected by a small research team. The early Commission proposals were difficult to acquire because they were not available on the internet nor in the hands of the relevant ministries or information offices. However, with the help of the 'Historical Archives of the Commission', we managed to also collect the early original proposals, allowing us to carry out a 'law attainment' examination for the entire period. Chapter 3 will further detail the analytical steps for the analysis of judicial influence over time.

Structure of the Book

This book is divided into seven chapters, including this introduction. Chapter 2 sets out the theoretical framework to examine and explain judicial

of EU law, such as environmental policy, justice and home affairs, taxation, financial regulation, education, and agriculture, we should expect similar degrees of political contestation.

8 This respondent from the Council refused to have the interview recorded; accordingly, notes were taken instead.

9 A small number of interviews deemed less important were not transcribed.

influence on legislative outputs. It presents the scholarly debate from the 1990s onwards on the power of courts to alter politics, unfolding in a somewhat dichotomous span between a 'dynamic' and a 'constrained' court view. This point of departure is found insufficient to capture and explain when and why jurisprudence does and does not affect legislation. To theoretically and analytically identify different types of judicial influence, a taxonomy of judicial influence is developed. In part, the taxonomy is derived from the existing scholarly debate on judicial impact; however, it presents additional types of political response with implications for judicial influence. The taxonomy presents four types of legislative response that—if occurring—cause variation in judicial influence: codification, modification, non-adoption, and override. The rest of the chapter discusses what may condition judicial influence. Why should this influence vary over time and in context when we generally rely on the progressive narrative of legal integration? Scholarly work has refuted the ability of legislative politics to condition judicial influence for two general reasons: (1) EU politics is too fragmented to be able to respond, and (2) politicians have a shorter time horizon than judges and therefore tend to disregard what might be longer-term implications of judicial decisions. I argue for the need to revisit these more general assumptions. Four explanatory factors that may account for variation in judicial influence are derived: time as a factor, decision-making rules, the role of the Commission, and political positions. Chapter 2 presents these factors as expectations as to the conditions under which jurisprudence may influence policy outputs.

Chapter 3 turns to the policy field under examination—social policy, including healthcare. It presents the achievements, dynamics, and tensions of the policy area as it has unfolded over time. After setting out the state of an EU social policy, the chapter initiates the empirical analysis of *the extent to which and the conditions under which judicial decisions influence EU social policy outputs*. Judicial influence over time is examined by using the 'law attainment' approach that I have developed, as presented above. Variation in judicial influence is identified, and explanations as to why are sought out. The statistical associations among key factors, such as time, political disagreements, and the likelihood of codification, are tested. The analysis over time proceeds by means of qualitative examinations of three decision-making processes that led, individually, to codification, modification, and legislative override of judicial decisions. Among other findings, Chapter 3 demonstrates 'time' and 'politics' to condition the likelihood of codifying jurisprudence into policy outputs.

Judicial influence on EU working time regulation is examined in Chapter 4. The chapter traces the dynamics between law and politics as they unfolded between the early 1990s and 2014. The analysis first sets out the process through which the working time directive was initially adopted, establishing SQ_{reg}^{1} but subsequently challenged by CJEU case law. Political disagreements over how to respond to the case law of the Court became severe within and between institutions. The political responses to SQ_{Court} are investigated by tracing why judicial influence on the policy output was ultimately rejected despite intense and prolonged interaction between political actors and institutions. Political gridlock and non-adoption became the policy response, creating a state of legal uncertainty marked by a considerable discrepancy between SQ_{reg}^{1} and SQ_{Court} and 'rules that nobody follows'.

Chapter 5 conducts the second case study on patients' rights in cross-border healthcare. It examines how EU integration of cross-border healthcare has unfolded in the exchange between law and politics. The chapter takes a long historical view, covering the period from the 1970s, when the original regulatory status quo SQ_{reg}^{1} was adopted; it was then challenged by early Court rulings but re-established by political override. The chapter then turns to the next sequence of Court interpretations SQ_{Court}, when internal market principles were applied to the healthcare sector and severely disturbed SQ_{reg}^{1}. Politics responded first by requesting a Treaty amendment, then by demanding that the Court be reined in by means of secondary legislation. The chapter analyses how the Commission and different political actors interpreted and responded to the jurisprudence through the bits and pieces of daily decision making. This process unfolded with much dispute within and between institutions; however, the patients' rights directive in cross-border healthcare was finally adopted. The political actors thereby managed to agree upon a new regulatory status quo SQ_{reg}^{2}, modifying the impact of judicial decisions and re-establishing a considerable degree of national control over where to seek healthcare. Chapter 5 also identifies subsequent judicial adaptation to the political correction of past legal integration.

Chapter 6 contains the third case study—EU regulation of the posting of workers. The chapter traces the process of regulation back in time. It sets out the fundamental regulatory dilemmas contained in the posting of workers' directive as it was originally adopted in 1996. The chapter analyses the process through which the directive was first adopted and how member states originally codified the early case law of Rush Portuguesa into the directive as a justification for applying national labour laws to posted workers. This regulatory status quo SQ_{reg}^{1} was, however, severely disrupted by the 'Laval quartet' case law. The subsequent sections of the chapter examine how legislative politics responded to the Commission's proposals to adopt the Court's interpretations into secondary law. First, the national parliaments rejected the Monti II proposal. Then, the European legislators managed to establish a compromise with the enforcement directive that modified judicial influence. However, with the non-adoption of the Monti II proposal, the discrepancy between SQ_{reg}^{1} and SQ_{Court} on the right to collective action *versus* free movement principles remains a wide one; consequently, there remains a loud call for political responses to legal integration.

Chapter 7 concludes on the findings. The analysis has demonstrated variable judicial influence on EU policy outputs and presented political responses as the overall condition for the legislative impact of judicial decisions. The findings contest the two general claims in studies of EU law and politics—that EU politics is not too fragmented to respond to litigation and that EU political actors engage in and correct legal integration as persistent actors rather than individuals with short time horizons. Time, decision-making rules, political positions, and interaction within and across institutions come to condition judicial impact on EU policies. The European Commission is the important first mover to decide which judicial decisions qualify for political adoption or correction. Its ability to steer the process to completion is, however, crippled by its own internal disagreements on the way forward and inter-institutional conflicts on how to respond. As a result of these day-to-day judicial–legislative interactions, the scope and limits of European integration are set. These findings invite us to revisit the image of progressive judicialization beyond political control. The findings demonstrate that both codification and overriding of judicial decisions are unlikely in the contemporary EU28 of fragmented politics. However, modification and non-adoption constitute other political responses where modification is able to attenuate unwelcome jurisprudence and constrain the legislative impact of judicial decisions.

References

Alter, K. (1998) 'Who are the 'Masters of the Treaty'? European governments and the European Court of Justice', *International Organization* 52(01): 121–47.

Alter, K. (2001) *Establishing the Supremacy of European Law: The Making of an International Rule of Law in Europe*, Oxford: Oxford University Press.

Alter, K. (2009) 'The European Court's political power across time and space', *Revue Française de Science Politique* 59: 1–24.

Alter, K. and Meunier-Aitsahalia, S. (1994) 'Judicial politics in the European Community: European integration and the pathbreaking Cassis de Dijon decision', *Comparative Political Studies* 26(4): 535–61.

Alter, K.J. and Vargas, J. (2000) 'Explaining variation in the use of European litigation strategies. European Community law and British gender equality policy', *Comparative Political Studies* 33(4): 452–82.

Armstrong, K.A. (1998) 'Legal integration: theorizing the legal dimension of European integration', *JCMS: Journal of Common Market Studies* 36(2): 155–74.

Bailey, M.A. and Maltzman, F. (2011) *The Constrained Court: Law, Politics, and the Decisions Justices Make*, Princeton, NJ: Princeton University Press.

Beach, D. and Pedersen, R.B. (2013) *Process-tracing Methods: Foundations and Guidelines*, Ann Arbor, MI: University of Michigan Press.

Blauberger, M. (2012) 'With Luxembourg in mind .... the remaking of national policies in the face of ECJ jurisprudence', *Journal of European Public Policy* 19(1): 109–26.

Blauberger, M. (2014) 'National responses to European Court jurisprudence', *West European Politics* 37(3): 457–74.

Blauberger, M. and Krämer, R.U. (2014) 'Europeanisation with many unknowns: national company law reforms after Centros', *West European Politics* 37(4): 786–804.

Burley, A.-M. and Mattli, W. (1993) 'Europe before the Court: a political theory of legal integration', *International Organization* 47(01): 41–76.

Campbell, J.L. (2002) 'Ideas, politics, and public policy', *Annual Review of Sociology* 28: 21–38.

Carrubba, C. and Gabel, M. (2015) *International Courts and the Performance of International Agreements: A General Theory with Evidence from the European Union*, Cambridge: Cambridge University Press.

Carrubba, C.J., Gabel, M., and Hankla, C. (2008) 'Judicial behavior under political constraints: evidence from the European Court of Justice', *American Political Science Review* 102(04): 435–52.

Carrubba, C.J., Gabel, M., and Hankla, C. (2012) 'Understanding the role of the European Court of Justice in European integration', *American Political Science Review* 106(01): 214–23.

Cichowski, R.A. (2007) *The European Court and Civil Society, Litigation, Mobilization and Governance*, Cambridge: Cambridge University Press.

Conant, L. (2006) 'Individuals, courts, and the development of European Social rights', *Comparative Political Studies* 39(1): 76–100.

Conant, L.J. (2002) *Justice Contained, Law and Politics in the European Union*, Ithaca, NY: Cornell University Press.

Davies, B. (2012a) 'Pushing back: what happens when member states resist the European Court of Justice? A multi-modal approach to the history of European law', *Contemporary European History* 21(Special Issue 03): 417–35.
Davies, G. (2012b) 'Activism relocated. The self-restraint of the European Court of Justice in its national context', *Journal of European Public Policy* 19(1): 76–91.
Davies, G. (2014) 'Legislative control of the European Court of Justice', *Common Market Law Review* 51(6): 1579–607.
De Búrca, G. (2005) 'Rethinking law in neofunctionalist theory', *Journal of European Public Policy* 12(2): 310–26.
Dür, A. (2008) 'Measuring interest group influence in the EU. A note on methodology', *European Union Politics* 9(4): 559–76.
Epp, C.R. (1998) *The Rights Revolution: Lawyers, Activists, and Supreme Courts in Comparative Perspective*, Chicago: University of Chicago Press.
Ferrera, M. (2005) *The Boundaries of Welfare: European Integration and the New Spatial Politics of Social Protection*, Oxford: Oxford University Press.
Fisher, L. (1988) *Constitutional Dialogues: Interpretation as Political Process*, Princeton, NJ: Princeton University Press.
Garrett, G., Kelemen, R.D., and Schulz, H. (1998) 'The European Court of Justice, national governments, and legal integration in the European Union', *International Organization* 52(1): 149–76.
George, A.L. and Bennett, A. (2005) *Case Studies and Theory Development in the Social Sciences*, Cambridge, MA: MIT Press.
Gerring, J. (2004) 'What is a case study and what is it good for?', *American Political Science Review* 98(02): 341–54.
Ginsburg, T. (2014) 'Political constraints on international courts', in C. Romano, K.J. Alter and Y. Shany (eds), *The Oxford Handbook of International Adjudication*, Oxford: Oxford University Press, pp. 483–502.
Hatzopoulos, V. and Hervey, T. (2013) 'Coming into line: the EU's Court softens on cross-border health care', *Health Economics, Policy and Law* 8(01): 1–5.
Hay, C. (1997) 'State of the art: divided by a common language: political theory and the concept of power', *Politics* 17(1): 45–52.
Herzog, R. and Gerken, L. (2008) 'Stop the European Court of Justice', *EU Observer*, 10. September.
Hirschl, R. (2009) 'The realist turn in comparative constitutional politics', *Political Research Quarterly* 62(4): 825–33.
Höpner, M. and Schäfer, A. (2012) 'Embeddedness and regional integration: waiting for Polanyi in a Hayekian setting', *International Organization* 66(03): 429–55.
Kagan, R.A. (2008) 'The "non-Americanisation" of European law', *European Political Science* 7(1): 21–31.
Kelemen, R.D. (2008) 'The Americanisation of European law? Adversarial legalism *à la Européenne*', *European Political Science* 7(1): 32–42.

Kelemen, R.D. (2013) 'Judicialisation, democracy and European integration', *Representation* 49(3): 295–308.
Klüver, H. (2011) 'The contextual nature of lobbying: explaining lobbying success in the European Union', *European Union Politics* 12(4): 483–506.
Larsson, O. and Naurin, D. (2016) 'Judicial independence and political uncertainty: How the risk of override impacts on the Court of Justice of the EU', *International Organization*, 70(2).
March, J.G. (1955) 'An introduction to the theory and measurement of influence', *American Political Science Review* 49(02): 431–51.
Marks, G. and Steenbergen, M. (2002) 'Understanding political contestation in the European Union', *Comparative Political Studies* 35(8): 879–92.
Martinsen, D.S. (2011) 'Judicial policy-making and Europeanization: the proportionality of national control and administrative discretion', *Journal of European Public Policy* 18(7): 944–61.
McCann, M. (1994) *Rights at Work: Pay Equity, Reform and the Politics of Legal Mobilization*, Chicago: The University of Chicago Press.
McCann, M. (2009) 'Interests, ideas, and institutions in comparative analysis of judicial power', *Political Research Quarterly* 62(4): 834–9.
Miller, M.C. (1992) 'Congressional committees and the Federal courts: a neo-institutional perspective', *The Western Political Quarterly* 45(4): 949–70.
Miller, M.C. (2009) *The View of the Courts from the Hill: Interactions between Congress and the Federal Judiciary*, Charlottesville, VA: University of Virginia Press.
Nowak, T. (2010) 'Of garbage cans and rulings: judgments of the European Court of Justice in the EU legislative process', *West European Politics* 33(4): 753–69.
Panke, D. (2007) 'The European Court of Justice as an agent of Europeanization? Restoring compliance with EU law', *Journal of European Public Policy* 14(6): 847–66.
Pollack, M.A. (2003) *The Engines of European Integration, Delegation, Agency, and Agenda Setting in the EU*, Oxford: Oxford University Press.
Rasmussen, M. (2013) 'Rewriting the history of European public law: the new contribution of historians', *American University International Law Review* 28(5): 1187–223.
Rosenberg, G.N. (2008) *The Hollow Hope: Can Courts Bring About Social Change?*, Chicago: University of Chicago Press.
Schmidt, S.K. (2014) 'Judicial Europeanisation: the case of Zambrano in Ireland', *West European Politics* 37(4): 769–85.
Seikel, D. (2014) 'Nationale Anpassungsstrategien an das Fallrecht des Europäischen Gerichtshofes. Europäisierung durch Richterrecht und innenpolitische Veto-Positionen', in WSI-Diskussionspapier, no. 189: 1–26.
Seikel, D. (2015) 'Class struggle in the shadow of Luxembourg. The domestic impact of the European Court of Justice's case law on the regulation of working conditions'. *Journal of European Public Policy* 22(8): 1166–85.

Slepcevic, R. (2009) 'The judicial enforcement of EU law through national courts: possibilities and limits', *Journal of European Public Policy* 16(3): 378–94.

Stone Sweet, A. (1995) 'Governing with judges: the new constitutionalism', in J. Hayward and E.C. Page (eds), *Governing the New Europe*, Cambridge: Polity Press, pp. 286–315.

Stone Sweet, A. (2000) *Governing with Judges: Constitutional Politics in Europe*, Oxford: Oxford University Press.

Stone Sweet, A. (2004) *The Judicial Construction of Europe*, Oxford: Oxford University Press.

Stone Sweet, A. and Brunell, T. (2012) 'The European Court of Justice, state noncompliance, and the politics of override', *American Political Science Review* 106(01): 204–13.

Vanberg, G. (2005) *The Politics of Constitutional Review in Germany*, Cambridge: Cambridge University Press.

Wasserfallen, F. (2010) 'The judiciary as legislator? How the European Court of Justice shapes policy-making in the European Union', *Journal of European Public Policy* 17(8): 1128–46.

Weiler, J. (1991) 'The transformation of Europe', *Yale Law Journal* 100: 2403–83.

Wincott, D. (2001) 'The Court of Justice and the European policy process', in J. Richardson (ed.), *European Union, Power and Policy-Making*, London: Routledge, 179–97.

Wind, M. (2010) 'The Nordics, the EU and the reluctance towards supranational judicial review', *JCMS: Journal of Common Market Studies* 48(4): 1039–63.

2

The Court of Justice of the European Union: Master of Integration?

> Parliamentary supremacy, understood by most students of European politics to be a constitutive principle of European politics, has lost its vitality. After a polite, nostalgic nod across the Channel to Westminster, we can declare it dead.
>
> (Stone Sweet, *Governing with Judges*, [2000: 1])

> The 'harder' the law in terms of its binding effect both on and within states, the less willing states are to give up their prerogative to control the emergence of such law or the law's 'opposability' to them. When the international law is 'real', when it is 'hard' in the sense of being binding not only on but also in states, and when there are effective legal remedies to enforce it, *decision making suddenly becomes important, indeed crucial.*
>
> (Weiler, 'The transformation of Europe', [1991: 2426], emphasis added)

The ability of courts to generate political change is a theme of ample theoretical and empirical relevance. It questions the transfer of decision-making power to a non-majoritarian institution. It addresses the impact of judicial decisions beyond the courtroom. It concerns the ability of majoritarian powers to respond to and ultimately decide the scope and limits of judicial decisions. The international scholarly debate on law and politics has contributed various articulated positions on the ways and extent to which court decisions may further change. Studies of the US Supreme Court and other national and international courts thus share puzzles and offer views on the CJEU's legislative impact (Staton and Moore [2011: 569]). Can court decisions change the direction of politics (Alter [2014]), and if so, to what extent and under which conditions? Why would legislative politics subordinate to a 'juristocracy' (Hirschl [2009a])? Can politics respond to law and roll unwanted judicialization back? Indeed, international academia presents different positions and findings unfolding between two poles of the 'dynamic court view', according to which courts are powerful and vigorous in making change, and the 'constrained court view', according to which the courts have no automatic impact, but they are conditioned by a large set of factors (Rosenberg [2008]).

This chapter sets forth the theoretical framework for understanding the relationship between legal and political integration. It presents different scholarly interpretations of this relationship, first as presented in international and comparative politics, then as presented specifically in EU studies.

The chapter begins by presenting the scholarly debate from the 1990s onwards on the power of courts to alter politics. The interpretations of courts' ability to generate political change are initially contrasted by distinguishing between the 'dynamic' and the 'constrained' court views, both in comparative and in EU studies. This more dichotomous understanding of judicial influence is found to be insufficient for both theoretical and analytical purposes, for which a taxonomy is developed that allows more variation on judicial influence. The taxonomy is derived from our preceding theoretical knowledge but develops alternative expectations to help refine our understanding of law–politics dynamics. The taxonomy presents four types of legislative response with different implications for judicial influence on policy outputs: codification, modification, non-adoption, and override. Against this background, different expectations of what may condition judicial influence are formulated. Four factors explaining what might condition judicial influence are derived from the literature and presented: time as a factor, decision-making rules, the role of the Commission, and political positions. With the taxonomy and the factors explaining variance as the theoretical framework, an empirical analysis is conducted in the subsequent chapters.

The Dynamic Court View

According to the dynamic court view, we have experienced a fundamental change in the relation between judicial and legislative politics in which a 'judicialisation' of politics has taken place (Alter [2014]; Cichowski [2007]; Kelemen [2013]; Stone Sweet [2000]). Constitutionalization and constitutional supremacy have take form as a global trend in which courts carry out a judicial review of legislative acts, and have therefore become powerful institutions of modern democracies. There is broad agreement that increased judicial involvement in policy making has taken place at both the national and international levels (Woods and Hilbink [2009]). In this process, judges act independently from pressures of partisan politics. They operate 'above' politics and instead focus on protecting the rights of minorities and individual liberties. This process of increasing the power of courts as non-majoritarian institutions has often been 'portrayed as a reflection of progressive social or political change, or simply as the result of societies' or politicians' devotion to a 'thick' notion of democracy and their uncritical celebration of human rights' (Hirschl [2009b: 825]).

The political power of courts is partly explained by politics lacking the capacity to override unwanted jurisprudence (Stone Sweet and Brunell [2012]). If jurisprudence goes against political preferences, politicians are paralysed by their inability to establish majorities sufficient to correct court interpretations. Therefore, courtrooms can make successful inroads for generating change that is not possible to achieve in parliaments. By taking new cases to court or by fighting for the general applicability of their cases on the street, societal actors, including lawyers, are key to pushing for a judicial decision to gain wider implications. A test case can be a successful strategy in which an individual action prepares the ground for broader social and political purposes. In this way, parliaments and legislation might no longer have the final word, as they had within the framework of parliamentary sovereignty (Harlow and Rawlings [1992: 322]).

This global trend towards increased judicial power has had severe consequences for politics. Parliamentary sovereignty is no longer the constitutive principle of democratic politics, as parliaments have to subordinate to judicial interpretations of their statutes in the light of bills of rights and constitutions. The work on constitutional politics by Stone Sweet points to increased judicial power with severe consequences for politics; in fact, through the 'judicialisation of politics', parliamentary supremacy has lost its vitality, and it can be declared 'dead' (Stone Sweet [1995: 287]; [2000: 1]). Studying the constitutional courts in France, Germany, Italy, Spain, and the European Community, Stone Sweet finds that constitutional judges routinely intervene in policy making by establishing limits to legislative behaviour and to legislation (Stone Sweet [1995: 286]). Over time, the influence of law on politics has increased and intensified:

> In consequence, the influence of constitutional judges over legislative outcomes has widened and deepened. Indeed, it can be argued that within legislative processes constitutional courts function as specialized legislative chambers. In consequence, legislators have come to behave 'judicially'. (Stone Sweet [1995: 294])

In this version of the dynamic court view, judicial power grows over time. Relying on Dahl's classic definition of power, A (the constitutional court) has power over B (the government and its parliamentary majority) when 'B anticipates A's interest and constrains its behaviour accordingly' (Stone Sweet [1995: 301]; for the same definition, see also Stone Sweet [2000: 75]). The power of law increases over time to the detriment of politics. The interests of A become more precise, and B increasingly conforms to these interests (Stone Sweet [1995: 301]; repeated in Stone Sweet [2000: 75]). The governing majority is pushed into compliance with the law, and it abstains from formulating legislative proposals that contradict what the constitutional court has laid down or is likely to lay down. In consequence, as judicial power grows, political power shrinks, and parliamentary supremacy withers. This understanding of governing 'with and like judges' (Stone Sweet [2000: 204]) portrays politics as unable to respond to an unwanted direction of litigation and instead as subordinate to it.

The Constrained Court View

By contrast, according to the 'constrained court view' the judiciary has little independent impact on politics. In an international and comparative context, scholars from the 'constrained court view' find that courts have only a limited impact on political change if they are not supported by an extremely strong network of legal activists who see the advantage of a new doctrine (Epp [1998]). However, a successful push for change by means of litigation is more the exception than it is the rule. Ultimately, the judiciary depends on the executive branch to carry out and comply with its rulings. At the end of the day, courts cannot enforce the law, and they depend on the executive to do so:

> (The judiciary) has no influence over either the sword or the purse; no direction either of the strength or of the wealth of the society; and can take no active

resolution whatsoever. It may truly be said to have neither FORCE nor WILL, but merely judgement; and must ultimately depend upon the aid of the executive arm even for the efficacy of its judgments. (A. Hamilton [1961], as quoted in Conant [2002: 219])

Rosenberg's seminal study of the 'hollow hope' of litigation brings political institutions into the equation of what conditions courts' abilities to catalyse change. His 1991 book 'hit a raw nerve' in the American debate on law and politics, as he argues that American courts are severely limited and are not all-powerful institutions (Rosenberg (2008: 429–30]).[1] Rosenberg's study of the US Supreme Court noted that even that court, acting from atop the hierarchical structure, depends on social, administrative, and political responses to its rulings to have an impact that extends beyond an individual lawsuit. Courts rely primarily on consent, and in its absence they face a considerable compliance problem (Conant [2002: 221]). Individual litigation is not influential by itself, but it may create 'hollow hopes', high expectations and/or severe concerns among societal actors on unjustified grounds. The piecemeal nature of litigation necessitates that judges rely on 'episodic case-to-case remedies for complex social problems' (Rosenberg [2008: 20]). In and of themselves, judicial decisions are not sufficiently strong to be considered general remedies; instead, they rely on political institutions to give them further impact. Thus, a victory in court does not automatically bring about the desired change. Only when institutional, structural, and ideological barriers to change are weak can courts help produce significant social change:

The structural constraints of the constrained court view, built into the American judicial system, make courts virtually powerless to produce change. They must depend on the actions of others for their decisions to be implemented. (Rosenberg [2008: 420])

The two court views interpret the impact of the same court ruling fundamentally different. In the American scholarly debate, one landmark case found to have proven 'pressure through law' is the 1954 Brown case.[2] In the dynamic court view, this US Supreme Court case has been interpreted as a primary example of the broader impact of litigation, in this case as the key to ending racial segregation in the US public educational system (Harlow

[1] The second edition of Rosenberg's book came out in 2008. The second edition updates the author's findings. Its main argument, findings, and conclusions, however, remain unchanged from the first edition.

[2] Brown v Board of Education of Topeka (1954) 347 US, 483.

and Rawlings [1992: 12]). From the constrained court viewpoint, the famous Brown case did not, however, constitute a landmark case for its ability to produce change (Staton and Vanberg [2008: 504]), i.e. the case itself did not generate change. When US southern states rejected the desegregation doctrine that the Supreme Court set forth in Brown, then-president Eisenhower and the rest of the country reacted at first with indifference (Conant [2002: 221]). The continued resistance from the southern states pushed political reaction and mobilized the civil rights movement. Social mobilization—not the Supreme Court's ruling in Brown—led to broader civil rights reforms (Conant [2002: 229]). Along this line, Rosenberg criticizes the dynamic court view for overstating the effectiveness of courts as catalysts for change. By assuming that courts are effective instruments of change, the focus of analysis is reduced to court actions in their own light. As noted by McCann, it 'is not surprising that scholars who focus on courts and make them the center of attention tend to conclude that courts and judicial initiative matter' (McCann [2009: 838]). The constrained court view thus invites us to examine the limitations and constraints sited beyond the courtroom, in which politics are a main factor explaining the constraints on judicial power:

> American courts are not all-powerful institutions. They were designed with severe limitations and placed in a political system of divided powers. To ask them to produce significant social reforms is to forget their history and ignore their constraints. It is to cloud our vision with a naive and romantic belief in the triumph of rights over politics. (Rosenberg [2008: 429])

Law depends on politics to execute its decisions. Politics can overturn court rulings if rulings counteract political preferences and the courts, and judges are well aware of the threat of override, which causes them to consider politics when ruling (Bailey and Maltzman [2011]; Fisher [1988]; Hirschl [2009b]; Miller [2009]). The constrained court view refuses to see the judicialization of politics as a global trend. Instead, this view finds that social and political impact is generally very conditioned. International courts' effectiveness depends on whether court rulings are consistent with the preferences of governments (Carrubba and Gabel [2015: 191ff.]). A court ruling against such preferences will be ineffectual. Domestic courts face similar problems of effectiveness (Miller [2009]; Vanberg [2005]). Domestic courts lack executive means and therefore depend on the national executive to implement their rulings (Staton and Moore [2011: 560–1]). In the relation between courts and congresses, the latter remain powerful and able to override or quell unwanted judicial rulings (Fisher [1988]; Miller [2009]).

Taken in a European context, the constrained court view suggests that the broader influence of the CJEU depends on a large set of institutions, actors, and mechanisms outside the courtroom. Foremost, it depends on politics. The CJEU is likely to face more constraints than its cross-Atlantic counterpart. The CJEU operates in a system in which the use of judicial review varies between member states (Wind et al. [2009]). The CJEU faces a quasi-federal system in which national interests and national institutional legacies are considerable (Kagan [2008]). Furthermore, it does not enjoy the popular support that the US Supreme Court does, and it therefore does not enjoy the same legitimacy in its relevant population and constituencies as its US counterpart (Conant [2002: 218]). Nevertheless, the European Court has had the ability to transform the legal order of the community (Alter [1998]). It is regarded as the 'supreme' or 'constitutional' court of the European Union (Stone Sweet [1995: 287]; Weiler [1991: 2428]) and the most powerful and influential existing international court (Alter [2009: 3]). It has been concluded to be the most legitimate supranational institution in the EU (Caporaso and Tarrow [2009: 615]). It has also been argued that the EU and the US political systems resemble one another because of the fragmented nature of each, which makes political institutions in both systems ill-equipped to contest legalism (Kelemen [2008: 35]; [2011]). The relationship between law and politics in the EU is thus likely to share important characteristics with the same relationship in the US. Furthermore, as the CJEU stands out as the most powerful court among its international counterparts, its influence on politics can cast a more general light on the ability of other international courts to develop similar experiences. If the CJEU is successful in influencing policy outputs, other international courts may follow suit. If it is unsuccessful despite being comparatively powerful, other international courts are likely to face even greater obstacles.

In a similar vein, scholars studying the relationship between law and politics in the EU disagree about the degree of power wielded by the CJEU and its ability to generate change.

The Dynamic Court View on EU Integration

The dynamic court view has become highly influential in studies of European integration. American scholars first noted the decisive role of the European Court, using neo-functional logic to argue that case law causes political integration and that it is incorporated into political decisions. The dynamic court view of European integration finds the Court to be a significant producer of change that has irrevocably transformed the European community (Burley and Mattli [1993]; Mattli and Slaughter [1995]; Stein [1981]; Stone Sweet [2004, 2010]; Stone Sweet and Brunell [1998]; Weiler [1991]).[3]

The work of Stone Sweet and co-authors presents a causal relationship between law and politics and finds a self-sustaining dynamic with the European Court as a key actor:

> Once fixed in a given domain, European rules—such as the relevant Treaty provisions, secondary legislation, and the European Court of Justice's (ECJ) case-law generate a self-sustaining dynamic that leads to a gradual deepening of integration in that sector and, not uncommonly, to spill-overs into other sectors. (Sandholtz and Stone Sweet [1998: 4–5])

The forward move towards integration occurs in a process of mutually constitutive stages in which transnational activity as the first stage leads to subsequent stages of rule creation and expansion. Judicial decisions cause political integration, and they will be incorporated into political decisions (Burley and Mattli [1993]; Mattli and Slaughter [1995]; Stone Sweet [2004, 2010]; Stone Sweet and Brunell [1998, 2012]). The integration dynamic is presented using a stage model that suggests a clear causal link among the following phases: (1) interaction or contracting between social actors creates a social demand for third-party dispute resolution, i.e. litigation; (2) dispute resolutions will push for legislation; and (3) such legislation will stimulate more contracting and interactions and more dispute resolution and legislation (Cichowski [2007: 21]; Stone Sweet [2000: 194–203; 2004, 2010]; Stone Sweet and Brunell [1998]). The causal link between dispute resolution and legislation concerns how legal decisions influence policy outputs. According to Stone Sweet, a 'judicialisation of politics' has gained traction in the European Union (Stone Sweet [2010: 7]). In his view, the 'judicialisation of politics'

> concerns how judicial lawmaking—defined as the law produced by a judge through normative interpretation, reason-giving, and the application of legal norms to facts

[3] As part of his work on the transformation of Europe, Weiler also hypothesizes a supranational, intergovernmental equilibrium in which politics may increasingly oppose Court activism, possibly leading to politics restraining law (Weiler [1991, 1994]. Weiler's supranational–intergovernmental equilibrium will be discussed further below.

in the course of resolving disputes—influences the strategic behavior of non-judicial agents of governance. (Stone Sweet [2010: 7])

A causal logic or 'virtuous circle' defines the relationship between judicial decisions and politics; in this relationship, CJEU rulings are followed by a legislative process that codifies how the Court ruled. Political decision making has become judicialized, which means that non-judicial actors are guided by court-developed rules. Judicialization creates a new type of legislative politics in which legislators

routinely take decisions that they would not have taken in the absence of review, and governing majorities anticipate likely decisions of the court and constrain their behavior accordingly. (Stone Sweet [2000: 202])

The causal assumptions in the stage model are clearly presented: transnational activity causes Court rulings, Court rulings push for more supranational legislative rules, more supranational legislation causes more transnational activity and more judicial references in an increasing number of domains (Stone Sweet and Brunell [1998: 66–7]). The progressive narrative is strong. Together, the three factors—transnational activity, judicial activity, and the production of European legislation—evolve interdependently and drive European integration in a predictable direction, i.e. towards more integration. The causal dynamic is inherently expansive, and further institutionalization and spill-overs between policy areas is the dominant logic (Stone Sweet [2010: 18]).

Governments and parliaments have their work structured 'by an ever-expanding web of constitutional constraints' that has judicialized European policy making (Stone Sweet [2000: 1]). The EU suffers from a fragmented institutional structure both vertically between the EU and its member states and horizontally between the institutions at the EU level (Kelemen [2011: 8]). Owing to the fragmented power structure of the EU, the CJEU is shielded from political sanctions, and this power 'emboldens it to make expansive interpretations of EU rights, to stand up to laggard member states and *to play an active role in the policy process more generally*' (Kelemen [2008: 35], emphasis added). Political fragmentation in the EU has increased judicial power:

Divisions between the Council, the Parliament, and the Commission make it difficult for these political branches to act in concert to rein in the ECJ. The European Court of Justice can take an assertive stance in expanding the scope of EU law and enforcing EU law against noncompliant member states, with little fear of political backlash. (Kelemen [2011: 27])

The process of judicialization is set forth as an onward and irreversible move. According to the theory of judicialization, politics is inexorably placed in the 'shadow' of constitutional review, and this 'shadow' can be expected to lengthen over time to cover policy areas in which interaction between the constitutional court and the legislative branch is most intense (Stone Sweet [2000: 202]). Parliamentary sovereignty, understood as majoritarian rule, has lost 'its grip' and has been 'steadily undermined' by the counter-ideology of modern constitutionalism (Stone Sweet [2000: 196]). Judicial activity conditions politics, rather than the other way around.

> ... Governments and parliaments have developed new practices designed to accommodate the constitutional law, as it is progressively elaborated by the court. Judicialisation provokes the emergence and institutionalisation of a new kind of legislative politics. (Stone Sweet [2000: 202–3])

Politicians must generally act consistently within the dictates of the case law and employ the same modes of reasoning as those laid down by constitutional courts (Stone Sweet [2000: 74]). The dynamic court view as applied to the EU polity regards the CJEU as the most important driver of integration, with fundamental implications for politics. This position, however, is juxtaposed with the 'constrained' view of the CJEU's power and impact.

The Constrained Court View on EU Integration

Other EU scholars emphasize the power of politics and question the court-driven logic of integration. According to this group of scholars, power remains under member states' control, and judicial decisions have no or only modest impact on politics when contradicting political preferences. Member states ultimately control the Court, the Court does not have the autonomy to rule against the more powerful states, and the Court must generally bend to the interests of these states (Garrett [1992: 537, 552]). In a set of articles written in the 1990s, Geoffrey Garrett and co-writers argue that the course of integration has not escaped national control but continues to unfold in accordance with an intergovernmental logic. Member states possess instruments to alter or limit the role of the Court. An unwanted course of legal integration may sometimes require a constitutional amendment in which the Court interprets the Treaty. Typically, however, the Court interprets secondary legislation, which can be corrected by altering the relevant statute

(Carrubba et al. [2008: 438; 2012]; Garrett and Weingast [1993: 201]). Thus ultimately the political power of the Court depends on 'the tolerance of the countervailing powers' (Garrett et al. [1998: 149]).

The Court has a self-interest in taking political preferences into account because its legitimacy is closely linked with member states' willingness to comply with its rulings. Therefore, the constrained court view argues that international courts are sensitive to political positions and reactions. The reasoning of the Court becomes contextual rather than independent and autonomous. The power of the Court is constrained by the preferences of strong member states in particular (Garrett [1992, 1995]; Garrett and Weingast [1993]; Garrett et al. [1998]). Courts are strategic actors because they wish to maintain their legitimacy. If member states 'defy or ignore the judgments of a supranational court, they undermine the court's status as the authoritative voice of the law and resolver of disputes' (Kelemen [2001: 624]). Kelemen has developed two hypotheses on the limits of judicial power (Kelemen [2001]). (1) The more likely politics are to defy a controversial ruling, the more likely the court is to take political preferences into account. However, the political assertiveness of a court also depends on legal certainty. (2) Thus, if precedents have been established with respect to a given subject matter and if legal interpretations have been fine-tuned over time, the Court is less likely to take political preferences into account.

Whether supranational courts take politics into account thus depends on, first, the likelihood of political disobedience and, second, the degree of legal certainty; both of these factors condition court behaviour. The first hypothesis highlights the importance of political reactions to judicial rulings. It assumes that politics do not automatically accept litigation but respond to legal integration. If judicial interpretations overstep what member governments can accept, politicians will ultimately overturn or evade the legal decision in a 'legal politics game' (Garrett et al. [1998: 152–4]). The second hypothesis states that political obedience is a matter of how clear and well-developed the course of legal integration is. Vague rulings are open to political discretion (Staton and Vanberg [2008]). The greater the degree of legal clarity, the more likely member states are to respond to jurisprudence (Garrett et al. [1998: 158]; Kelemen [2001: 625]). When a CJEU legal precedent has had time to mature and has developed consistently in the same direction, the legal clarity of jurisprudence increases, and it will be more difficult for member states to ignore it.

According to the constrained court view, EU member states have the power to change treaties and to adopt secondary legislation, which constitute the political means to override unwanted CJEU case law (Carrubba et al. [2008: 438]). Member states are not regarded as powerless in the 'legal-politics' game. Overturning or defying a legal decision means refusing its general impact and damages the legitimacy and authority of the Court; therefore, the judiciary wants to avoid such political reactions. The threat of legislative override restrains Court behaviour (Carrubba and Gabel [2015]; Carrubba et al. [2008, 2012]; Larsson and Naurin [2016]). Thus, contrary to the dynamic court view, the judiciary is responsive to politics.

A Taxonomy of Judicial Influence on Policy Outputs

Both the dynamic and the constrained court views shed light on the relationship between law and politics in the European Union, albeit with different conclusions. Two different types of political response to legal integration can be derived from the ongoing dispute between these views. The dynamic court view envisions EU legislators as receptive to the jurisprudence of the Court and willing to adopt judicial decisions into legislation. That legal integration will lead to political integration is a key causal assumption in the stage model presented above, according to which dispute resolutions will push for legislation (Cichowski [2007: 21]; Stone Sweet [2000: 194–203]). Politics will thus respond by *codifying* judicial decisions in subsequent legislation.

The constrained court view, on the other hand, suggests that when the course of legal integration goes against political preferences, politics will override judicial decisions. Member states, even in constitutional matters, may manage to respond to the Court and to overturn the Court's ruling. This capacity is demonstrated by the Barber protocol attached to the Maastricht Treaty in 1992, which restricted the impact of the Court's ruling in the Barber case concerning the early payment of retirement pensions.[4] According to Wincott, the protocol 'amounted to a manipulation of the judicial process by politicians—a clear indication that the Community legislators are prepared to restrict the judicial independence of the Court' (Wincott [2001: 191]). While *overriding* the Court by means of such a Treaty amendment is very difficult, politics may also steer legal integration by means of secondary legislation.

[4] Case C–262/88 Douglas Harvey *Barber* v Guardian Royal Exchange Assurance Group *GRE* [1990] ECR I–01889.

Although an override by secondary legislation does not overturn judicial interpretations in constitutional terms, it can still be a powerful correction of the course of legal integration, as the Court typically interprets secondary legislation, which can be responded to with a simple statute (Carrubba et al. [2008]; Garrett and Weingast [1993]).[5]

However, the EU legislator might not respond to jurisprudence simply by either codification or override. Judicial influence on policy output might be conditioned by more diverse types of response. To enable an analysis that captures how judicial influence on policy outputs may vary, a taxonomy of judicial influence has been constructed.[6] This taxonomy serves to classify different political responses that produce different outputs, i.e. different degrees of judicial influence. The taxonomy of judicial influence sets out four types of political response, leading to four different implications for and degrees of judicial influence: codification, modification, non-adoption, and override. The first two responses, *codification* and *override*, are derived from the existing scholarly debate. The second two responses, *modification* and *non-adoption*, are added to enable me to capture more diverse types of response should they occur. Politics may respond to a new status quo generated by the Court (SQ_{Court}) by adopting a statute that modifies the principles or reasoning generated by the Court. Through this response, the impact of jurisprudence is modified. A modification implies that parts of the Court's reasoning are incorporated in subsequent EU decision making and simultaneously restrained. Thus, *modification* implies that the acceptance of the Court-generated principle is only partial. Court interpretations are 'ruled in' but not fully 'overridden' or 'codified'. Politics may also respond with *non-adoption*. Politicians respond with non-adoption when legislators are unable to respond collectively to legal integration because no sufficient majority can be established to codify, modify, or override judicial decisions. Non-adoption constitutes legislative gridlock, producing a

[5] It has been argued that, de facto, politics are unable to override the Court because many Court rulings are based on the Treaty, and an override would thus require a Treaty amendment (Davies [2014]). However, in the political science discussion on the relationship between law and politics, 'override' is defined more broadly, including when secondary legislation corrects legal integration.

[6] For examples of the use of taxonomies that consider the classification of different forms and degrees, see, for example, Barnett and Duvall's taxonomy of power (Barnett and Duvall [2005]) and Radaelli's taxonomy of the different degrees of Europeanization (Radaelli [2003: 34–6]). Lisa Conant's work on the implementation of CJEU case law uses a typology with six types of national response, which explains the 'variable reach of the law' (Conant [2002: 15ff.]).

Table 2.1 A Taxonomy of Judicial Influence on EU Policy Outputs

Type of political response	Judicial influence on policy output
Codification	SQ_{Court} is incorporated in the EU policy output. SQ_{reg}^2 equals SQ_{Court}. Strongest type of judicial influence on policy outputs.
Modification	SQ_{Court} is ruled in by the EU policy output. SQ_{reg}^2 modifies SQ_{Court}. The impact of judicial decisions is reduced. Weaker form of judicial influence on policy outputs.
Non-adoption	No political agreement, i.e. no SQ_{reg}^2 on how to respond to SQ_{Court}, is adopted. No sufficient majority can be established on how to respond to judicial decisions. Legal uncertainty and suboptimality result.
Override	SQ_{Court} is overturned by the EU policy output SQ_{reg}^2. No judicial influence on policy outputs.

stalemate between the EU legislators in which no legislation is adopted (Binder [1999]). Non-adoption implies a political deadlock, resulting in a non-decision. In the wake of a non-adoption, legal uncertainty arises.

The four types of political response set out in the taxonomy of judicial influence , and the different implications for and degrees of judicial influence that they lead to, are set out in Table 2.1 above. The different political responses will be traced in the empirical analysis of the following chapters.

The Judicial Transformation of Europe

The important role of the CJEU in building up the European Community and constitutionalizing the European legal order is generally acknowledged. Scholars of European integration appear to agree on the overall conclusion that the Court has managed to further integration, albeit disagreeing on the extent to which and under which conditions it has done so (Alter [1998: 121]; Burley and Mattli [1993]; Carrubba et al. [2012]; Garrett et al. [1998: 149];

Moravcsik [1993: 513]; Pollack [2003]; Stone Sweet and Brunell [2012]; Wind [2001]). The Treaty's article 267 TFEU and article 258 TFEU represent the most important means to legally further integration.

Article 267 TFEU constitutes the preliminary reference procedure whereby national courts can send preliminary references to the CJEU to obtain its interpretations of EU law (Stone Sweet and Brunell [2012: 206]). Article 267 authorizes the Court to give preliminary rulings on the interpretation of the Treaty, on secondary legislation, and on the relation between Community law and national law (Craig and De Búrca [1998: 406–7]). Through article 267, the relationship between the Community and national legal systems has been defined. The article on preliminary ruling has enabled private individuals to challenge the compatibility of national law with Community law. Whereas lower national courts *can* refer a question on the interpretation of Community law to the CJEU, national courts of last resort *are obliged to do so* in certain contexts.

Furthermore, the CJEU can be requested by the Commission to judge whether a member state fulfils its Treaty obligations. Article 258 TFEU authorizes the Commission to initiate infringement proceedings against any of the member states and ultimately gives the Court the final word in determining whether the member state has complied (Tallberg [2002]). The powers assigned to the Court by means of articles 267 and 258 are the most important means of judicial integration.

In part, the power ascribed by scholars to the CJEU is historically deduced. When the member states signed the Treaty of Rome and thereby adopted article 177 (now article 267 TFEU) on preliminary ruling, their intention was neither to give individuals the opportunity to sue their own governments nor to declare the supremacy of Community law. The case law of the Court itself established the doctrines of direct effect and supremacy, and thereby, in the words of Weiler, initiated the transformation of Europe and transformed the relationship between the Community and its member states (Weiler [1991]).

The Court's ruling in the van Gend case of 1963 gave Community law direct effect.[7] The doctrine of direct effect means that certain provisions confer direct rights on individuals and equally impose obligations on national authorities, without these necessarily having been implemented by national

[7] Case 26/62, NV Algemene Transport- en Expeditie Onderneming van Gend & Loos v Netherlands Inland Revenue *Administration* [1963] ECR 1.

law.[8] With the principle of direct effect, individuals became subjects of Community law. The establishment of direct effect thus made Community law different from traditional international law, as the latter's only subjects are states. By conferring direct rights on individuals, laws adopted in Brussels became directly enforceable as if they had been adopted by national parliaments (Weiler [1994: 513]; Wind [2001: 138]).

The legal doctrine of direct effect gave private litigants a supranational opportunity to challenge national policies. The later doctrine of supremacy established by the Costa case in 1964 reinforced this possibility.[9] While federal constitutions normally specify that in the case of conflict, federal law is supreme to the law of lower states, the Treaty did not define the relation between Community law and national law (Rasmussen [1998: 263]). In the Costa case, the Court laid down that if national law conflicts with Community law, the latter is supreme.[10] The doctrine made European law superior to subsequent changes to national law, meaning in principle that member states cannot adopt policies that contradict their Community obligations (Alter [2001: 17]). In the Costa case, the Court concluded that, by being part of the

[8] In the conclusions of van Gend, the Court stated:

> The European Economic Community constitutes *a new legal order of international law* for the benefit of which the states have *limited their sovereign rights*, albeit within limited fields, and the subjects of which comprise *not only the member states but also their nationals*. Independently of the legislation of the member states, community law not only imposes obligations on individuals but is also intended to confer upon them rights which become part of *their legal heritage*. These rights arise not only where they are expressly granted by the Treaty but also by reasons of obligations which the Treaty imposes in a clearly defined way upon individuals as well as upon the member states and upon the institutions of the Community (emphasis added).

[9] Case 6/64 Flaminio *Costa* v E.N.E.L. [1964] ECR 585.

[10] In the conclusions of Costa, the Court stated:

> The integration into the laws of each member state of provisions which derive from the Community and more generally the terms and the spirit of the Treaty, make it impossible for the states, as a corollary, to accord precedence to a unilateral and subsequent measure over the legal system accepted by them on the basis of reciprocity. Such a measure cannot therefore be inconsistent with that legal system. The law stemming from the Treaty, an independent source of law, could not because of its special and original nature, be overridden by domestic legal provisions, however framed, without being deprived of its character as Community law and without the legal basis of the Community itself being called into question. *The transfer by the states from their domestic legal system to the Community legal system of the rights and obligations arising under the Treaty carries with it a permanent limitation of their sovereign rights* (emphasis added).

Community legal system, the member states had permanently limited their sovereign rights.

Whereas the Treaty nowhere stated the principles of direct effect and supremacy, the legal reasoning of the Court brought about this conclusion. The European Court thereby transformed the preliminary ruling system and the Community legal order from a system in which individuals could question Community law to a system allowing them to question national law in national courts (Alter [1998: 126]; Alter and Vargas [2000: 456]). The Court's early legal actions integrated the national and supranational legal systems (Stone Sweet and Brunell [1998: 65–6]). By allying itself with the citizens of the member states, granting them direct rights beyond their own states, the Court made sure that individuals would take a private interest in monitoring state compliance with supranational law. By allying itself with national courts, the Court ensured a decentralized mechanism for enforcing Community law. The transformation of the Community's legal system thus improved the effectiveness of European law. The questions how far and under which conditions it did so, however, remain.

Conditions of Judicial Influence

From this early jurisprudence, the Court embarked on its reputation as independent and effective in promoting integration. The Court's reasoning and methodology has been described as teleological or purposive, where law is interpreted in the service of an objective. That is, the goal is the motor of law (Alter [2001: 20]; Craig and De Búrca [1998: 89]). This notion has been described as the application of a method of 'gap filling', where the line of a legal principle is gradually drawn and extended to new situations using, for example, the proportionality test to examine whether the objectives of national restrictions are proportional to Community goals (Martinsen [2011]). The gradual establishment of a legal principle means establishing a precedent where the content or conclusive parts of a former case are applied to a subsequent case.

Teleological interpretations of Community law and a creative case-by-case establishment of precedent support a proactive and independent position by the Court of Justice. However, legal scholars have also noted that this form of judicial activism, in which the Court moves forward European integration, may not be all that general:

> The Court has at times been reactive, at times proactive, and at times a mixture of both. In other words, the Court has not pursued a project of integration growing

> more or less 'activist' all the time. At times it appears cautious in one area of law and ambitious in another, responding perhaps to external events and to the position of the member states or other institutions. (Craig and De Búrca [1998: 78–9])

The position of the Court is here presented as ambiguous and complex. This quotation rejects the idea of the Court as being generally proactive and instead suggests a Court that acts contextually and that is capable of both moving integration forwards and showing political caution. This mixed behaviour of the Court calls for a further exploration of the conditions of judicial influence, particularly influence on the relationship between judicial decisions and political responses (De Búrca [2005: 323]).

As a particular consequence of (1) the fragmented character of EU politics, in which the diffusion of legislative power shields the CJEU from political sanctions, and/or (2) the shorter time horizon of politicians, who focus on electoral cycles and short-term outcomes rather than long-term judicial consequences, legislative politics tends to be rejected as a factor conditioning judicial influence. Judges and politicians have different time horizons, which largely insulates the CJEU from political responses:

> Because of these different time horizons, the ECJ was able to be doctrinally activist, building legal doctrine based on unconventional legal interpretations and expanding its own authority, without provoking a political response. Politicians have shorter time horizons because they must deliver the goods to the electorate in order to stay in office. The focus on staying in office makes politicians discount the long-term effects of their actions or, in this case, inaction. (Alter [1998: 130])

Judicial Influence as Contingent and Disordered

The taxonomy presented in Table 2.1 above allows for variation in judicial influence caused by different types of political response. It thus brings the political component into focus. From different disciplines of law, history, and political science, scholars have suggested the need for further exploration of what might condition judicial influence. Wincott argues that the Court's role in making substantive policies is frequently overstated (Wincott [2001: 192]). The Court is one actor among many in the EU policy process; moreover, its influence is 'conditional and contingent' (Wincott [2001: 180–1]) and depends on the way in which a larger set of forces may align to overcome member states' resistance. Historians have recently called for a 'new history of EU law' and have posited that, from Stein's seminal work onwards (Stein [1981]; Rasmussen [2013: 1195]), our understanding of the historical role of the European Court has relied too firmly on a core narrative of progressive and successful constitutionalization grounded in the constitutional paradigm. Informed by this narrative, scholars have come to rely on an unproven assumption that member states have progressively accepted European public law and that a firmly established European rule of law existed by the early 1990s (Rasmussen [2013: 1211]). However, more recent historical research by Rasmussen and colleagues investigates the period between the 1960s and the 1980s and notes that national administrations and national courts sidestepped or ignored European law at crucial moments:

> ...the classical historical narrative of the constitutional paradigm needs to be replaced with a new history of European public law. A history that reveals the deeper legal, social, and political nature of the constitutional practice and a history that does not assume that member states progressively accepted the constitutional practice and a European rule of law. (Rasmussen [2013: 1218])

In a debate with scholars of this new history of European law, Pollack notes that member states have indeed clipped the wings of the Court at important historical moments of primary law by such practices as limiting private parties' access to the Court in the Treaty of Rome and restricting, in the Maastricht Treaty, the Court's jurisdiction over the two new pillars of Justice and Home Affairs and Common Foreign and Security Policy (Pollack [2013: 1289]). Rasmussen and co-writers note that we must not only recognize how politics responded during those important political events but also develop systematic and comparative analyses of how national courts and administrations generally apply European law (Rasmussen [2013: 1220–1]). The new history of European law thus invites us to pay more careful attention to 'the deeper legal, social, and political' conditions of Court influence and how it has been contested over time (Rasmussen [2013: 1218]).

Other scholars have added the need to examine the more contemporary interplay between judicial and legislative politics. Genschel's research on corporate taxation notes that, despite decades of intrusive CJEU jurisprudence and Commission pressure to formulate a legislative response, the Council has refused to do this. Instead, the Court has softened its approach and accommodated its rulings towards political positions (Genschel [2011: 60–1]; Genschel et al. [2011: 598–600]). Bonjour and Vink's examination of the Europeanization of migration policies looks into the *ex post* judicial and political reactions to the family reunification directive (Bonjour and Vink [2013]).[11] Applying this book's analytical framework for examining judicial influence, the dynamic between law and politics unfolded as the family reunification directive was adopted in 2003, and a $SQ_{reg}{}^{1}$ was thereby established. This $SQ_{reg}{}^{1}$ was later challenged by expansive judicial interpretations, SQ_{Court}, which constituted an unwelcome course of legal integration for some member states. The judicial Europeanization process, however, was not simply accepted politically, but 'backfired'. The Dutch government became increasingly interested in opting out of EU migration policies, and member states collectively demanded that the Commission come up with a proposal modifying the impact of jurisprudence (Bonjour and Vink [2013: 403–4]).

Other scholars find the Court's influence on EU policies to be anything but automatic or forward-moving. Instead of developing along clear causal logic, as suggested by the stage model of neo-functionalism, Nowak finds that the relationship between law and politics instead resembles a garbage can, being piecemeal and disorganized as a process (Nowak [2010]). He posits that the political impact of Court rulings is conditional and highly disordered, and he criticizes the neo-functional understanding of a 'judicialisation of politics' as depicting 'order and causality where there is none' (Nowak [2010: 754]). In contrast, the garbage can approach depicts the relationship between law and politics as chaotic and steered by chance and coincidence instead of by strategies or logic. The timing and interpretation of judicial decisions are important with regard to whether a ruling is discovered to solve a problem and brought into the political process (Nowak [2010: 759]). Rulings of the Court may be influential, but not necessarily as a given or in a predetermined way.

The call to develop a 'more subtle, nuanced and temporally sensitive analytical framework' to understand and explain the ways in which judicial decisions take political effect remains highly relevant (De Búrca [2005: 323]). Below, I present four factors, likely to condition judicial influence on legislative politics and outputs: time as an explanatory factor, decision-making rules, the role of the Commission, and the positions of political actors. For each factor, expectations are formulated about the conditions under which judicial decisions influence EU policy outputs.

[11] *Council Directive 2003/86/EC* of 22 September 2003 on the right to family reunification.

Increases in Political Voice over Time

The work of Joseph Weiler is primarily known for its seminal understanding of the constitutionalization of the EU legal order and of the 'silent revolution'. A transformative process made EU law both 'the law of the land' and 'the higher law of the land', i.e. when doctrines established direct effect and supremacy (Weiler [1991, 1994, 1999]). However, Weiler's early work also hypothesizes that judicial integration is not necessarily a forward move (Weiler [1991, 1994]). In his original work, Weiler hypothesises that the 'quiet revolution' of law might over time be met by the loud voices of politics (Weiler [1991: 2408]). Drawing on Hirschman (Hirschman [1970]), Weiler presents the categories 'exit' and 'voice' as the two ways in which member states might respond to the unsatisfactory performance of the Community they created. Exit means leaving the organization, and it has been considered unlikely.[12] Alternatively, voice is the mechanism of correction and recuperation, representing the 'messy world of politics' (Weiler [1991: 2411]; see also Ginsburg [2014: 491–3], on the mechanism of 'voice'). When the possibility of exit is foreclosed, the importance of voice increases. Weiler presents a hypothesis of a supranational-intergovernmental equilibrium. The hypothesis posits that the harder and more binding EU law becomes, the more we should expect member states to respond to it, i.e. voicing against mal-performance. Thus, as the fog clears around the binding and substantive effect of European law and the Court's interpretation of it, we should expect politicians to respond and eventually correct EU law. The hypothesis posits the relationship between law and politics as follows:

> The 'harder' the law in terms of its binding effect both on and within states, the less willing states are to give up their prerogative to control the emergence of such law or the law's 'opposability' to them. When the international law is 'real', when it is 'hard' in the sense of being binding not only on but also in states, and when there are effective legal remedies to enforce it, decision making suddenly becomes important, indeed crucial. (Weiler [1991: 2426])

[12] The likelihood of using the exit option, however, increased in 2014, when the British Conservative David Cameron promised to hold a referendum on the UK's membership of the European Union if re-elected as prime minister (*The Guardian*, 'David Cameron: in-out referendum on EU by 2017 is cast-iron pledge', 11 May 2014).

According to Weiler's hypothesis, we should indeed expect member states to respond when they find that the CJEU 'mal-performs'. An 'increase in voice' is the natural reaction to hardened law (Weiler [1991: 2427]). After a long, continuous period in which the European Community was legally transformed in silence, the Single European Act marked a turning point. The unanimity rule prior to the Single European Act had established a supranational-intergovernmental equilibrium in which member states felt that they were in control because they maintained veto rights. This equilibrium was disturbed by the introduction of qualified majority voting (QMV) (Weiler [1991: 2453ff.]). According to Weiler, the turn to QMV constituted a dramatic change in the relationship between law and politics in the Community. With QMV, the 'honeymoon' was over and the supranational-intergovernmental equilibrium broken (Weiler [1994: 532]). The CJEU has entered a different epoch in which fierce reactions from its interlocutors should be expected. After 'the quiet revolution', we should expect political responses to the increased public visibility of Community law. The social and politically sensitive reach of Community law is ever-widening (Weiler [1994: 532]). In 1994, Weiler also noted that it was not the Court that had become more confrontational and more politicizing. Instead, the conditions of politics had changed. According to Weiler, changing the decision rule constituted one explaining factor; the other was the increased heterogeneity of Community members because of many more member states had joined (Weiler [1991: 2456]). On the dramatic change in the relationship between the Court and member states in the early 1990s, Weiler notes:

> [m]y argument is that it is not the Court that has taken some bold new step against which Mr. Kohl was reacting.[13] The Court has been on an even keel. It is the conditions of acceptance that have been changing. (Weiler [1994: 533])

More than twenty years have passed since Weiler first presented his hypothesis of a broken supranational-intergovernmental equilibrium. Since then, the conditions of politics have taken other decisive turns. The logic of Weiler's argument remains highly important, so that, twenty years after it was formulated, we should expect a political response and correction to be even more

[13] Weiler refers to the former German Chancellor's fierce reaction against the European court in October 1992, expressing his views as follows: 'If one takes the Court of Justice ... it does not only exert its competencies in legal matters, but goes far further. We have an example of something that was not wanted in the beginning' (Kohl as quoted in Weiler [1994: 533].

likely.[14] Decision-making rules have changed again to count the European Parliament more and more as a veto actor that further conditions the power of individual member states. Furthermore, socio-economic heterogeneity has increased considerably in an EU of twenty-eight member states (Höpner and Schäfer [2012: 436–8]). In sum, Weiler's early work suggests that, over time, EU legislators have learned their lesson and realised the binding character of EU law; meanwhile, member states have lost their power to overturn this law by veto. Member states should therefore be less willing to accept judicial decisions and use their voices more forcefully against them.

The expectation derived from Weiler's early work and hypothesis is that *over time, EU legislators will be less willing to codify the case law of the Court in EU policy outputs.*

Rules of Decision Making

In Weiler's words, we must unfold the 'messy world of politics' to explain when judicial decisions are likely—or unlikely—to generate political change (Weiler [1991: 2411]). In the daily decision-making processes of the EU, the EU legislatures to be taken into account are the European Commission, the Council of the European Union, and the European Parliament. Together these constitute EU legislative politics, each with a formal role to play in the decision-making process. These collective institutions of EU politics contain multiple actors with their own perspectives and positions who are obliged to interact with one another, according to the rules of the game. The decision-making rules set the frame for institutional and political interactions. These rules define the thresholds to be crossed before responding to the case law of the Court.

If the CJEU interprets primary law, i.e. treaties of the European Union, such interpretations can only be overturned by a unanimous decision of all member states in an intergovernmental conference, which subsequently must be ratified at the national level. The likelihood of EU politics overturning Court decisions increases with the Court's interpretation of secondary legislation. Judicial decisions interpreting a regulation or a directive can be

[14] Stone Sweet notes that Weiler's hypothesis on the supranational-intergovernmental equilibrium has never been rigorously tested but has been implicitly rejected by himself, Burley and Mattli, and Cichowski, i.e. scholars with a dynamic court view (Stone Sweet [2010: 20]).

overturned by a statute, which generally must be decided by a qualified voting majority in the Council and by a majority in the European Parliament. In this institutional setting, the likelihood of legislative override depends on (a) the number of veto points and (b) the ability of political actors to act in a sufficiently unified manner to mobilize such a veto point (Cooter and Ginsburg [1996]; Pollack [2003]). As the European Parliament increasingly acts as a co-legislator, a legislative overturn of a Court's ruling is confronted with three veto points: (1) the Commission must first present a proposal to override a judicial decision, (2) the Council must adopt a common position that overturns the Court's decision, and (3) the European Parliament must also adopt this overturning legislation. As noted by Pollack, the voting rules of the European Union raise the institutional thresholds even further. A qualified majority voting in the Council requires a supermajority of more than two-thirds of Council votes. In addition, the European Parliament can either approve the Commission's proposal and the common position of the Council by a simple majority, or reject the Council's common position by an absolute majority. In sum, the EU thresholds to correct an unwanted CJEU decision by means of secondary legislation are lower than those of primary law but still 'higher than the thresholds for constitutional amendment in most democratic states', and they are higher than those of 'the proverbial home of judicial activism, the United States' (Pollack [2003: 171]).

Owing to considerable institutional barriers, the judicial discretion of the CJEU is deemed high, which, at first glance, seems to confirm the neo-functional version of the 'judicialisation of politics', in which politics tends to codify what the Court has previously decided. However, for such codification to occur, the same institutional thresholds condition the Court's influence on EU legislation. The same three veto points and the same voting rules apply to CJEU decisions that are to be codified in secondary legislation: (1) the Commission must present a proposal to codify the case law of the Court, (2) the Council's common position must adopt this codification and be able to mobilize a qualified majority among the member states, and (3) the European Parliament must adopt the codification of judicial decision making by a plenary majority. Thus institutional rules do not favour the codification of judicial decision making to the legislative override of judicial decision making. Both outputs face extremely high thresholds or 'consensus hurdles' (Blauberger [2012: 110]). We can thus expect that the high threshold in EU decision-making processes makes both codification and override less likely.

Against this background, I expect that *EU decision-making rules in EU28 make both override and codifications of judicial decisions less likely to occur.*

Institutional Positions: The Role of the Commission

When jurisprudence challenges the established regulatory status quo, the Commission has the first move and decides whether the new SQ_{Court} requires a legislative response. The European Commission functions as both a legislature with the sole responsibility for drafting bills and a bureaucracy with important executive functions (Tsebelis and Garrett [2001: 358]). It thus has a double function but, in its legislative role, it has a crucial function as an agenda-setter. It decides whether to bring judicial decisions into the legislative process. Subsequently, the European Parliament and the Council step into the process as majoritarian decision makers.

As noted by Wincott, the way in which the Commission may make legislative use of case law is thus likely to be decisive (Wincott [2001: 189]). In addition, Nowak points to the entrepreneurial role of the Commission in this regard but applies a garbage can perspective to the relationship between law and politics. The Commission may choose to make a ruling an important driver of change. Thus, judicial decisions can sometimes be used as a medium for change (Nowak [2010: 754]). According to Nowak, the difference in influence depends on the political conditions under which jurisprudence occurred rather than on its legal content or legal certainty. The use of jurisprudence to justify change is not a process that is steerable by the Commission or by one set of actors. The broader impact of Court rulings is not rationally decided, but it has an element of chance and coincidence. Comparing the Dassonville case with the Cassis de Dijon case,[15] Nowak finds that Dassonville had no traceable political impact, while Cassis de Dijon led to the principle of mutual recognition being written into the Single European Act six years after the ruling. In the latter case, the Commission pushed hard for political codification. The Cassis de Dijon ruling was issued five years after the Dassonville ruling, and the political conditions at that later point in time supported the political codification of its principles. The political timing was simply better.

Nowak's finding suggests that the entrepreneurial usage of a ruling and its political timing are central to the broader effect of judicial decisions. The Commission here becomes a key player in 'upgrading' a case or a cluster of

[15] Case 8/74, Procureur du Roi v Benoît and Gustave *Dassonville* [1974] ECR 837. Case 120/78, Rewe-Zentral AG v Bundesmonopolverwaltung für Branntwein [*Cassis de Dijon*] [1979] ECR 649.

cases for codification to have a general impact as binding legislation. The Commission, however, may be much more strategic than Nowak's garbage can interpretation envisions (Schmidt [2000, 2004]). According to Schmidt, the Commission's powers in making policy extend beyond its agenda-setting role; thus, it has the capacity to force member states to adopt proposals that they might have initially opposed (Schmidt [2000]). The Commission can use its role as guardian of the Treaty to coax member states into adopting secondary legislation. In manipulating member states into action, the Commission can use the CJEU as a threat, convincing member states that they are better off adopting legislation than allowing the Court to steer the process by means of judicial policy-making. Political regulation becomes the 'lesser evil' compared to legal integration. Schmidt's findings provide more systematic insight into how the Commission may put pressure on Council negotiations and succeed in influencing these negotiations by acting strategically and pushing member states into action with reference to the Court (Schmidt [2000: 42, 44]). The Commission assumes a crucial monitoring role in decision-making processes by pushing case law forward into Council decision making.

We should thus expect the position of the Commission to be decisive regarding judicial influence (Pollack [2003]; Schmidt [2000]). The Commission constitutes the gatekeeper for jurisprudence to be incorporated into the political process. The Commission is thus the agenda-setter that proposes an appropriate response to legal interpretations. By bringing in the voice of the judiciary, the Commission may acquire a particularly strong position in steering decision making in a specific direction, capitalizing on the legitimacy of the Court (Alter and Meunier-Aitsahalia [1994: 542]). The Commission's institutional position on how to bring the case law forward can be strategic. When acting strategically, its position will serve a particular integrative purpose. However, the institutional position of the Commission can also be role-based, i.e. serving the role of guardian of the Treaty. In a rule-of-law-based system such as the EU, the Commission should have a particularly strong position in steering negotiations when it justifies a proposal based on the 'voice of law' as stated by the Court (Martinsen [2009]; Martinsen and Falkner [2011]). Along this line of reasoning, the Commission's institutional position towards and usage of CJEU jurisprudence becomes crucial. The expectation derived states that *judicial decisions will be adopted in policy outputs as the Commission proposes.*

Political Positions: Disagreements on Legal Integration

Adopting judicial decisions into EU legislation is a process characterized by many steps. Making secondary legislation in the EU tends to be a lengthy process through which political positions are formed and delicate compromises are made. *First*, the Commission must agree internally on how to formulate and present a proposal. To coordinate the positions internally in the Commission, i.e. inside the college of commissioners, the different directorates general, and the various units is difficult in itself, and it is a process through which compromises must be made (Hartlapp et al. [2014]). How this coordination is undertaken and the balances established between different and sometimes contradictory EU objectives can be crucial to the viability of a proposal. *Second*, the Council negotiates a common position on the grounds of unanimity or, increasingly, qualified majority voting among the twenty-eight member states. *Third*, the Council normally must establish an agreement with the European Parliament through the ordinary legislative procedure. However, before an inter-institutional compromise can be reached, the European Parliament, which now numbers 751 members organized into various political groups, must find an internal compromise. A European Parliament rapporteur is assigned to the proposal. He or she drafts a report, and the relevant European Parliament committee must agree on it. The committee votes on amendments, and a final report is published. Against this background, the rapporteur and shadow rapporteurs from the largest political groups in the European Parliament initiate negotiations with the Council. The Council presidency negotiates on behalf of the Council, and the Commission has a seat at the negotiating table, from which it can advise legislators, but it has no competence to decide. If a compromise is found between the representatives from the Council and the European Parliament, Council members and the European Parliament plenary must approve the final text. These processes are normally lengthy and typically involve many changes to the Commission's proposal.

This institutional frame constitutes the political context through which judicial decisions must pass to have legislative impact. Through the many steps of this decision-making process, the crux of the matter becomes political positions for or against the case law of the Court. If judicial decisions invoke the key political conflict lines, disagreements on how to respond to litigation are likely to loom large. The extent to which interaction can diminish political disagreements thus becomes crucial for the ability to form compromises between such different positions.

Recent studies of EU decision-making note that ideological congruence affects the duration of the decision-making process in the EU, i.e. the degree of political contestation, within and between legislative bodies (Klüver and Sagarzazu [2013]). When political institutions have similar positions, proposals are quickly adopted. However, if legislative institutions disagree politically, it will take longer to find common ground, and the adoption of a policy proposal will be protracted or blocked. The durability of a decision-making process tells us something about its political sensitivity. We can thus use decision-making speed as a proxy for the political controversy of a proposal.

For judicial decisions to be overridden by or adopted into political decisions, they must be supported by the Commission and then by a sufficient winning coalition in the Council and European Parliament. Many judicial decisions are not politically neutral; they are likely to serve some interests or ideological convictions more than others. Political actors are likely to understand, argue, and interpret judicial decisions in line with their ideological views and interests. Judicial decisions contain and inform politics. If political actors have divergent positions on how to respond to the case law of the Court, a blocking minority in the Council or a simple majority in the European Parliament can block a common response to the case law of the Court. The institutional and socio-economic conditions of the EU28 differ remarkably from those during past times of European integration. In the current setting of increased socio-economic heterogeneity and new veto players, diverging positions for and against the case law of the Court are likely to arise. Political contestation in response to legal integration is likely to occur in a two-dimensional space (Marks and Steenbergen [2002]):[16] a *left–right dimension* of, for example, EU social rights *versus* liberal free movement principles and a *more integration versus less integration dimension*, i.e. European regulation *versus* subsidiarity. In identifying political positions and contestation, we should be able to capture their dynamic moves. Political positions and the views, interests, and rationality behind them are not necessarily fixed; they may change as a result of their contextual conditions (Grimmel [2012, 2014]).

[16] For a one-dimesional examination of law–politics interaction, see Bailey and Maltzman's examination of US Court–Congress interactions (Bailey and Maltzman [2011]; see in particular chapter 6).

Thus, political positions and contestation may change over time, i.e. between T_1 and T_2.

In sum, bringing political positions and decision making into focus invites us to identify how positions differ in a two-dimensional space and over time. I argue that it is important to try to identify judicial decisions and political positions on these two dimensions as well as over time because only by doing so can we carve out the political substance of Court rulings and understand the way in which politics mobilize as well as the likelihood of establishing a common political response to legal integration, i.e. of establishing sufficient majorities for or against the case law of the Court. I expect that *the more political actors disagree within and between institutions and the more fixed their positions are, the less likely override, modification, and codification become.* The political implications of judicial decisions are crucial in this regard. In addition, it becomes important to examine the ability or willingness of political actors to establish compromises about how to respond to the Court. When sufficient majorities on how to respond cannot be established, non-adoption results, and with it, legal uncertainty, since the discrepancy between SQ_{reg}[1] and SQ_{Court} remains.

Political Positions in Focus

This study thus adds the political content of judicial decisions and the responding political positions as likely important conditions for the broader impact of legal integration. In substance—and especially in the eyes of politicians—judicial decisions are not apolitical in nature. According to McCann, legal conventions have built-in biases and tend to validate certain voices while silencing others (McCann [1994: 305]), which implies that law filters out some meaning while privileging other perspectives. Miller finds that in the interaction between the US federal courts and Congress, court-stripping legislation is principally pushed by social conservatives to assert legislative power over courts, whereas liberals have opposed such actions, instead seeing federal courts as protectors of individual rights (Miller [2009]). In the EU, political attitudes towards legal integration may be more mixed, depending on the political content of litigation. In addition, law may be open to interpretation. The use and meaning of law are likely to depend on how actors interpret it. Not all actors read jurisprudence in the same way. The actors that are the focus in this study are politicians and civil servants, not judges. Sometimes, these actors may behave and treat legal interpretations in rather unorthodox ways. Furthermore, Court decisions may lack clarity and clear rationality, and they may instead be contextually conditioned (Grimmel [2012, 2014]). Judicial interpretations and precedence may change over time. In addition, lawyers may disagree on the meaning and impact of a decision. Thus, jurisprudence informs political struggles, but it may do so in conflicting ways. Law is both an enabling and a constraining force (De Búrca [2005: 319]), but it does not enable or constrain the same set of actors. Different interpretations and uses of judicial decisions might mirror both cognitive and normative orientations as well as different interests.

To study the extent to which and the conditions under which judicial decisions influence EU policy outputs, we need an analytical perspective that disaggregates political institutions into the actors and subgroups they comprise. The analytical framework must take into account the importance of actor behaviour, perceptions, and positions and capture these factors in a policy process that is

> driven by the interaction of individual and corporate actors endowed with certain capabilities and specific cognitive and normative orientations, within a given institutional setting and within a given external situation. (Scharpf [1997: 37])

To analyse how politics responds to law as an institution, I examine how political actors behave in response to judicial decisions. Thus, how they read, interpret, and use the case law from the Court becomes important; of course, who does so is also crucial.

How political actors respond to judicial decisions ties into the debate regarding how far actors are bound by institutions. To what extent does the institution of law determine the action of politicians? Beginning in the 1980s, different versions of new institutionalism have dominated interpretations of the ways in which actors' behaviours are conditioned by and embedded in institutions (March and Olsen [1983]; North [1990]; Pierson [1996]). From the institutionalist perspective, actors are expected to constrain their behaviour in accordance with the dictates of the institution, i.e. jurisprudence, in this case (Stone Sweet [2000: 202]).

To examine this relationship between the institution of law and the behaviour, positions, and interactions of political actors, I combine an actor-centred institutional approach with insights from sociological institutionalism and 'bounded rationality' (March and Olsen [1998]; Scharpf [1997]; Simon [1985]). This combination allows me to understand and explain how actors' behaviour is structured in multi-faceted ways. Rationality is considered to be 'bounded'. Political actors are not irrational (Simon [1985]). We see many examples of rational, strategic usages of the case law of the Court. However, attention spans are limited, and in the wide blend of interests, attitudes, convictions, interpretations, and compromises towards jurisprudence, political responses may tend to be satisfactory rather than optimal (Jones [1999]; Martinsen and Vollaard [2014]).

Political responses to judicial decisions are conditioned not only by the bounded rationality of individual actors but also by institutional rules and the positions, behaviour, and interaction of other political actors. Institutional rules define the framework and guide actors' behaviour, but not in a deterministic sense or by a simplistic causal relationship (Scharpf [1997: 42]; Weiler [1991: 2426]). Political positions are made up not only of actors' preferences but also of their perceptions and interpretations of Court case law. Such positions may be fixed or dynamic. Important here is that the rules of decision making require interaction between political actors. Such interaction might change positions and produce a different policy output than would be the case if positions remained fixed (Scharpf [1997: 46]). The committees, departmental offices, working groups, and trialogues all debate the meaning of law and what should be appropriate responses to it. As Miller notes on US congressional committees' responses to judicial decisions, we cannot regard Congress, an assembly, the European Parliament, or the Council of Ministers as monolithic institutions that have the same response to the law:

> Thus committees' reactions to the courts are a function of both the goals and behaviour of the committee's individual members and the norms or broader political culture of the committee. (Miller [1992: 951])

The work of Miller provides evidence that the impact of federal court decisions depends on the day-to-day interaction between political actors in their institutional context:

> In other words, the impact of court decisions of course involves highly complex interactions with actors outside the judicial system. (Miller [1992: 963])

Thus, the behaviour, interpretations, usages, normative orientations, and preferences of actors as well as their ability to carry these through in a continuous interaction with other political actors should be the centre of the analysis. As a result, responses to the institution of law are formed, which decide whether judicial decisions influence policy outputs.

Analytical Steps

To examine the relationship between the institution of law and the responses of political actors, I *first* examine how the case law of the Court is brought into the political process. At this juncture, the Commission is the gatekeeper that decides whether and in what way it will craft a legislative proposal with reference to the Court. This again depends on how the Commission interprets previous case law. It can use the 'voice of law' as a reference point to justify its proposals and to specify which solutions are consistent with previous Court decisions (Martinsen [2009]; Martinsen and Falkner [2011]). *Second*, I investigate how the political actors respond to the Commission's reasoning. Such responses depend on how the political actors interpret the same Court decision and how they use this decision in political negotiations. In this way, CJEU rulings can become a decisive point of orientation in the legislative process and a 'focal point' upon which to decide the scope, condition, and direction of European politics (Wasserfallen [2010: 1143]). However, using judicial reviews as a reference point in politically salient negotiations is anything but technical or neutral. Instead, this use promotes certain policy ideas and solutions and strengthens the bargaining positions of some political groups and actors (Wasserfallen [2010: 1134]). The 'voice of law' may be used out of conviction as a type of indisputable norm, or it may be used for strategic reasons. In both ways, it can be used to convince other political actors that political options are constrained or restricted by previous judicial decisions. Regardless of whether the law is used out of conviction or for strategic reasons, it is important whether actors interpret and use the law in a similar way. The more open or unclear jurisprudence is to politicians, the more they may disagree on how to respond.

In the case studies to follow, I examine whether such normative and strategic struggles over the interpretation of law occur among actors, as they might not. It may be that politicians tend to regard Court interpretations as authoritative and legitimate and as a last word to which they must bend. On the other hand, different interpretations and usages of judicial decisions would substantiate the view that in the hands of politicians law becomes more plural, pragmatic, and political than a strict legal reading of it might suggest. It might demonstrate a considerable gap between 'law in the books' and 'law as politicized'. In the words of Wincott, politicians 'manipulate', i.e. ignore, restrict, or modify the course of integration as laid down by the Court

(Wincott [2001: 191]). If politicians read the case law of the Court more flexibly, scope would be created in which to negotiate the meaning of law within its constitutional limits. If law is treated with a certain pragmatism, it may enable compromises on how judicial decisions should influence political decision making. What constitutes law-abiding behaviour becomes open to interpretation.

Political Conditions of Judicial Influence

The subsequent chapters will analyse how judicial decisions have influenced EU social policy outputs over time and for the three case studies (working time, patient rights' in cross-border healthcare, and the posting of workers). While the analysis over time takes a broad view of judicial influence, the three case studies examine judicial influence in a post-Lisbon Treaty setting. Most scholarly work on legal and political integration has addressed judicial and legislative interactions before the great enlargement of 2004. However, both the institutional and the socio-economic conditions of European integration have changed fundamentally since 2004. According to Weiler, we should expect the changed institutional and socio-economic reality to have a substantial impact on the relationship between law and politics and to have a stronger political voice as a result (Weiler [1991, 1994]). Consistent with the expectations developed above, I expect modification and non-adoption to be more likely political responses to the Court's case law in EU28 than codification or override. Times have changed since the quiet revolution of the Community legal order.

References

Alter, K. (1998) 'Who are the 'Masters of the Treaty'? European governments and the European Court of Justice', *International Organization* 52(01): 121–47.

Alter, K. (2001) *Establishing the Supremacy of European Law: The Making of an International Rule of Law in Europe*, Oxford: Oxford University Press.

Alter, K. (2009) 'The European Court's political power across time and space', *Revue Française de Science Politique* 59: 1–24.

Alter, K. (2014) *The New Terrain of International Law: Courts, Politics, Rights*, Princeton, NJ: Princeton University Press.

Alter, K.J. and Meunier-Aitsahalia, S. (1994) 'Judicial politics in the European Community: European integration and the pathbreaking Cassis de Dijon decision', *Comparative Political Studies* 26(4): 535–61.

Alter, K.J. and Vargas, J. (2000) 'Explaining variation in the use of European litigation strategies. European Community law and British gender equality policy', *Comparative Political Studies* 33(4): 452–82.

Bailey, M.A. and Maltzman, F. (2011) *The Constrained Court: Law, Politics, and the Decisions Justices Make*, Princeton, NJ: Princeton University Press.

Barnett, M. and Duvall, R. (2005) 'Power in international politics', *International Organization* 59(01): 39–75.

Binder, S.A. (1999) 'The dynamics of legislative gridlock, 1947–96', *American Political Science Review* 93(03): 519–33.

Blauberger, M. (2012) 'With Luxembourg in mind ... the remaking of national policies in the face of ECJ jurisprudence', *Journal of European Public Policy* 19(1): 109–26.

Bonjour, S. and Vink, M. (2013) 'When Europeanization backfires: the normalization of European migration politics', *Acta Politica* 48(4): 389–407.

Burley, A.-M. and Mattli, W. (1993) 'Europe before the Court: a political theory of legal integration', *International Organization* 47(01): 41–76.

Caporaso, J.A. and Tarrow, S. (2009) 'Polanyi in Brussels: supranational institutions and the transnational embedding of markets', *International Organization* 63(04): 593–620.

Carrubba, C. and Gabel, M. (2015) *International Courts and the Performance of International Agreements: A General Theory with Evidence from the European Union*, Cambridge: Cambridge University Press.

Carrubba, C.J., Gabel, M., and Hankla, C. (2008) 'Judicial behavior under political constraints: evidence from the European Court of Justice', *American Political Science Review* 102(04): 435–52.

Carrubba, C.J., Gabel, M., and Hankla, C. (2012) 'Understanding the role of the European Court of Justice in European integration', *American Political Science Review* 106(01): 214–23.

Cichowski, R.A. (2007) *The European Court and Civil Society, Litigation, Mobilization and Governance*, Cambridge: Cambridge University Press.

Conant, L.J. (2002) *Justice Contained, Law and Politics in the European Union*, Ithaca, NY: Cornell University Press.

Cooter, R. and Ginsburg, T. (1996) 'Comparative judicial discretion: an empirical test of econometric models', *International Review of Law and Economics* 16: 295–314.

Craig, P. and De Búrca, G. (1998) *EU Law. Text, Cases and Materials*, Second edition, Oxford: Oxford University Press.

Davies, G. (2014) 'Legislative control of the European Court of Justice', *Common Market Law Review* 51(6): 1579–607.

De Búrca, G. (2005) 'Rethinking law in neofunctionalist theory', *Journal of European Public Policy* 12(2): 310–26.

Epp, C.R. (1998) *The Rights Revolution: Lawyers, Activists, and Supreme Courts in Comparative Perspective*, Chicago: University of Chicago Press.
Fisher, L. (1988) *Constitutional Dialogues: Interpretation as Political Process*, Princeton, NJ: Princeton University Press.
Garrett, G. (1992) 'International cooperation and institutional choice: the European Community's internal market', *International Organization* 46(2): 533–60.
Garrett, G. (1995) 'The politics of legal integration in the European Union', *International Organization* 49: 171–181.
Garrett, G. and Weingast, B. (1993) 'Ideas, interests, and institutions: constructing the European Community's internal market', in J. Goldstein and R.O. Keohane (eds), *Ideas and Foreign Policy: Beliefs, Institutions, and Political Change*, Ithaca, NY: Cornell University Press, pp. 173–206.
Garrett, G., Kelemen, R.D., and Schulz, H. (1998) 'The European Court of Justice, national governments, and legal integration in the European Union', *International Organization* 52(1): 149–76.
Genschel, P. (2011) 'One trap, many exits, but no free lunch: how the joint-decision trap shapes EU tax policy', in G. Falkner (ed.), *The EU's Decision Traps. Comparing Policies*, Oxford: Oxford University Press, pp. 54–73.
Genschel, P., Kemmerling, A. and Seils, E. (2011) 'Accelerating downhill: how the EU shapes corporate tax competition in the single market', *JCMS: Journal of Common Market Studies* 49(3): 585–606.
Ginsburg, T. (2014) 'Political constraints on international courts', in C. Romano, K.J. Alter, and Y. Shany (eds), *The Oxford Handbook of International Adjudication*, Oxford: Oxford University Press, pp. 483–502.
Grimmel, A. (2012) 'Judicial interpretation or judicial activism? The legacy of rationalism in the studies of the European Court of Justice', *European Law Journal* 18(4): 518–35.
Grimmel, A. (2014) 'The uniting of Europe by transclusion: understanding the contextual conditions of integration through law', *Journal of European Integration* 36(6): 549–66.
Harlow, C. and Rawlings, R. (1992) *Pressure Through Law*, London: Routledge.
Hartlapp, M., Metz, J., and Rauh, C. (2014) *Which Policy for Europe?: Power and Conflict inside the European Commission*, Oxford: Oxford University Press.
Hirschl, R. (2009a) *Towards juristocracy: the origins and consequences of the new constitutionalism*. Harvard: Harvard University Press.
Hirschl, R. (2009b) 'The realist turn in comparative constitutional politics', *Political Research Quarterly* 62(4): 825–33.
Hirschman, A.O. (1970) *Exit, Voice and Loyalty. Responses to Decline in Firms, Organizations, and States*, Cambridge, MA: Harvard University Press.
Höpner, M. and Schäfer, A. (2012) 'Embeddedness and regional integration: waiting for Polanyi in a Hayekian setting', *International Organization* 66(03): 429–55.

Jones, B.D. (1999) 'Bounded rationality', *Annual Review Of Political Science* 2(1): 297–321.

Kagan, R.A. (2008) 'The "non-Americanisation" of European law', *European Political Science* 7(1): 21–31.

Kelemen, R.D. (2001) 'The limits of judicial power: trade–environment disputes in the GATT/WTO and the EU', *Comparative Political Studies* 34(6): 622–50.

Kelemen, R.D. (2008) 'The Americanisation of European law? Adversarial legalism *à la Européenne*', *European Political Science* 7(1): 32–42.

Kelemen, R.D. (2011) *Eurolegalism: The Transformation of Law and Regulation in the European Union*, Cambridge, MA: Harvard University Press.

Kelemen, R.D. (2013) 'Judicialisation, democracy and European integration', *Representation* 49(3): 295–308.

Klüver, H. and Sagarzazu, I. (2013) 'Ideological congruency and decision-making speed: the effect of partisanship across European Union institutions', *European Union Politics* 14(3): 388–407.

Larsson, O. and Naurin, D. (2016) 'Judicial independence and political uncertainty: How the risk of override impacts on the Court of Justice of the EU', *International Organization*, 70(2).

March, J.G. and Olsen, J.P. (1983) 'The new institutionalism: organizational factors in political life', *American Political Science Review* 78(03): 734–49.

March, J.G. and Olsen, J.P. (1998) 'The institutional dynamics of international political orders', *International Organization* 52(4): 943–69.

Marks, G. and Steenbergen, M. (2002) 'Understanding political contestation in the European Union', *Comparative Political Studies* 35(8): 879–92.

Martinsen, D.S. (2009) 'Conflict and conflict management in the cross-border provision of healthcare services', *West European Politics* 32(4): 792–809.

Martinsen, D.S. (2011) 'Judicial policy-making and Europeanization: the proportionality of national control and administrative discretion', *Journal of European Public Policy* 18(7): 944–61.

Martinsen, D.S. and Falkner, G. (2011) 'Social policy: problem-solving gaps, partial exits, and court-decision traps', in G. Falkner (ed.), *The EU's Decision Traps. Comparing Policies*, Oxford: Oxford University Press, pp. 128–45.

Martinsen, D.S. and Vollaard, H. (2014) 'Implementing Social Europe in times of crises: re-established boundaries of welfare?', *West European Politics* 37(4): 677–92.

Mattli, W. and Slaughter, A.-M. (1995) 'Law and politics in the European Union: a reply to Garrett', *International Organization* 49(1): 183–90.

McCann, M. (1994) *Rights at Work: Pay Equity, Reform and the Politics of Legal Mobilization*, Chicago: University of Chicago Press.

McCann, M. (2009) 'Interests, ideas, and institutions in comparative analysis of judicial power', *Political Research Quarterly* 62(4): 834–9.

Miller, M.C. (1992) 'Congressional committees and the Federal courts: a neo-institutional perspective', *The Western Political Quarterly* 45(4): 949–70.
Miller, M.C. (2009) *The View of the Courts from the Hill: Interactions between Congress and the Federal Judiciary*, Charlottesville, VA: University of Virginia Press.
Moravcsik, A. (1993) 'Preferences and power in the European Community: a liberal intergovernmentalist account'. *Journal of Common Market Studies*, 31(4): 473–523.
North, D.R. (1990) *Institutions, Institutional Change, and Economic Performance*, Cambridge: Cambridge University Press.
Nowak, T. (2010) 'Of garbage cans and rulings: judgments of the European Court of Justice in the EU legislative process', *West European Politics* 33(4): 753–69.
Pierson, P. (1996) 'The path to European integration a historical institutionalist analysis', *Comparative Political Studies* 29(2): 123–63.
Pollack, M.A. (2003) *The Engines of European Integration, Delegation, Agency, and Agenda Setting in the EU*, Oxford: Oxford University Press.
Pollack, M.A. (2013) 'New EU legal history: what's new, what's missing', *American University International Law Review* 28: 1257–311.
Radaelli, C.M. (2003) 'The Europeanization of public policy', in K. Featherstone and C.M. Radaelli (eds), *The Politics of Europeanization*, Oxford: Oxford University Press, pp. 27–57.
Rasmussen, H. (1998) *EU-ret i kontekst*, Copenhagen: GadJura.
Rasmussen, M. (2013) 'Rewriting the history of European public law: the new contribution of historians', *American University International Law Review* 28(5): 1187–223.
Rosenberg, G.N. (2008) *The Hollow Hope: Can Courts Bring About Social Change?*, Chicago: University of Chicago Press.
Sandholtz, W. and Stone Sweet, A. (1998) *European Integration and Supranational Governance*, New York: Oxford University Press.
Scharpf, F.W. (1997) *Games Real Actors Play: Actor-centered Institutionalism In Policy Research*, Boulder, CO: Westview Press.
Schmidt, S.K. (2000) 'Only an agenda setter?: The European Commission's power over the Council of Ministers', *European Union Politics* 1(1): 37–61.
Schmidt, S.K. (2004) 'The European Commission's powers in shaping European policies', in D.G. Dimitrakopoulos (ed.), *The Changing European Commission*, Manchester: Manchester University Press, pp. 105–21.
Simon, H.A. (1985) 'Human nature in politics: the dialogue of psychology with political science', *American Political Science Review* 79(02): 293–304.
Staton, J.K. and Moore, W.H. (2011) 'Judicial power in domestic and international politics', *International Organization* 65(3): 553–87.
Staton, J.K. and Vanberg, G. (2008) 'The value of vagueness: delegation, defiance, and judicial opinions'. *American Journal of Political Science* 52(3), 504–19.

Stein, E. (1981) 'Lawyers, judges and the making of a transnational constitution', *American Journal of International Law* 75(1): 1–27.

Stone Sweet, A. (1995) 'Governing with judges: the new constitutionalism', in J. Hayward and E.C. Page (eds), *Governing the New Europe*, Cambridge: Polity Press, pp. 286–315.

Stone Sweet, A. (2000) *Governing with Judges: Constitutional Politics in Europe*, Oxford: Oxford University Press.

Stone Sweet, A. (2004) *The Judicial Construction of Europe*, Oxford: Oxford University Press.

Stone Sweet, A. (2010) 'The European Court of Justice and the judicialization of EU governance', *Living Reviews in European Governance* 5(2): 1–50.

Stone Sweet, A. and Brunell, T.L. (1998) 'Constructing a supranational constitution: dispute resolution and governance in the European Community', *American Political Science Review* 92(1): 63–81.

Stone Sweet, A. and Brunell, T. (2012) 'The European Court of Justice, state noncompliance, and the politics of override', *American Political Science Review* 106(01): 204–13.

Tallberg, J. (2002) 'Paths to compliance: enforcement, management, and the European Union', *International Organization* 56(03): 609–43.

Tsebelis, G. and Garrett, G. (2001) 'The institutional foundations of intergovernmentalism and supranationalism in the European Union', *International Organization* 55(02): 357–90.

Vanberg, G. (2005) *The Politics of Constitutional Review in Germany*, Cambridge: Cambridge University Press.

Wasserfallen, F. (2010) 'The judiciary as legislator? How the European Court of Justice shapes policy-making in the European Union', *Journal of European Public Policy* 17(8): 1128–46.

Weiler, J. (1991) 'The transformation of Europe', *Yale Law Journal* 100: 2403–83.

Weiler, J. (1999) *The Constitution of Europe: Do the New Clothes Have an Emperor? And Other Essays on European Integration*, Oxford: Oxford University Press.

Weiler, J.H.H. (1994) 'A quiet revolution: the European Court of Justice and its interlocutors', *Comparative Political Studies* 26(4): 510–34.

Wincott, D. (2001) 'The Court of Justice and the European policy process', in J. Richardson (ed.), *European Union, Power and Policy-Making*, London: Routledge, pp. 179–97.

Wind, M. (2001) *Sovereignty and European Integration: Towards a Post-Hobbesian Order*, Basingstoke: Palgrave Macmillan.

Wind, M., Martinsen, D.S., and Rotger, G.P. (2009) 'The uneven legal push for Europe: questioning variation when national courts go to Europe', *European Union Politics* 10(1): 63–88.

Woods, P.J. and Hilbink, L. (2009) 'Comparative sources of judicial empowerment: ideas and interests', *Political Research Quarterly* 62(4): 745–52.

3

A Social Policy for the European Union

> In the early years of the European Economic Community (EEC), interest in equality between the sexes coincided with both second-wave feminism and the development of socio-economic conditions conducive to women's emancipation. Economic reconstruction, expanding educational opportunities and changes in family structure all contributed to producing an environment in which national governments were receptive to proposals for promoting greater gender equality.
>
> (Hantrais, *Social Policy in the European Union*, [2007: 123])

> ...the general shift to legalization in international politics, the fact that the ECJ is the most legitimate supranational institution in the EU, and the growing socialization of national courts and lawyers into the acceptance of the integration of European law into domestic jurisprudence convinces us that the ECJ is not without resources in building a tissue of embedded liberalism.
>
> (Caporaso and Tarrow, 'Polanyi in Brussels: supranational institutions and the transnational embedding of markets', [2009: 615])

The social responsibilities and competences of the European Union continue to be disputed and controversial. The organization of welfare remains primarily a national responsibility, and heads of states have generally resisted the delegation of this responsibility to the supranational level (Ferrera [2005]; Leibfried [2010]). The EU has long been regarded as a market-making entity, whereas social policies remain national prerogatives.

The EU continues to face a deep sovereignty dilemma, since on one hand member states formally deny supranational responsibilities, and on the other hand they adopt policies that deeply impact welfare regulation. On close examination, never, probably has there been a full separation between a supranational market and national social policies (Leibfried [2010: 254]). The two regulatory levels have been interwoven from the start, and their reciprocity and interdependence have only increased over time.

This chapter presents the achievements, dynamics, and challenges of EU social policy. It first presents the dynamics of EU social integration, distinguishing between negative and positive integration as well as open methods of coordination. The chapter then takes a historical view and sets out the development of EU social policies, including healthcare, in the face of a weak Treaty mandate and political contestation. After this presentation of the policy area, begins the analysis of *the extent to which and the conditions under which judicial decisions influence EU social policy outputs*. In this chapter, the analysis of judicial influence over time is carried out. All social and healthcare proposals as well as major amendments adopted between 1957 and 2014 have been compiled. For this compilation, I first examine the extent to which the Commission refers to case law in its policy proposals and the extent to which judicial decisions are used to justify or supply a reason for a specific provision or principle in these proposals. Second, the Commission's response to the case law of the Court is examined in accordance with the typology presented in chapter 2. Third, the political responses to the Commission's proposals on how to respond to SQ_{Court} are investigated. I then turn to explanations of the variance in judicial influence. The statistical association between key factors, such as time and political disagreements, and the likelihood of codification, is examined. The analysis proceeds by means of qualitative examinations of three decision-making processes leading to different types of judicial influence: codifying, modifying, and overriding the case law of the Court.

Dynamics of EU Social Integration

The scope and limits of EU social policies are the results of different constitutive and occasionally contradictory integration dynamics. In the current European Union, we can identify at least three dynamics of social integration: (1) negative social integration, (2) positive social integration, and (3) the open methods of coordination, which are increasingly subordinated to a 'policy of restraint' as a result of economic crisis (Armstrong [2013]; De la Porte and Natali [2014]). Negative and positive integration are identified by Scharpf as the fundamental asymmetry characterizing EU social integration (Scharpf [1996]). On one hand, free movement principles of the internal market and EU anti-discrimination provisions promote a form of negative social integration where national barriers to the free circulation of goods, services, capital, and persons must be removed. These principles, which are inscribed in the Treaty framework as fundamental principles, are guarded by the European Commission and are applied by the CJEU in its judicial decisions. Negative integration dynamics thus increase market integration by abolishing national restraints to trade and free competition (Scharpf [1996: 15]). National social, labour, and health policies must abide by the supremacy of Treaty principles to avoid becoming obstacles in an internal market. On the other hand, positive integration, in which EU social policy legislation is adopted by the Council of Europe and the European Parliament, corrects the markets of the European Union. Here, common EU policies are adopted to correct or shape market conditions (Scharpf [1996: 15]). However, such market-correcting dynamics encounter many obstacles and suffer from the intergovernmental character of EU decision making (Martinsen and Falkner [2011]). Although unanimity is no longer the main rule within social-policy decision-making (Leibfried [2010: 258–60]), thresholds to establish a common position in both the Council and the European Parliament remain very high. Thus, the social policy asymmetry between negative and positive integration continues to be considerable.

Since the late 1990s, the Open Method of Coordination (OMC) has increasingly been seen as the new governance approach to EU social policy and as a solution to the sovereignty dilemma. The apparent solution was that the EU was assigned a stronger role in coordinating national social policies while accepting the member states' prerogative to design, organize, and finance their own welfare states (Armstrong [2010]; Büchs [2007]; De la Porte [2012]; De La Porte and Pochet [2002] ; Hervey [2010]; Zeitlin [2011]). The OMC does not produce binding regulation but coordinates by means of soft law. Recommendations and best practices are the steering mechanism of this integration dynamic, and the effectiveness of OMC has been questioned. As a result of the 'Great Recession', which affected most parts of the Union after 2008, new governance dynamics have taken a different turn and have increasingly become policies of restraint (Armstrong [2013]). As noted by De la Porte and Natali, the economic crisis has had a significant impact on the content and effect of soft law regulation in social policy (De la Porte and

Natali [2014]). The classic version of the OMC has lost importance since the crisis, while national politicians have become more responsive to the policy recommendations of the stability and growth pact demanding financial sustainability. Thus, the leverage of EU pressure negatively affects the scope of national welfare policies and severely constrains policy options. These new EU policies of restraint have implications similar to the dynamics of negative integration because these policies ultimately reduce social sovereignty at the national level, while avoiding compensation by means of positive EU integration. This process of dismantling the EU policy of restraint intensifies the call for positive integration if a European social model is to be maintained.[1]

This book examines the dynamics of negative and positive social integration and specifically focuses on the relation between them. The third dynamic—OMC and the policy of restraint—are important parts of the full picture, but because they are not binding law, they will not be examined here. The book assumes a broad definition of social policy, defined according to a wider spectrum of welfare policies, including labour market policies, healthcare, gender equality, and welfare redistributive policies, but not education.

The interaction between negative and positive integration is detrimental to the emerging properties of social Europe (Hemerijck [2013: 292]). Negative integration describes the dynamic spurred by the CJEU. It is the principal institution in action here. However, the research question of this book goes beyond the interpretation of the Court and particularly examines the subsequent, receptive or corrective dynamics of positive integration. Here, political actors may respond actively to negative integrative steps taken by the judiciary. The tensions and interaction between the two forces constitute the main scope of and limits to EU social integration.

The History of an EU Social Policy

When the Treaty of Rome established the European Economic Community (EEC) in 1957, its founding idea was to build a common market between the six original states (Hantrais [2007]). The EEC should focus on the economic opening of national markets, while social policies should remain national

[1] A European social model is often defined, in contrast to the socio-economic order of the USA, as a social order in which improving living standards and supporting the socio-economically weak are of great public concern (Alber [2006]; Martinsen and Vollaard [2014: 679]).

(Hemerijck [2013: 303]). Gerard Veldkamp, the Dutch minister of social affairs from 1961 to 1967, observed the following:

> [The authors of the Treaty of Rome] based themselves on the principle that it was necessary to regulate everything which might artificially disturb the rules of competition, in other words, everything which might lead to distortions on the economic plane, but that the regulation of social conditions and social policy as such—i.e. independently of the efforts to bring about economic unity—was not necessary. (G. Veldkamp [1968] as quoted in Holloway [1981: 41])

However, two social provisions inserted in the Treaty of Rome became of major importance to the subsequent regulation of social policy. Italy pushed to have an article on the free movement of workers and the coordination of social security (Holloway [1981]; Romero [1993]). Article 51 of the EEC Treaty (now article 48 TFEU) indicates that a worker moving from one member state to another has the right to access the social security schemes of other member states and to export previously earned social security rights to other member states. On the initiative of France, article 119 (now article 157 TFEU) also became part of the original treaty, laying down that men and women are entitled to equal pay for equal work (Anderson [2015: 111–34]; Cichowski [2001: 116–17]; Falkner [1994: 81–3]; Hantrais [2007: 123–4]).

Coordinating Social Security for Migrant Workers

Both articles were constitutive for two main social policy achievements of the European Union, demonstrating how supranational regulation has gradually expanded into the welfare prerogative of member states. The Council adopted regulation no. 3 in 1958, addressing migrant workers' social security rights, as the first social regulation. In 1971, the original regulation was reformed as regulation 1408/71.[2] In 2004, regulation 1408/71 became regulation 883/2004, which covers not only workers and self-employed individuals but also all EU citizens and their family members. That the original regulation was adopted back in 1958 substantiates the founding idea of the EEC and the firm political commitment to create the conditions necessary so that workers could circulate freely between member states. National barriers—including

[2] Regulation (EEC) No 1408/71 of the Council of 14 June 1971 on the application of social security schemes to employed persons and their families moving within the Community.

nation-bound welfare provisions—that prevent such free circulation should be abolished. The 1950s—before the adoption of the Treaty of Rome—has been termed 'the era of bilaterally organised interdependence' (Romero [1993: 49]). At that time, national social security provisions were firmly built on territorial principles and discriminating rules, social risks were regarded as occurring within national borders, and social sharing took place between members of the nation (Pennings [1998: 5]). Bilateral agreements were sometimes adopted to regulate social security matters between two states, but these were more unstable and limited means of regulation than was the multilateral agreement that the EEC put into place.

Thus, the regulation coordinating social security rights across borders constituted a first crucial intervention in the national prerogative to define the members of social communities (Cornelissen [1996]; Ferrera [2003, 2005]; Van der Mei [2003]). It was soon after supplemented by the other early Regulation, no. 1612/68 (now regulation 492/2011), which established that migrant workers have the same rights as national citizens do to the social advantages of hosting member states in which they work.[3] Over time, the CJEU has played an important role in defining the personal and material scope of and limits to these two regulations, interpreting who should have rights to which types of social benefit (Blauberger and Schmidt [2014]; Martinsen [2005]). However, the CJEU has not acted independently. As will be demonstrated below in relation to special non-contributory benefits, regulation 1408/71 has featured in its own battles between legal and political integration. The scope of the regulation has increasingly been criticized in light of the economic crisis. The fundamental idea of cross-border welfare as as a means to facilitate the free movement of persons is up for political contestation. A free movement–welfare cleavage between old and new member states has become increasingly marked. On one side, the UK prime minister, David Cameron, declared that EU free movement needs to be less free and that access to cross-border welfare should be limited (*Financial Times*, 'Free movement within Europe needs to be less free', 26 November 2013). One year later, Cameron added a fresh attack on the EU social security regulations, demanding further cutbacks of EU migrants' access to British welfare. This time, the British prime minister even stated that he was prepared to force the UK to leave the Union if he did not get his way in Brussels (*The Guardian*,

[3] Regulation (EEC) No 1612/68 of the Council of 15 October 1968 on the freedom of movement for workers within the Community.

'Cameron to tell EU: cut all tax credits to migrants', 28 November 2014). On the other side of the cleavage, the former Polish president Lech Walesa has criticized the UK for acting in an 'irrational and short-sighted way' (*Financial Times*, 'Poland attacks Cameron view on migrants', 23 December 2013). Never before has the political debate on the EU and the welfare state been so heated.

Gender Equality

Article 119 EEC (now article 157 TFEU) was the other original Treaty provision that became a constitutional basis for expanded social competences within the Community. Like article 51 EEC (now article 48 TFEU), article 119 was inserted into the Treaty for economic reasons. France pushed to have a Treaty provision on equal pay for equal work between men and women because it had enshrined a principle of equal pay in its own 1946 constitution (Hantrais [2007: 123]). France thus feared competitive disadvantage, as it was the only one of the original six member countries to have introduced legislation for equal pay (Cichowski [2001: 116–17]).

The provision in the Treaty called for member states to implement equal pay before 31 December 1962, which was the date set for the completion of the first stage of the Common Market. However, none of the member states had implemented the provision by the required date (Warner [1984]) and, throughout the 1960s, the article remained a mere Treaty declaration with no real national implications.

Jurisprudence became a key driver of integration in EU gender equality. The case of gender equality has thus come to exemplify the integrative power of the European Court (Alter and Vargas [2000]; Anderson [2015]; Caporaso and Jupille [2001]; Cichowski [2001, 2007]; Pierson [1996]; Pollack and Hafner-Burton [2000]). The Defrenne cases were crucial in defining the meaning and effect of the Treaty's declaration on equal pay.[4] In the Defrenne II case,

[4] Case C–80/70 Gabrielle *Defrenne* v Belgian State [1971] ECR 445 (Defrenne I) and case C–43/75 Gabrielle *Defrenne* v Société anonyme belge de navigation aérienne Sabena [1976] ECR 455 (Defrenne II). The Defrenne cases concerned discriminatory practices in Sabena, a Belgian national airline. Male and female stewards had exactly the same job responsibilities, but the male stewards earned more. Furthermore, female stewards were obliged to retire when they turned forty, while their male colleagues could continue working another fifteen years and then became entitled to Sabena's special pension scheme.

the Belgian Court questioned whether article 119; (1) introduced the principle of equal pay directly into national law and (2) had become applicable to the internal policies of the member states by virtue of the Treaty or had to be applied first by national authorities. The UK and Ireland submitted their opinions to the Court, arguing that while the Treaty article implied a commitment to a constitutional principle, it nevertheless required national implementating legislation in order to take effect. Member states thereby claimed that article 119 lacked direct effect. The Court did not agree, but concluded that article 119 had direct effect from the date of applicability. In order to meet the financial concerns of the member states, the CJEU stated that no claims to equal pay could be made retrospectively, i.e. having effect before the date of the judgement (Craig and De Búrca [2011: 859]).

The long-awaited political initiatives came almost two decades after the adoption of the equal pay provision in the Treaty. The first EC Social Action Programme of 1974 included a section on women, and shortly afterwards the Council of Ministers adopted a first wave of secondary legislation. Between 1975 and 1986 five new directives were adopted. The first concerned *equal pay*, detailing and extending the scope and meaning of article 119 of the Treaty by stating that men and women are entitled to equal pay for equal work *and for work of equal value*.[5] The subsequent four directives went beyond the principle of equal pay to address the broader principle of equal treatment. The equal treatment directive extended the principle of non-discrimination to vocational training, access to employment and working conditions.[6] Directive 79/7 extended equal treatment to social security,[7] with the exception of occupational schemes, which were eventually included by the occupational social security directive of 1986.[8] In the same year, a directive extending equal treatment to the self-employed was introduced.[9]

Despite political commitments to gender equality during the 1970s and 1980s, implementation proceeded slowly (Martinsen [2007]). In various cases the Court found that national provisions and practices did not comply with the equal pay and equal treatment principles.[10] These cases were indeed stepping

[5] Council Directive 75/117/EEC of 10 February 1975.

[6] Council Directive 76/207/EEC of 9 February 1976.

[7] Council Directive 79/7/EEC of 19 December 1978.

[8] Council Directive 86/378/EEC of 24 July 1986.

[9] Council Directive 86/613/EEC of 11 December 1986.

[10] See for example case 129/79, Macarthys Ltd v Wendy *Smith* [1980] ECR 1275; case 96/80 J.P. *Jenkins* v Kingsgate (Clothing Productions) Ltd [1981] ECR 911; case 109/88, Handels- og

stones for extending the equal pay and equal treatment provisions to cover indirect and disguised forms of discrimination in which, although there was no *direct* gender-based discrimination, a discriminatory effect nevertheless resulted (Craig and De Búrca [1998: 809–15]). The progressiveness of the gender equality case law is striking. In the 1990s, maternity rights and rights during pregnancy were instigated by jurisprudence. The Court first considered the rights of pregnant workers in the case C–177/88 Dekker.[11] Ms Dekker had applied for a job when she was three months pregnant. Although she was found to be the most qualified person for the job, she did not get it. The Court found that a refusal of employment on the grounds of pregnancy constituted direct sex discrimination. The Court's jurisprudence thus extended to pregnant women the right to equal treatment, laying down a wider interpretation of sex discrimination to include a situation in which a woman is disadvantaged per se rather than disadvantaged only in comparison to a man (Cichowski [2001: 124]; Cichowski and Stone Sweet [2004: 178]).

From the 1990s onwards, the Council adopted a second wave of supranational equality policies. In 1992, the maternity leave directive was adopted,[12] and from 1992 onwards, additional directives were introduced concerning the organization of working time,[13] parental leave,[14] burden of proof in sex discrimination cases,[15] and framework agreements on part-time work.[16] As will be demonstrated below, the burden of proof directive codified previous case law of the Court. Regarding the general development of equal opportunity regulation in the EU, legal interpretations were indeed important first moves to prepare political actors to regulate.

However, political counter-responses have also been part of this development. In the Bilka and Barber cases,[17] the CJEU brought occupational pension schemes within the Treaty's article on equal pay. Directive 79/7 on equal

Kontorfunktionærernes Forbund i Danmark v Dansk Arbejdsgiverforening, acting on behalf of *Danfoss* [1989] ECR 3199.

[11] Case C–177/88 Elisabeth Johanna Pacifica *Dekker* v Stichting Vormingscentrum voor Jong Volwassenen (VJV-Centrum) Plus [1990] ECR I–03941.

[12] Council Directive 92/85/EEC of 19 October 1992.

[13] Council Directive 93/104/EC of 23 November 1993.

[14] Council Directive 96/34/EC of 3 June 1996.

[15] Council Directive 97/80/EC of 15 December 1997.

[16] Council Directive 97/81/EC of 15 December 1997.

[17] Case 170/84 *Bilka-Kaufhaus GmbH* v Karin Weber von Hartz [1986] ECR 1607. Case C–262/88 Douglas Harvey *Barber* v Guardian Royal Exchange Assurance Group *GRE* [1990] ECR I–01889.

treatment for men and women in social security had exempted pensionable age from equal treatment.[18] Pensionable ages that discriminated between men and women could thus be maintained despite EU regulation on gender equality. However, in the Barber case, the Court laid down that the principle of equal treatment also applies to the age of retirement. Member states and employers argued strongly against the conclusions in the Barber case. In order to confine the impact of jurisprudence, the member states unanimously adopted a Barber protocol in the Maastricht Treaty, which limited the retrospective effects of the judgment (Craig and De Búrca [2011: 864]). The political response to the Barber case has taken forward as to exemplify the political ability to override the Court, even in constitutional matters. According to Wincott, the Barber protocol

> amounted to a manipulation of the judicial process by politicians—a clear indication that the Community legislators are prepared to restrict the judicial independence of the Court. (Wincott [2001: 191])

In summary, EU regulation on gender equality has moved from a Treaty provision with no national impact to become one of the EU's most important social policy achievements. Over time, it has developed from being justified on economic grounds and for competitive reasons to becoming a fundamental part of the protection of EU citizens (Chalmers et al. [2014: 571–3]). Gender equality and equal opportunity in general were reinforced in constitutional terms by the Treaty of Amsterdam's article 13 EC (now article 19 TFEU). Currently, article 19 TFEU grants the Union the ability to take action against discrimination based on 'sex, racial or ethnic origin, religion or belief, disability, age or sexual orientation'. In the 1970s, the Court's interpretations of the Treaty's article on gender equality gave the Community a key role ensuring equal pay and equal treatment between the sexes. In large part, the political actors accepted the jurisprudence of the Court. However, it has to be noted that this successful legal push for gender equality coincided with a more general political and societal push for equality. As noted by Hantrais:

> In the early years of the European Economic Community (EEC), interest in equality between the sexes coincided with both second-wave feminism and the development of socio-economic conditions conducive to women's emancipation. Economic reconstruction, expanding educational opportunities and changes in

[18] See article 7 of Directive 79/7.

family structure all contributed to producing an environment in which national governments were receptive to proposals for promoting greater gender equality. (Hantrais [2007: 123])

This receptiveness cannot be identified in the present socio-economic and political setting of the European Union. In 2008, the Commission proposed a revision of the maternity leave directive to extend paid maternity leave from fourteen to eighteen weeks.[19] The European Parliament wanted to extend paid maternity leave to twenty weeks, and the proposal was stalled for almost three years with no progress between the Council and the Parliament. In July 2014, the Commission finally decided to withdraw its proposal (*EU Observer*, 'Controversial maternity leave bill scrapped', 16 July 2014). In November 2012, the Commission proposed a directive to improve the gender balance on the boards of stock exchange-listed companies, obliging these companies to have 40 per cent female board members.[20] On 20 November 2013, the European Parliament voted strongly for the proposal, with 459 MEPs in favour, 148 voting against, and 81 abstaining. Despite this strong signal from the Parliament, the proposal was confronted with considerable opposition from the Council. Led by the UK, an alliance of member states opposed EU integration on the issue and, so far, the Council has been unable to agree on a common position. As described by a British government spokesman,

[w]e and a significant number of other EU governments also think it's far more appropriate for action to deal with this issue to be decided at the national level, not EU level, in part because of the different business structures and cultures. (*The Independent*, '"The first cracks in the glass ceiling": EU votes to impose legal quotas for women in the boardroom', 20 November 2013)

In the socio-economic and political setting of the current EU28, an EU push for further gender equality faces much starker opposition than it did in the heyday of progressive Community case law and legislation.

[19] *COM (2008) 600/4* proposal for a Directive of the European Parliament and of the Council amending Council Directive 92/85/EEC on the introduction of measures to encourage improvements in the safety and health at work of pregnant workers and workers who have recently given birth or are breastfeeding.

[20] *COM (2012) 614* proposal for a directive of the European Parliament and of the Council on improving the gender balance among non-executive directors of companies listed on stock exchanges and related measures.

Health and Safety and Public Health

In 1987, the Single European Act introduced a new article, article 118A (article 153(1) a TFEU), granting the Community the ability to adopt measures to regulate health and safety at work with qualified majority voting. This meant that, for the first time, social policy initiatives could be advanced on the basis of QMV, which provided 'an escape route out of the unanimity requirement' (Falkner [2010: 270]). As will be analysed in chapter 4, the Treaty's article 118A constituted the basis for adopting the working time directive in 1993 (Anderson [2015: 52–70]).

The Maastricht Treaty introduced the Social Protocol, of which the UK was able to opt out. In 1997, the newly elected Labour government ended the British opt-out from that protocol. The social protocol extended social regulation to include working conditions (article 153(1) b TFEU). The ability to regulate working conditions has subsequently led to a number of directives, including the temporary agency directive.

The Maastricht Treaty also introduced a separate article 152 (now article 168 TFEU) on public health, which became important for the negotiations of the patients' rights directive, as will be demonstrated in chapter 5. Based on this Treaty provision and on other EU measures, a patchy EU health policy has emerged since the early 1990s, addressing different major health issues such as cancer and BSE, pharmaceuticals, and medical devices as well as the free movement of health professionals, services, and patients (Hervey and McHale [2015]; Martinsen and Vollaard [2014]; Steffen et al. [2005]; Vollaard et al. [2013, 2015]). Finally, while the Amsterdam Treaty did not extend the EU's social commitments much, the charter of fundamental rights was written into the constitution with the Lisbon Treaty.

Extension of EU Regulation over Time

The willingness to adopt binding measures on EU social policy and healthcare has been regarded as reluctant (Leibfried [2010: 256–7]). Nevertheless, binding regulations on EU social and health policies have gradually expanded. By means of an advanced EUR-Lex search using the search codes 5.20 for social policy and 15.30 for health protection, we compiled all adopted directives

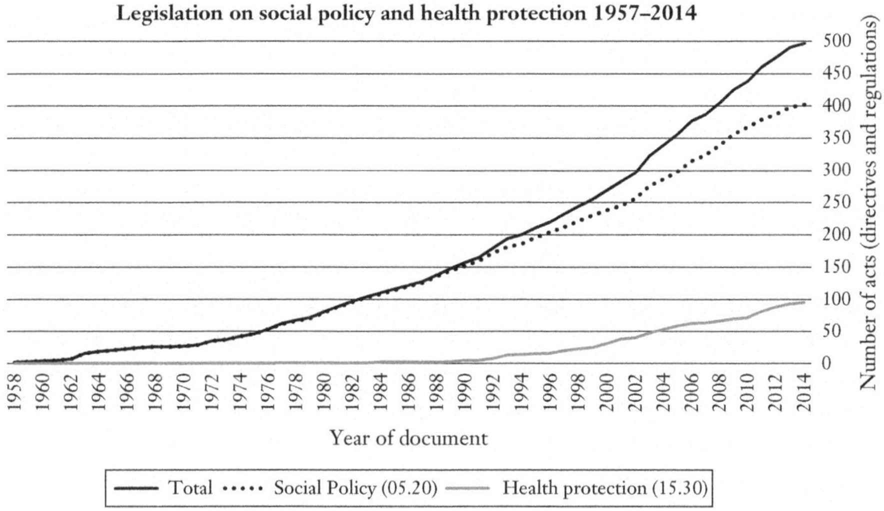

Fig. 3.1 Directives and Regulations on Social and Health Policies, 1957–2014 (absolute numbers. X-axis year of adoption)

and regulations. Between 1 March 1957 and 1 July 2014, 497 binding acts were adopted in the areas of social and health policies.[21]

Figure 3.1 above shows the full scope of the regulations and directives adopted between 1 March 1957 and 1 July 2014 within these policy areas.

This compilation of all legislative development, however, contains legislative acts of minor importance. In order to obtain a better overview of the main developments within the field, we removed minor amendments, application rules, and extensions from the compilation as well as acts addressing statistics, acts concerning the establishment and operation of European agencies or foundations, and acts amending and/or detailing individual articles of existing directives, as we considered these minor amendments.[22] This process left us with a dataset of 120 adopted acts plus 3 non-adopted policy proposals. Figure 3.2 below shows the development of major pieces of EU legislation

[21] Data compiled by means of EUR-Lex advanced search. Search code: (Directory_code = 1530+ OR 0520+) AND (Form = regulation NOT proposal OR directive NOT proposal).

[22] In their description of the evolution of legal instruments in EU social policy, Treib et al. distinguish the adopted hard law between (1) new directives and regulation and (2) amendments, applications, and extensions (Treib et al. [2011]). In the present study's compilation, major amendments of regulations and directives are included in the sample, as they may deal with the case law of the CJEU. Like Treib et al., we do not restrict our dataset to legislation in force.

for social and health policies disaggregated into six subcategories: gender equality and non-discrimination, social security, working conditions, health and safety, healthcare, and freedom of establishment and residence.

The development of these main binding acts gives us a crude overview of the regulatory history of a social Europe intending to facilitate the free movement of workers and to establish equal pay for equal work, while gradually expanding with new initiatives, increasingly making social and health policies irrevocable parts of European integration. Figure 3.2 shows a policy area in regulatory growth. Social security for migrant workers remains the area generating the most legislation in the EU social policy. By now working conditions and healthcare have generated more legislation than gender equality, but the social provisions in regulating the freedom of establishment and residence remain relatively low. In general, EU regulation of social and health policies has grown over the years, from the first regulation no. 3/58 on the coordination of social security for migrant workers, later becoming Regulation 1408/71, followed by the equal pay and equal treatment directives

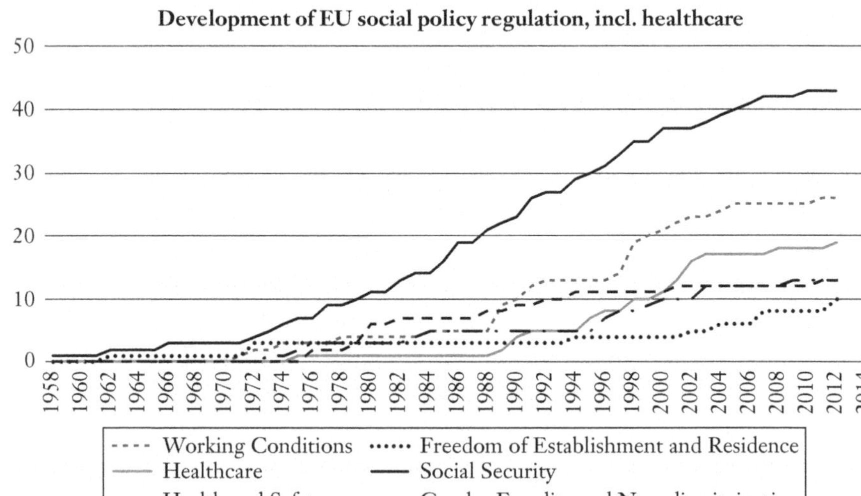

Fig. 3.2 Major Legislative Acts Adopted on Social and Health Policies,1957–2014 (absolute numbers. X-axis year of proposal).[24]

[24] The legislative acts have been classified on the basis of proposal dates. Where traceable proposals include non-adopted policy proposals that were not part of the original selection. We identified three non-adopted policy proposals.

of the 1970s. In 1993, the working time directive was decided. In the same year, a first key text on healthcare was developed, namely the directive on medical devices. In 1996, the posting of workers directive came forth and in 2011, the directive on patient rights in cross-border healthcare was adopted. In summary, over time social Europe has extended its regulatory scope. The continuous growth of legislative outputs is a first marker that not all EU social regulation is left to the courts and the market (Leibfried [2010]).

The European Court and Social Integration

The CJEU has often been interpreted as the driver of social integration that is able to advance what politics cannot. When examining judicial decision-making, the Court has undoubtedly moved individual social rights forward in areas such as disability rights, gender equality, cross-border healthcare, working time, and occupational pensions, among others (Hemerijck [2013]; Mabbett [2005, 2014]; Martinsen [2007, 2009]; Nowak [2008]). According to Caporaso and Tarrow, legal integration in the European Union has managed to embed the free market, and the CJEU has 'emerged as a regulatory arbiter of compromises between international openness and social concerns' (Caporaso and Tarrow [2009: 595]). Examining the case of social security for migrant workers, the authors conclude that judicial decision-making has established an EU social policy in which social considerations are broadly conceived. They conclude that

> ... the general shift to legalization in international politics, the fact that the ECJ is the most legitimate supranational institution in the EU, and the growing socialization of national courts and lawyers into the acceptance of the integration of European law into domestic jurisprudence convinces us that the ECJ is not without resources in building a tissue of embedded liberalism. (Caporaso and Tarrow [2009: 615])

The work of Caporaso and Tarrow, however, does not pay attention to the political responses to judicial decisions, nor do they examine whether the identified judicial embedding of the market is subsequently implemented at the national level. Thus, the broader impact and ultimate effectiveness of legal integration is not explored but merely assumed.

Another group of scholars points to the weakness of positive social integration and posits that as a result 'social Europe' will remain 'the road not taken'

(Scharpf [2002: 645]; see also Höpner and Schäfer [2012]; Leibfried [2010]; Scharpf [2010]; Von Maydell [1999]). Judicial law-making may expand non-discriminatory rights, but legal integration cannot bring social sharing to the EU (Höpner and Schäfer [2012: 450]). Höpner and Schäfer find that market-correcting CJEU case law is a very limited part of judicial decisions that, in their view, dismantles mainly social rights and the national welfare state. Market-enforcing dynamics are foremost at play in the EU, and the impact of the market on national and European social policies is considerable (Höpner and Schäfer [2012: 441–5]).

As presented in chapter 2 of this book, disagreements on the Court's role and power thus loom large in general studies of European integration, as they do in studies inquiring into the more specific scope and dynamics of social Europe. This invites the question how we can examine the influence of the Court. We now turn to the empirical analysis of judicial influence.

Analysing the Influence of the Court on EU Policy Outputs over Time

To what extent and under which conditions judicial decisions influence EU policy outputs will be examined in the subsequent chapters: chapter 4 addresses the regulation of working time, chapter 5 addresses patients' rights in cross-border healthcare, and chapter 6 addresses the regulation of the posting of workers. The three case studies provide insight into the current dynamics, scope, and limits on social Europe of EU28.

In addition to being examined in these detailed case studies, the Court's influence on EU social policy outputs has been examined over time using the 'law attainment' approach. As presented in figure 3.1 above, all new regulations, directives, and subsequent major amendments adopted between 1 January 1958 and 1 July 2014 were compiled. Where they were possible to trace, rejected policy proposals were also included in the compilation. All original Commission proposals were then collected. The early Commission proposals were difficult to acquire, as these are not available online or in the hands of relevant ministries or information offices. However, with the help of the 'Historical Archives of the Commission', DG EMPL, and EUR-Lex, we managed to collect early original proposals, allowing us to work with the full compilation of major legislative initiatives.

All the original Commission proposals in the compilation were then coded for their reference to the jurisprudence of the Court (see annex 2).[24] The proposals were coded for whether the Commission referred to the case law of the CJEU in its justifications for a proposal, i.e. in the explanatory memoranda and recitals of a proposal. The coding was binary: no = 0, yes = 1 (see annex 2, 4th column).[25] The coding was performed manually: three researchers examined all proposals in turn to ensure intercoder reliability. Unlike studies of 'preference attainment', we chose not to rely on quantitative text-analysis programs such as 'wordfish'[26] or similar computer programs so as to be able to distinguish between when a proposal *referred* to the Court and when it *justified* or *reasoned* a specific policy change on the basis of jurisprudence. Forty policy proposals referred to the Court's jurisprudence.

The Court as Justification

As the second analytical step, the forty proposals referring to the Court were examined to determine whether references to the Court were given in the proposal as the reason or justification for the formulation or change of a specific provision or principle. In twenty-two of the forty proposals, the Commission used references to the Court as a justification for how provisions or principles were proposed, often in the form of a reference to specific case law of the Court (see Annex 1, column on reference to specific case law). These twenty-two proposals were further classified using the taxonomy presented in chapter 2. As a first step, the response of the Commission was examined, i.e. whether the Commission proposed to codify, modify, or override the new status quo established by the Court (see Annex 1, column on the Commission's response). The taxonomy's category 'non-adoption' was irrelevant in relation to the Commission's proposals.

[24] Annexes 2, 3, and 4 are available at the the author's webpage at www.politicalscience.ku.dk as well as at the OUP webpage for this book at http://ukcatalogue.oup.com/product/academic/law/employment/9780198753391.do.

[25] The coding is CJEU (0 = No; 1 = Yes). The following search words were used as proxies for references to case law: 'Court of Justice', 'European Court of Justice', 'case law', 'jurisprudence', 'judgments', 'the Court', 'ECJ', 'CJEU', and reference to specific judgments. In those proposals only available in French, the following words were used as proxies: 'la cour de justice', 'la cour', 'jurisprudence'.

[26] As an example of the use of 'wordfish' to measure influence, see Klüver (2011).

In seventeen of the twenty-two proposals, the Commission proposed to *codify* the case law of the Court, demonstrating that the Commission often, but not always, proposes to codify case law when referring to previous jurisprudence. Three proposals were aimed at *modifying* the case law and two at *overriding* a Court ruling. We observe that, in some proposals, the Commission made extensive reference to the case law of the Court (annex 1, column on the number of references). In the proposal for a *patients' rights directive COM (2008) 414*, the *Monti II* proposal *COM (2012) 130*, the proposal for an *enforcement directive on the posting of workers COM (2012) 131*, the proposal for *amending regulation 1408/71 COM (2003) 468*, the proposal for *amending the equal treatment directive COM (2000) 334*, the proposal for *amending the insolvency directive COM 80/987*, and the proposal for a *burden of proof directive COM (96) 340*, the Commission used jurisprudence as a main justification for why the initiative was taken. In other proposals, case law served as justification, but it was referred to much less often by the Commission; for example, the proposal to *amend the working time directive COM (2004) 607* only mentioned the Court twice.

To exemplify the way the Commission justifies a proposal's general principle or a specific provision, we can examine three different proposals:

(a) *COM (88) 27* proposed in February 1988 to *amend regulation 1408/71 on social security for migrant workers*,

(b) *COM (2000) 334* proposed June 2000 to *amend the equal treatment directive* and

(c) *COM (2004) 2* proposed March 2004 on a *service directive*.

In *COM (88) 27*, the Commission referred once to the judicial decision 41/84 Pinna,[27] to justify the amendment of article 73 of regulation 1408/71 to clarify the exportability of family benefits, i.e. that workers in France were entitled to family benefits although their children resided in another member state. In *COM (2000) 334*, the Commission justified its initiative to amend the equal treatment directive in order to take 'account of the case law of the European Court of Justice, which comprises 40 judgments in the last 25 years' (*COM (2000) 334*, 2). The Commission reasoned that the proposal was necessary to establish legal certainty and made dense reference to Court-generated principles on equal treatment and specific judicial decisions. With reference to three specific judicial decisions, the Commission argued that it was necessary

[27] Case 41/84 Pietro *Pinna* v Caisse d'allocations familiales de la Savoie [1986] ECR 1.

to change article 2.2 of the directive. Justifications for the proposed amendments on the basis of jurisprudence formed the core of the proposal, worded as 'the Court has stressed', 'the Court has ruled', 'the Court has concluded', and 'in accordance with the case law of the Court', among other formulae. The Commission's justifications on the basis of legal interpretations were subsequently accepted by the European legislators and codified into the directive (see annex 1, the column on political response). In *COM (2004) 2* on the service directive, the Commission justified article 23 on the basis of judicial decisions. In the explanatory memorandum, the Commission put forward jurisprudence as an indisputable rationale: 'Article 23 of the proposal incorporates the distinction between hospital and non-hospital care that has been clearly established by the consolidated case-law of the Court of Justice' (*COM (2004) 2*, 14). In chapter 5, the Commission's limited success in drawing on an assumed legitimacy of the Court in this regard will be explored further.

The Commission does not always push for a full-scale codification of jurisprudence. In the proposal for a Posted Workers Directive *COM (91) 230*, the Commission attempted to modify the implications of the Rush Portuguesa case,[28] finding that the case had extended social protection to such a degree that it would hinder the free movement of services. The posting of workers case will be further analysed in chapter 6. The Commission also suggested modification of the case law of the Court in the proposal for a Patients' Rights Directive *COM (2008) 414*, which will be discussed further in chapter 5. In *COM (88) 27*, the Commission proposed modifying the implications of the Pinna case by demarcating which French family benefits could be exported and which could not.[29] Finally, in the *COM (85) 396* proposal, the Commission proposed to override the case law of the Court that had extended the range of social benefits that migrant workers could export across borders (Conant [2002: 192–4]). This process will be detailed further below. As will be further analysed in chapter 4, in the *COM (2004) 607* proposal on the revision of the Working Time Directive the Commission proposed to overturn the new definition of working time that the Court had established.

In sum, these findings confirm the Commission's important role as gatekeeper. Only those judicial decisions that the Commission wants to bring into the political process find their way there. The Commission constitutes the first threshold

[28] Case C–113/89, *Rush Portuguesa* Ld^{a} v Office national d'immigration [1990] ECR I–01417.

[29] See note 29 above.

for the Court's influence on policy outputs. In addition, the findings demonstrate that the Commission often sides with the Court's interpretations, but does not always do so, and sometimes proposes to modify or even override the new status quo generated by the Court. This finding notes that the Commission has its own position on whether jurisprudence serves the course of integration.

Political Responses

The 'law attainment' analysis proceeded by analysing the European Parliament's and the Council's responses to the case law as proposed by the Commission. In this way, we bring into focus the European legislators as the subsequent thresholds for judicial influence. The specific formulation of these provisions or principles as proposed by the Commission was compared with the formulation of the same provision or principle in the final policy output. The degree of judicial influence on policy outputs ranging from codification, through modification and non-adoption to override could hereby be assessed. Annex 3 details this comparison from proposal to final policy act for all the proposals included in the medium-sized n-study of judicial influence over time.[30] We first examined whether the adopted provisions were largely identical to what the Commission had proposed. Against this background, I could identify whether the legislators supported how the Commission proposed to respond to the case law of the Court.

The political responses were subsequently analysed and classified using the taxonomy on judicial influence: in terms of whether the political institutions codified, modified, overturned, or did not adopt the Commission's proposal on how to respond to the case law of the Court (see Annex 1, the last column on political response).

Out of the twenty-two proposals, thirteen binding acts codified, five modified, and one overrode the influence of judicial decisions on EU legislation; three were not adopted. The examination of judicial influence over time thus demonstrates that EU legislators are capable of ruling in the case law of the Court and that they actively respond to judicial influence. Override is rare as a political response, but it became the policy output in 1992. Modification

[30] Annexes 2, 3, and 4 are available at the the author's webpage at www.politicalscience.ku.dk as well as at the OUP webpage for this book at http://ukcatalogue.oup.com/product/academic/law/employment/9780198753391.do.

and non-adoption are more likely outputs. Modification implies that the new court-generated status quo is partly taken into account, but its implications are limited by politics. Modification can be very similar to override. Non-adoption means that no sufficient majority could establish a common position in relation to how the Commission proposed to respond to the case law of the Court. Thus, the proposal to amend the working time directive *COM (2004) 607* failed, as did the Monti II proposal *COM (2012) 130*. Furthermore, the specific provision proposing to codify jurisprudence in the proposal for a service directive *COM (2004) 2* was not adopted. All three findings on non-adoption will be analysed in the case studies in the following chapters. Non-adoption implies legal uncertainty, where SQ_{Court} is contested but not overturned, modified, or codified.

However, thirteen binding acts codified the case law of the Court. Does this not confirm the 'judicialisation of politics' repeated by the dynamic court view, where politics is receptive to legal integration and adopts it into legislation? I assume that the willingness to codify depends on the political implications or salience of jurisprudence. Does SQ_{Court} matter to politics? Recent research on EU decision making concludes that the duration of the decision-making process crucially depends on ideological congruence, i.e. the degree of political conflict, within and between the legislative bodies (Klüver and Sagarzazu [2013]). Decision-making speed can thus be used as a proxy for the political importance of and conflicts generated by a proposal to codify the case law of the Court. Decision-making time suggests that in the majority of codification cases, it was largely politically uncontroversial or even technical to codify the case law of the Court, as evidenced in the many amendments to regulation 1408/71. Adopting codification where the EU legislators agreed with the Commission took an average of 1 year and 3 months (469 days), suggesting the presence of much less conflict than that present when responding by override, modification, or non-adoption. The proposals that ended in override, modification, or non-adoption, or those in which the Commission and the legislators disagreed, lasted 3 years and 1 month on average (1149 days) (see Annex 1, column on the length of the policy process).

When examining the substance of the codification proposed by the Commission, we find that, of the thirteen cases adopting legal integration, ten were minor/technical or uncontroversial from a political perspective. Among the thirteen cases of codification, there were only two in which judicial decisions pushed for considerable change of the regulatory status quo, being the adoption of the Burden of Proof Directive 97/80 and the amendment of regulation 1408/71 by *COM 647/2005*. Thus, we find two cases of substantive codification in which SQ_{reg}^{2} is unlikely to have been reached if SQ_{Court} had not happened. The third case in which codification of the case law implied a substantive change of SQ_{reg}^{1} was the Posting of Workers Directive 96/71, where the Commission and the legislators disagreed about how to respond to the case law of the Court. The Commission proposed to modify the course of legal integration, but the legislators wanted to codify it and extend social rights. This highly conflicting policy process and what happened afterwards will be analysed in chapter 6. It is important to note here that, in the large majority of codification cases, codifying jurisprudence is rather technical and has small political significance. It is also important to note that the majority of codification cases were adopted before the 2004 enlargement. In summary, the analysis over time demonstrates that the codification of judicial decisions in EU legislation is more likely to happen (1) when SQ_{Court} is less important to politics and/or (2) in a more socio-economically homogeneous setting with relatively fewer member states.

Examining the Probability of Codification

The above examination over time shows that the extent of judicial influence varies. EU legislators do not simply respond to legal integration by codification; modification, override, and non-adoption are other responses to be taken into account. Under which conditions does codification tend to happen? So far, it has been demonstrated that codification tends to take place when SQ_{Court} is less important to politics and in a more socio-economically homogeneous setting of fewer member states. The latter finding is in line with the expectation derived on the basis of Weiler's work that, over time, EU legislators will be less willing to codify the case law of the Court into policy outputs. Political voice will sound louder.

Although the research for this book is conducted mainly by qualitative methods, the data collected over time makes it possible to examine the statistical association between key factors and codification as an output. To determine whether several key characteristics affect the probability that a case is codified, and how, a probit model[31] was constructed that includes as

[31] A probit model is a type of regression where the dependent variable can only take two values, i.e. in this case *codification* or *not codification*. It thus explains the probability of codification as a function of several variables. I thank Gabriel Pons Rotger for help with this section.

explanatory variables the *year* that a proposal was adopted (or rejected), i.e. the importance of time; the *length of the decision-making process* as a proxy for political disagreement; the *co-decision procedure*, i.e. the European Parliament as a co-legislator; and *unanimity* in the Council. The results presented in table 3.1 below show that, of all these all case features, unanimity is the only one that is clearly insignificant (see column 1 of the table). When we exclude

Table 3.1 Estimated Coefficients in a Probit Model of Codification

Covariate	Coefficient (Standard Error) *p-value*	Coefficient (Standard Error) *p-value*
Adoption Year	-0.1072* (0.0551) *0.0520*	-0.1074** (0.0545) *0.0490*
Length of Decision-making Process	-0.0010 (0.0007) *0.1320*	-0.0010 (0.0006) *0.1170*
Co-decision	1.0781 (0.8447) *0.2020*	1.0730 (0.8154) *0.1880*
Unanimity	0.0167 (0.7193) *0.9810*	
Constant Term	214.95* (110.39) *0.0510*	215.36** (109.02) *0.0480*
Number of Cases	22	22
Prob<χ^2	0.16	0.08
LR <$\chi^2(k)$	6.64	6.64
Log Likelihood	-11.56	-11.56

Notes: (1) Adoption year is the year the proposal was adopted or rejected; (2) Length of decision-making process is the number of days between the presentation of a proposal and its adoption or rejection; (3) Co-decision indicates the involvement of the European Parliament in the decision-making procedure; (4) Unanimity denotes the voting rule in the Council.* indicates statistical significance at the 10 per cent level, and** indicates statistical significance at the 5% level. Prob<χ^2 shows the probability of rejecting the null hypothesis that all of the coefficients are simultaneously equal to zero. LR <$\chi^2(k)$ tests that at least one of the k predictors' regression coefficient is not equal to zero.

this variable from the model, the estimated coefficients of the remaining characteristics are practically unchanged (see column 2 of the table).

The estimated probit coefficients for the year of adoption of a proposal are negative and statistically significant at the 5 per cent level, the estimated coefficient of the length of the decision-making process is negative and borderline statistically significant at the 10 per cent level. The importance of co-decision as a decision-making procedure is positive, but the estimated coefficient is statistically insignificant at the 10 per cent level.

These results suggest that 'time' and, to some extent, 'politics' are important to the likelihood of codification. On the other hand, decision-making rules (unanimity in the Council and co-decision between the European Parliament and the Council) do not explain whether judicial decisions are codified. In line with Weiler's prediction, earlier judicial decisions are more likely to be codified than are those put forward later. The length of the decision-making process is borderline significant, but this may be due to some important outlier cases, such as the Monti II proposal *COM (2012) 131*, which was only on the table for 171 days before it was rejected by the national parliaments. This finding suggests that when political disagreements arise over how to respond to judicial decisions, they are less likely to be codified in secondary legislation.

We have identified that 'time' and, to some extent, 'politics' matter to the likelihood of codification. Over time, EU legislators are less willing to codify jurisprudence in secondary legislation. In addition, more politically contested proposals, estimated by reference to the length of the decision-making process, are also less likely to be codified. This suggests that as the institutional and socio-economic setting of the EU becomes increasingly heterogeneous, EU legislators are less willing to approve of codification. The case studies below will explore the political factor further through recent decision-making processes. The case studies thus examine the 'legal-political game' in the EU28, but through cases in which SQ_{Court} was characterized by a high degree of legal clarity. I will also go further and analyse whether and how the role of the Commission and political positions can explain variation in judicial influence.

Before turning to the legal-political game in EU28, findings on political responses of codification, modification, and override will be presented in more detail as they unfolded over time. Political responses of non-adoption will be analysed in the subsequent chapters.

Codifying the Case Law of the Court

The codification of judicial decisions was suggested by the Commission in seventeen proposals and adopted in thirteen, out of which only three appear to have been more politically important: regulation 647/2005 amending 1408/71 on coordination of social security for migrant workers, the Posting of Workers Directive 96/71, and the Burden of Proof Directive 97/80. Proposal *COM (96) 340* on the burden of proof in cases of sex discrimination is a clear example of how the Commission has been successful in reasoning and justifying its proposals on the basis of judicial decisions. In the burden of proof case, judicial decisions were used to push for political integration and to justify that secondary legislation was required to codify what the Court had established. On the basis of the case law of the Court, it became possible to adopt a directive, establishing that the burden of proof reverts to the defendant when the plaintiff has established that less favourable treatment of one gender exists. The previous case law of the Court, including Danfoss,[32] C–127/92 Enderby,[33] and C–400/93 Royal Copenhagen,[34] constituted the main points of reference and justification in the Commission's proposal. References to the Court occurred no fewer than twenty-seven times in that proposal. Article 4 of the directive was adopted on this basis, laying down that the burden of proof reverts to the defendant when the plaintiff has established discrimination based on gender.

The decision-making process on the burden of proof directive was established on the basis of a considerable degree of legal clarity since the Court had matured its position and established a precedent over time by means of a series of cases. The decision-making process took 517 days from the submission of the proposal to the adoption of the legislative act, and it was decided by the Council and the European Parliament in co-decision. In this way, the proposal was adopted by the EU legislators without much dispute. Again, it should be noted that this codification took place in a different political setting, with fifteen member states that were more socio-economically similar than the EU28 is currently.

[32] See note 10 above.

[33] C–127/92 Dr Pamela Mary *Enderby* v Frenchay Health Authority and Secretary of State for Health [1993] ECR I–05535.

[34] C–400/93 Specialarbejderforbundet i Danmark v Dansk Industri, formerly Industriens Arbejdsgivere, acting for *Royal Copenhagen* A/S [1995] ECR I–01275.

Modifying the Case Law of the Court

One of the first examples of the Commission citing previous case law as the reason for a specific provision concerned the Pinna case.[35] The case law addressed French family benefits as regulated by 1408/71 on the coordination of the social security of migrant workers. The Pinna case confirmed the broad interpretation of the principle of equal treatment, even when the praxis leading to actual discrimination of the migrant worker was in compliance with regulation 1408/71. When 1408/71 was adopted, the Council did not reach a unanimous decision on which state was to grant family benefits when the family of a migrant worker does not reside in the same member state as the migrant worker. Typical for that time was the migrant worker as male breadwinner whose wife and children remained in the member state of origin. The question of the exportability of family benefits has again become topical in the heated debate on 'welfare tourism' in EU28. Back in 1984, the general rule adopted by article 73(1) was that of *lex loci laboris*, which states that the state where the work is performed pays family benefits, regardless of where the family lives. However, a dual system was established for the sake of France, under which article 73(2) permitted a French exception. Article 73(2) allowed that if the family of a migrant working in France remained abroad, the family was to receive benefits according to the law of the state of residence. In the case of Pinna, however, the Court found that the French exception discriminated between French nationals and citizens of other member states. The Court made clear that the principle of equal treatment prohibits 'all covert forms of discrimination which, by applying other distinguishing criteria, in fact achieve the same result' (Summary of case 41/84, Pinna).

On this basis, the Court concluded not only that French legislation and praxis in fact discriminated against migrant workers but also that article 73(2) of regulation 1408/71 was invalid. Against this judicial review, in 1988 the Commission put forward an amending regulation. *COM (88) 27* proposed to amend article 73, so that family benefits would be paid according to the legislation of the member state of work, which was maintained when the family stayed abroad (Cornelissen [1997: 37]). However, in its proposal, the Commission inserted a new exception, implying that it did not propose to codify the case law of the Court in full but actually suggesting a modification of what the Court had

[35] See note 27 above.

stated in the Pinna case. The Commission proposed a demarcation of the exportability of family benefits by stating that the amendment to article 73 should be 'subject to the provisions of Annex VI'. The proposed annex VI then stated that certain French housing allowances would not be paid to family members of a migrant worker if they did not reside in France. This exception to the new rule on exportability was probably inserted by the Commission to overcome French opposition. Thus, the Commission proposed partial modification instead of full codification of the case law of the Court.

The Council, however—and particularly France—was unsatisfied with the scope of the proposed modification. Negotiations in the Council led to further modifications, in which annex VI came to state that not just housing allowances but also the home child-care allowance and the parental child-rearing allowance should not be paid to migrant workers' family members if they did not reside in France. The Commission's and the member states' responses to the Pinna case thus demonstrate a modification that was proposed by the Commission and further extended by the Council members. It is thus a first finding on how the Commission and subsequent political responses came to compromise the influence of the Court. They did not fully abide by its jurisprudence.

Overriding the Court

Regulation 1408/71 on the coordination of social security for migrant workers has been a core piece of EU social regulation. At first glance, its integration process appears to be legally driven, each year producing a considerable number of preliminary references before the European Court as well as infringement procedures. However, the development of the regulation has not been devoid of politics but marked by decisive political responses through which the regulatory scope and limits have been clarified (see also, in chapter 5, the political responses to the Pierik cases).[36] One of the most intense disputes between the European Court and legislators has been about drawing the line between social assistance and social security, especially distinguishing the benefits between the two categories. When 1408/71 was adopted, its substantive scope seemed reasonably clear. On one hand, social security

[36] Case 117/77, Bestuur van het Algemeen Ziekenfonds Drenthe-Platteland v G. *Pierik* [1978] ECR 825 and Case 182/78, Bestuur van het Algemeen Ziekenfonds Drenthe-Platteland v G. *Pierik* [1979] ECR 1977.

benefits were included, exhaustively listed by article 4(1) of the regulation. According to the regulation at the time, these benefits were both accessible and exportable for the persons to whom the regulation applied, i.e. migrant workers. The prime characteristics of national *'social security'* schemes again seemed fairly obvious. The general characteristic of social security was, and still is, that security is offered by public schemes through which specific categories of persons are compulsorily or voluntarily insured against defined social risks. The schemes are generally financed by collectively paid contributions. According to a legally defined position a beneficiary of social security schemes is entitled to benefits that mirror the individual contributions paid. The level of benefits is likewise legally specified and made independent of income (Van der Mei [2002: 553]).

On the other hand, there existed excluded *'social assistance'* benefits as established in article 4(4) of the regulation. Social assistance was and is different in nature, since it is what the state offers its citizens or long-term residents who are not able to provide for themselves and who have no alternative financial means. Social assistance is usually granted on a discretionary basis, within which a means test is likely to play a part. In contrast to social security, social assistance schemes are non-contributory and financed by tax revenues. However, previous payment of taxes is not a criterion of entitlement (Van der Mei [2002; 553]). Social assistance policies have traditionally been based on the principle of territoriality (Ferrera [2005]).

The distinction between the two benefit types has become increasingly blurred over the years. As national welfare systems have developed, they have increasingly combined aspects of the two benefit types. The new mixed nature of some benefits means that social security may currently be granted on the basis of a means test; meanwhile, social assistance may increasingly be a legally enforceable right (Pieters [1997: 207]). From the earliest case law, the Court admitted that certain benefits have a dual character somewhere between social 'security' and social 'assistance', while it simultaneously refused to draw an authoritative distinction between the two. From early on member states insisted that, owing to their affinities with social assistance, these 'hybrid' benefits were not exportable. The first case to consider this dual character of a benefit was the Italian Piscitello case on the social aid pension.[37] Despite the member states' warnings about the financial implications of exportability,

[37] Case 139/82 Paola *Piscitello* v Istituto nazionale della previdenza sociale (INPS)[1983] ECR 1427.

the Court concluded that the social aid pension was an old-age benefit within the meaning of article 4(1)(c) of regulation 1408/71. The benefit was granted following objective, legally defined criteria and was therefore exportable outside Italian borders as an old-age benefit. There followed the assessment of the French supplementary allowance in the joined cases 379 to 381/85 and 93/86 *Giletti* et al. from February 1987 (Christensen and Malmstedt [2000: 82]; Eichenhofer [2001: 80]).[38] The CJEU disregarded the national opinions submitted and stated that although the benefit was financed out of tax revenues and aimed to provide a minimum level of income for the recipient, it was an old-age benefit as listed in article 4(1)(c) of 1408/71 and was therefore exportable.

However, despite the Court's conclusions, France refused to comply, and the dispute on the supplementary allowance continued. The Commission initiated infringement procedures against France. While France continued to refuse, the Commission sought to find a political compromise. In 1985, it submitted a proposal to amend 1408/71, suggesting that certain non-contributory benefits were covered by the regulation but that they should not be exportable (*COM (85) 396*). In the proposal, the Commission suggested a new article 10a to the regulation, under which certain non-contributory benefits were made non-exportable. These benefits had to be adopted in an annex IIa and thus be defined by the Council as non-contributory. In this way, the Commission proposed to roll back the Court's rulings, which had applied exportability to these special benefits.

Although the Commission sided with the member states and was actually willing to correct the Court, the member states were not satisfied. Negotiations lasted almost seven years. On 30 April 1992, the Council of Ministers unanimously adopted Regulation 1247/92,[39] but annex IIa had become far more extensive than originally proposed by the Commission. Four member states had managed to insert more benefits into the annex than proposed by the Commission: Greece increased the single benefit proposed by the Commission to nine adopted, Ireland increased the original eleven to twelve, Italy's complement rose from four to seven, and the UK's from two proposed to seven adopted benefits. In addition, the new member states of

[38] Joined Cases 379 to 381/85 and 93/86 Caisse régionale d'assurance maladie Rhône-Alpes v Anna *Giletti*, Directeur régional des affaires sanitaires et sociales de Lorraine v Domenico Giardini, Caisse régionale d'assurance maladie du Nord-Est v Feliciano Tampan and Severino Severini v Caisse primaire centrale d'assurance maladie [1987] ECR 955.

[39] Council Regulation (EEC) No 1247/92 of 30 April 1992 amending Regulation (EEC) No 1408/71 on the application of social security schemes to employed persons, to self-employed persons and to members of their families moving within the Community.

Spain and Portugal inserted two and nine benefits in the annex, respectively. Thus, as a result of long Council negotiations, more benefits became tied to the national territory than the Commission had envisaged. The implications of the override were therefore extended.

The collective political response marked by regulation 1247/92 stood out clearly. The interpretations by the Court went far beyond its political intentions, and the override suggested by the Commission was not sufficient. The Council managed to overcome the significant threshold of unanimous political action, and the unintended case law development was reined in. The new SQ_{reg}^2 was a legislative override of SQ_{Court}.

Regulation 1247/92 as SQ_{reg}^2 amended 1408/71 and added a 'special rule' to the coordination system. The special rule exists today, and it is politically very important. The 'special rule' meant that special non-contributory benefits were included within the material scope of Regulation 1408/71, and rights awarded between member states could thus be aggregated. Additionally, the principle of equal treatment applied to these listed benefits. However, by virtue of article 10a, the benefits remained territorially bound. For a benefit to be coordinated under the 'special rule', it had to be listed in the annex. Its inclusion in the annex had to be approved in the Council. Among other benefits, annex IIa came to include the supplementary allowance from the French National Solidarity Fund,[40] Italy's social pensions for persons without means,[41] and the British attendance allowance,[42] disability living allowance,[43] and family credit (see Annex 4).[44] Previous Court rulings establishing the exportability of the French and Italian benefits were thus overturned.

Whether such a legislative correction was in line with the Treaty was ultimately for the Court to decide. Some years later, it had the opportunity to come back and invalidate the political correction of its previous interpretations. Five years after the adoption of the 'special rule' the Court was requested to consider whether this contradicted the Treaty's article 51 EEC (now article 48 TFEU). Case C–20/96 Snares of 4 November 1997 questioned the compatibility of the special rule and article 51 of primary law.[45] The facts of the case concerned a British national whose continued right to

[40] Law of 30 June 1956. [41] Law no 153 of 30 April 1969.

[42] As formulated in the Social Security Act 1975, sections 37A and 35.

[43] Disability Living Allowance and Disability Working Allowance Act 1991.

[44] Annexes 2, 3, and 4 are available at the author's webpage at www.politicalscience.ku.dk as well as at the OUP webpage for this book.

[45] Case C–20/96 Kelvin Albert *Snares* v Adjudication Officer [1997] ECR I–6057.

disability living allowance depended on his residence in Britain.[46] The case questioned whether the territorial binding of the benefit did not set aside the essence and purpose of article 51: to promote the free movement of migrant workers. The Snares judgment demonstrates that the Court was receptive to previous political correction, in this case, as codified by regulation 1247/92. The CJEU noted that the waiver of residence clauses should be taken into account unless 'otherwise provided in this Regulation' (paragraph 39 of the judgment). The Court reiterated existing case law but emphasized that regulation 1408/71 does not aim to harmonize social security matters and that it was the sole competence of the member state to define the conditions for granting social security benefits as long as these benefits were non-discriminatory (paragraph 45 of the judgment). The Court concluded that the special rule did not contradict the Treaty.

Case C–297/97 Partridge on 11 June 1998 followed up on the Snares case,[47] questioning the nature of another British disability allowance, the attendance allowance, which is a care benefit awarded to dependent people. The preliminary reference concerned whether the answer given by the Court in the case of Snares also applied to a benefit type such as the attendance allowance, and the facts of the case examined the situation of Mrs Partridge, whose attendance allowance was withdrawn when she went to live with her son in France. The British social security commissioner noted that, if Mrs Partridge had been awarded her benefit and had transferred residence before regulation 1247/92 had come into effect, she would have been entitled to take her allowance with her. Before 1247/92, the attendance allowance had been treated as an invalidity benefit within the meaning of 1408/71, article 4(1)(b) (ECR 1998, 3470). The judgment of the Court, however, reaffirmed the conclusions from the Snares case. The attendance allowance was a special non-contributory benefit exclusively governed by the rules established in article 10a and was therefore not exportable outside the territory of the UK.

[46] Albert Snares was a British national who paid contributions to the British social security scheme as an employee for almost twenty-five years. In 1993, he suffered a serious accident and obtained the British disability living allowance. Shortly after, he decided to leave the UK to live with his mother in Tenerife. The relevant institution informed him that, by moving to Spain, he was no longer entitled to the disability living allowance. The preliminary questions raised by the British Court first addressed whether that allowance fell within the material scope of 1408/71. Second, the reference questioned the validity of the new special rule codified by regulation1247/92.

[47] Case C–297/96 Vera A. *Partridge* v Adjudication Officer [1998] ECR I–3467.

Rule Discovery and Further Clarification

With the adoption of regulation 1247/92 and the legal approval thereof in the Snares and Partridge cases, 'special non-contributory' benefits seemed to have been definitively re-territorialized. Together, the Commission, the Court, and the Council institutionalized a compromise: the principle of exportability was not without deviations. In the absence of political guidance, at first the Court had expanded the material scope of the regulation, but its line of interpretation had been politically corrected, and the Court subsequently accepted the new regulatory status quo SQ_{reg}^{2}. Judicial behaviour thus proved receptive to politics.

Temporarily, the special rule seemed to have satisfied all parties and indeed became a politically popular solution. When examining the specific development of annex IIa over the years, it is evident that the initial impact of the annex varies to a great degree between the member states. As illustrated in this book's Annex 4, 'Adding to annex IIa over the years',[48] some member states reacted promptly and listed a large set of benefits in the annex, thus protecting the residence clauses of their social policies. Belgium, Spain, France, Greece, Ireland, Italy, Luxembourg, Portugal, and the UK all made prompt and quite intensive use of the new rule. Over the years, they added benefits to the annex, and even though Denmark and the Netherlands had no 'non-contributory special benefits' at the outset, they also came to make use of the 'special rule' of non-exportability. Adding benefits to annex IIa made it possible for member states to evade exportability, and as some governments made intense use of the opportunity, they incited others to do the same (interviews, member states' civil servants, 4 and 5 April 2001).

The praxis of adding benefits has had its own expansionary logic and ultimately reflects the member states' defence of the territorial principles of their social policies. As noted elsewhere (Martinsen and Falkner [2011]), member states have had a double motive for territorializing these special non-contributory benefits: preventing pensioners residing in the South from exporting costly long-term care benefits that were intended to support them in their home member states, and preventing workers from Eastern Europe and their family members from exporting 'generous' benefits from Northern and Continental Europe. These concerns have only increased over time, and they still prevail.

[48] Annexes 2, 3, and 4 are available at the the author's webpage at www.politicalscience.ku.dk as well as at the OUP webpage for this book.

Since its adoption in 1992, the special rule has been both contested and defended. Inter-institutional disagreements between the Commission, the Council, and the Court over its scope have intensified over the years. In the later judicial decisions of Jauch and Leclere,[49] the Court was again requested to clarify the scope of annex IIa. The case of Jauch concerned a German national who resided in Germany but worked in Austria, where he was affiliated with the social security scheme. The relevant Austrian institution had denied him long-term care because he did not regularly reside in Austria and because the care allowance was listed in annex IIa of 1408/71 and thus was non-exportable (see Annex 4 of this book). The CJEU, however, concluded that the Austrian care allowance ought to be classified as a sickness benefit in cash, for which reason, under Regulation 1408/71's article 19(1)(b), it was exportable; so its listing in annex IIa had been invalid.

The Leclere case interpreted the scope of annex IIa further. The case examined the rights of Mrs Leclere, whose husband had worked in Luxembourg while the couple resided in Belgium. The husband suffered an accident at work in 1981 and thereafter received an invalidity pension paid by the Luxembourg social security services. With the birth of their child, they applied for various allowances in Luxembourg, among which was the maternity allowance. The application was turned down because the couple did not meet the residence requirement for the benefit, which was one of the benefits explicitly listed in regulation 1408/71's annex IIa (see Annex 4).[50] Again, the Court ruled that the maternity allowance had been placed in the annex invalidly and, contrary to the opinion of the Luxembourg government, that its maternity benefit had to be exported.

Against this background, in *COM (2003) 468* (see Annex 1 of this book) the Commission proposed to amend annex IIa with the aim of reducing it substantially. The Commission proposed not only to codify the Jauch and Leclere cases and to remove the Austrian care allowance and the Luxembourgian maternity benefit from annex IIa but also to remove a long list of other benefits from the annex. After difficult negotiations, the Council and the European

[49] Case C–215/99 Friedrich *Jauch* v Pensionsversicherungsanstalt der Arbeiter [2001] ECR I–1901; Case C–43/99 Ghislain *Leclere* and Alina Deaconescu v Caisse nationale des prestations familiales [2001] ECR I–4265.

[50] Annexes 2, 3, and 4 are available at the author's webpage at www.politicalscience.ku.dk as well as at the OUP webpage for this book.

Parliament adopted Regulation 647/2005.[51] They introduced a new definition of special non-contributory benefits. As a result, annex IIa on special benefits was completely revised. Approximately forty benefits were removed and made exportable (interview, Commission, 20 February 2007).

Although European legislators codified judicial decisions in Regulation 647/2005, the Commission was not satisfied (Verschueren [2007]). It also proposed to remove the UK disability living allowance, attendance allowance, and carer's allowance, the Finnish child care allowance, and the Swedish disability allowance and care allowance for disabled children. The member states had not been willing to do this but maintained those benefits in the annex of Regulation 647/2005. For this reason the Commission took the Council and the European Parliament to Court, calling for the annulment of Regulation 647/2005. In October 2007, the Court ruled in support of the Commission. Regulation 647/2005 was annulled, and these specific British, Swedish, and Finnish benefits were removed from annex IIa.[52]

Despite the success of the Commission in both codifying later judicial decisions and achieving the inclusion of additional benefits annulled by the Court, the special rule currently applies to a large number of social benefits. In the codified version of regulation 883/2004 of November 2013, no less than sixty-eight benefits are listed and therefore cannot be exported outside the national territory (see Annex 4 of this book).[53] Non-exportability thus covers a wide range of benefits, such as the guaranteed income for elderly persons in Belgium, social allowance in the Czech Republic, accommodation expenses for pensioners in Denmark, basic subsistence income in Germany, the Spanish minimum income guarantee, supplementary allowances in France, Greek special benefits for the elderly, Irish unemployment assistance, social pensions for persons without means in Italy, social assistance pensions in Lithuania, non-contributory old-age allowances in Hungary, supplementary benefits in the Netherlands, social pensions in Poland, special assistance for immigrants in Finland, Swedish financial support for the elderly, and

[51] Regulation (EC) No 647/2005 of the European Parliament and of the Council of 13 April 2005 amending Council Regulations (EEC) No 1408/71 on the application of social security schemes to employed persons, to self-employed persons, and to members of their families moving within the Community, and (EEC) No 574/72 laying down the procedure for implementing Regulation (EEC) No 1408/71.

[52] Case C–299/05 Commission of the European Communities v European Parliament and Council of the European Union. [2007] ECR I–08695.

[53] With the adoption of regulation 883/2004, annex IIa became annex X.

income-based allowances for jobseekers in the UK, among many other types of benefit.[54]

Despite the efforts of the Commission to trim the special rule, the rule has had its own expansionary logic and constitutes a highly important instrument through which member states can exempt certain benefits from exportability. The rule was once adopted to rein in the Court. It is currently a rule of high political priority in the heated discussion of 'welfare tourism'. The Commission and the Court may remove a number of benefits in concerted action, but the special rule as such is here to stay.

Judicial Influence on EU Social Policy Outputs over Time

Over time EU integration of social policy has been a slow-moving process set in motion by two Treaty articles: negative integration as established by the Court and positive integration by means of regulations and directives as adopted by the EU legislators.

The Court of Justice of the European Union has undoubtedly been an important player in the forward moves towards social integration. However, the Court's influence has been strongest in the two well-known policy areas gender equality/equal treatment and the social security of migrant workers (Caporaso and Tarrow [2009]; Cichowski [2007]; Cichowski and Stone Sweet [2004]; Martinsen [2005]). In these two subfields of social integration, we have the large majority of findings on judicial influence on social policy outputs by means of codification. Ten out of thirteen of the codification findings concern gender equality/equal treatment or social security for migrant workers. However, as noted by Hantrais, progressive integration of gender equality coincided with a more general political and societal push for equality (Hantrais [2007: 123]). The political and socio-economic setting of the Community from the late 1970s to the late 1990s differs strikingly from the EU28 of today. After a difficult inception with the early cases, decades of greater political receptiveness followed, partly explaining the striking progressiveness and legislative effect of gender equality case law. The CJEU

[54] For the full list of benefits, see Annex 4 available at the author's webpage at www.politicalscience.ku.dk as well as at the OUP webpage for this book.

has also advanced social security for migrant workers, and the judicial clarification and extension of rights have been adopted into secondary legislation. However, most of the codification findings concerning social security for migrant workers have been of a more technical and/or apolitical nature. When political interest rose high, as in the case of the exportability of special non-contributory benefits, the Council managed to roll back the Court and ensure territoriality for these benefits. A long 'legal-political' dispute followed, on which the final word will probably never be spoken. It is clear, however, from this specific development over time that politics restrained the course of integration taken by the Court. Although not obliged to do so, the Court subsequently followed the legislators. Such adaptive judicial behaviour tends to be overlooked in the scholarly debate on judicial–legislative dynamics. However, according to Hervey and McHale, judicial adaptation to the legislator is a common response (Hervey and McHale [2015: 91]).

The 'law attainment' approach uncovered the variability of judicial influence on policy outputs. Furthermore, it identified inter-institutional disagreements between the Commission and the EU legislators over how to respond to the case law of the Court. The Commission is the first mover here. It acts as gatekeeper and filters the judicial decisions to which political actors are to respond and how they are to respond. The Commission is thus in a position to select, prioritize, and propose which judicial decisions should have a general legislative impact, and when. In this selection process, the Commission does not always side with the Court, but it has its own position on whether jurisprudence serves the course of integration. Legislators are next to move and decide. They do not simply follow what the Commission suggests but, while the Commission proposes to codify, they are able to modify, extending modification beyond that suggested by the Commission and sometimes refusing to adopt what the Commission proposes.

The analysis over time identified that 'time' and, to some extent, 'politics' condition the likelihood of codification. In line with Weiler's hypothesis (Weiler [1991, 1994]), the analysis shows that, over time, EU legislators are less willing to codify jurisprudence in secondary legislation. In addition, proposals that are politically contested are less likely to be codified. The quiet revolution of early integration, in which jurisprudence transformed the Community legal order and its polity, would face significantly more hurdles in the current EU setting with many more socio-economically heterogeneous member states.

In summary, the findings from the analysis over time question whether the 'judicialisation of politics' has been a general trend. Judicial influence takes place but tends to do so when jurisprudence is less controversial in political terms, and it tended to occur before the 2004 enlargement. The Commission does try to capitalize on the legitimacy of the Court (Alter and Meunier-Aitsahalia [1994: 542]), but it is often unsuccessful. This result questions the strategic capacity of the Commission regarding when to bring jurisprudence into decision making. However, it also questions the assumed legitimacy of the CJEU.[55] More political contestation of legal integration seems to be at play.

The following chapters will examine the processes and conditions of the legal-political game as they unfold between judicial decisions and policy outputs.

References

Alber, J. (2006) 'The European social model and the United States', *European Union Politics* 7(3): 393–419.

Alter, K.J. and Meunier-Aitsahalia, S. (1994) 'Judicial politics in the European Community: European integration and the pathbreaking Cassis de Dijon decision', *Comparative Political Studies* 26(4): 535–61.

Alter, K.J. and Vargas, J. (2000) 'Explaining variation in the use of European litigation strategies. European Community law and British gender equality policy', *Comparative Political Studies* 33(4): 452–82.

Anderson, K. (2015) *Social Policy in the European Union*, London: Palgrave Macmillan.

Armstrong, K. (2010) *Europeanization through Policy Coordination*, Oxford: Oxford University Press.

Armstrong, K. (2013) 'The new governance of EU fiscal discipline', *European Law Review* 5: 601–17.

Blauberger, M. and Schmidt, S.K. (2014) 'Welfare migration? Free movement of EU citizens and access to social benefits', *Research & Politics* 1(3): 1–7.

Büchs, M. (2007) *New Governance in European Social Policy: The Open Method of Coordination*, Basingstoke: Palgrave Macmillan.

Caporaso, J. and Jupille, J. (2001) 'The Europeanization of gender equality policy and domestic structural change', in M.G. Cowles, J. Caporaso and T. Risse (eds), *Transforming Europe*, Ithaca, NY: Cornell University Press, pp. 21–44.

[55] As noted above, Caporaso and Tarrow conclude that the CJEU is the most legitimate supranational institution in the EU (Caporaso and Tarrow [2009: 614]).

Caporaso, J.A. and Tarrow, S. (2009) 'Polanyi in Brussels: supranational institutions and the transnational embedding of markets', *International Organization* 63(04): 593–620.

Chalmers, D., Davies, G., and Monti, G. (2014) *European Union Law*, Third edition, Cambridge: Cambridge University Press.

Christensen, A. and Malmstedt, M. (2000) '*Lex loci laboris versus lex loci domicilii*—an inquiry into the normative foundations of European social security law', *European Journal of Social Security* 2(1): 69–111.

Cichowski, R.A. (2001) 'Judicial rulemaking and the institutionalization of European Union sex equality policy', in A.S. Sweet, W. Sandholtz and N. Fligstein (eds), *The Institutionalization of Europe*, Oxford: Oxford University Press, pp. 113–37.

Cichowski, R.A. (2007) *The European Court and Civil Society, Litigation, Mobilization and Governance*, Cambridge: Cambridge University Press.

Cichowski, R.A. and Stone Sweet, A. (2004) 'Sex equality', in A. Stone Sweet (ed.), *The Judicial Construction of Europe*, Oxford: Oxford University Press, pp. 147–97.

Conant, L.J. (2002) *Justice Contained, Law and Politics in the European Union*, Ithaca, NY: Cornell University Press.

Cornelissen, R. (1996) 'The principle of territoriality and the Community regulations on social security (Regulations 1408/71 and 574/72)', *Common Market Law Review* 33(3): 439–71.

Cornelissen, R. (1997) '25 Years of Regulation (EEC) No. 1408/71. Its achievements and its limits', in *25 Years of Regulation (EEC) No. 1408/71 for Migrant Workers—Past Experiences, Present Problems and Future Perspectives*, Stockholm: Swedish National Social Insurance Board, 27–68.

Craig, P. and De Búrca, G. (1998) *EU Law. Text, Cases and Materials*, Second edition, Oxford: Oxford University Press.

Craig, P. and De Búrca, G. (2011) *EU Law. Text, Cases and Materials*, Fifth edition, Oxford: Oxford University Press.

De la Porte, C. (2012) 'The EU and the welfare state: addressing policy challenges through the OMC', in B. Greve (ed.), *The Routledge Handbook on the Welfare State*, London: Routledge, pp. 171–90.

De la Porte, C. and Natali, D. (2014) 'Altered Europeanisation of pension reform in the context of the great recession: Denmark and Italy compared', *West European Politics* 37(4): 732–49.

De La Porte, C. and Pochet, P. (2002) *Building Social Europe through the Open Method of Co-Ordination*, Brussels: PIE-Peter Lang.

Eichenhofer, E. (2001) *Sozialrecht der Europäischen Union*, Berlin: Erich Schmidt Verlag.

Falkner, G. (1994) *Supranationalität trotz Einstimmigkeit?: Entscheidungsmuster der EU am Beispiel Sozialpolitik*, Bonn: Europa Union Verlag.

Falkner, G. (2010) 'The European Union's social dimension', in M. Cini and N.P.-S. Borragán (eds), *European Union Politics*, Oxford: Oxford University Press, pp. 268–81.

Ferrera, M. (2003) 'European integration and national social citizenship: changing boundaries, new structuring?', *Comparative Political Studies* 36(6): 611–52.
Ferrera, M. (2005) *The Boundaries of Welfare*, Oxford: Oxford University Press.
Hantrais, L. (2007) *Social Policy in the European Union*, Basingstoke: Palgrave Macmillan.
Hemerijck, A. (2013) *Changing Welfare States*, Oxford: Oxford University Press.
Hervey, T. (2010) '" Adjudicating in the shadow of the informal settlement?": The Court of Justice of the European Union, new governance and social welfare', *Current Legal Problems* 63(1): 92–152.
Hervey, T. and McHale, J. (2015) *European Union Health Law: Themes and Implications*, Cambridge: Cambridge University Press.
Holloway, J. (1981) *Social Policy Harmonisation in the European Community*, Westmead: Gower.
Höpner, M. and Schäfer, A. (2012) 'Embeddedness and regional integration: waiting for Polanyi in a Hayekian setting', *International Organization* 66(03): 429–55.
Klüver, H. (2011) 'The contextual nature of lobbying: explaining lobbying success in the European Union', *European Union Politics* 12(4): 483–506.
Klüver, H. and Sagarzazu, I. (2013) 'Ideological congruency and decision-making speed: the effect of partisanship across European Union institutions', *European Union Politics* 14(3): 388–407.
Leibfried, S. (2010) 'Social policy: left to the judges and the markets?', in H.S. Wallace, W. Wallace, M.A. Pollack, H. Wallace and A.R. Young (eds), *Policy-Making in the European Union*, Oxford: Oxford University Press, 253–83.
Mabbett, D. (2005) 'The development of rights-based social policy in the European Union: the example of disability rights', *JCMS: Journal of Common Market Studies* 43(1): 97–120.
Mabbett, D. (2014) 'Polanyi in Brussels or Luxembourg? Social rights and market regulation in European insurance', *Regulation & Governance* 8(2): 186–202.
Martinsen, D.S. (2005) 'The Europeanization of welfare—the domestic impact of intra-European social security', *Journal of Common Market Studies* 43(5): 1027–54.
Martinsen, D.S. (2007) 'The Europeanization of gender equality—who controls the scope of non-discrimination?', *Journal of European Public Policy* 14(4): 544–62.
Martinsen, D.S. (2009) 'Conflict and conflict management in the cross-border provision of healthcare services', *West European Politics* 32(4): 792–809.
Martinsen, D.S. and Falkner, G. (2011) 'Social policy: problem-solving gaps, partial exits, and court-decision traps', in G. Falkner (ed.), *The EU's Decision Traps. Comparing Policies*, Oxford: Oxford University Press, pp. 128–45.
Martinsen, D.S. and Vollaard, H. (2014) 'Implementing Social Europe in times of crises: re-established boundaries of welfare?', *West European Politics* 37(4): 677–92.
Nowak, T. (2008) 'The Working Time Directive and the European Court of Justice', *Maastricht Journal of European and Comparative Law* 15(4): 447–71.
Pennings, F. (1998) *Introduction to Social Security Law*, The Hague: Kluwer Law International.

Pierson, P. (1996) 'The path to European integration: a historical institutionalist analysis', *Comparative Political Studies* 29(2): 123–63.

Pieters, D. (1997) 'Towards a radical simplification of the social security co-ordination', in P. Schoukens (ed.), *Prospects of Social Security Co-ordination*, Louvain: Uitgeverij Acco, pp. 117–225.

Pollack, M.A. and Hafner-Burton, E. (2000) 'Mainstreaming gender in the European Union', *Journal of European Public Policy* 7(3): 432–56.

Romero, F. (1993) 'Migration as an issue in European interdependence and integration: the case of Italy', in A.S. Milward (ed.), *The Frontier of National Sovereignty, History and Theory 1945–1992*, London: Routledge, pp. 35–59.

Scharpf, F.W. (1996) 'Negative and positive integration in the political economy of European welfare states', in G. Marks, F.W. Scharpf, P.C. Schmitter and W. Streeck (eds), *Governance in the European Union*, London: Sage Publications, pp. 15–40.

Scharpf, F.W. (2002) 'The European social model: coping with the challenges of diversity', *Journal of Common Market Studies* 40(4): 645–70.

Scharpf, F.W. (2010) 'The asymmetry of European integration, or why the EU cannot be a "social market economy"', *Socio-Economic Review* 8(2): 211–50.

Steffen, M., Lamping, W., and Lehto, J. (2005) 'Introduction. The Europeanization of health policies', in M. Steffen (ed.), *Health Governance in Europe. Issues, challenges and theories*, London: Routledge, pp. 1–18.

Treib, O., Bähr, H., and Falkner, G. (2011) 'Social policy and environmental policy: comparing modes of governance', in W.R.a.W.W. Udo Diedrichs (ed.), *The Dynamics of Change in EU Governance*, Cheltenham: Edward Elgar, pp. 103–31.

Van der Mei, A.P. (2002) 'Regulation 1408/71 and co-ordination of special non-contributory benefit schemes', *European Law Review* 5: 551–66.

Van der Mei, A.P. (2003) *Free Movement of Persons within the European Community. Cross-Border Access to Public Benefits*, Oxford, Portland, OR: Hart Publishing.

Verschueren, H. (2007) 'European (internal) migration law as an instrument for defining the boundaries of national solidarity systems', *European Journal of Migration and Law* 9(3): 307–46.

Vollaard, H., Bovenkamp, H.v.d., and Martinsen, D.S. (2015) 'The making of a European healthcare union: insights from comparative federalism', *Journal of European Public Policy*, doi:10.1080/13501763.2015.1034160.

Vollaard, H., van de Bovenkamp, H.M., and Vrangbæk, K. (2013) 'The emerging EU quality of care policy: from sharing information to enforcement', *Health Policy* 111(3): 226–33.

Von Maydell, B.B. (1999) 'Auf dem Wege zu einem gemeinsamen Markt für Gesundheitsleistungen in der Europäischen Gemeinschaft', *Vierteljahresschrift für Sozialrecht* 1: 3–19.

Warner, H. (1984) 'EC social policy in practice: Community action on behalf of women and its impact in the member states', *JCMS: Journal of Common Market Studies* 23(2): 141–67.

Weiler, J. (1991) 'The transformation of Europe', *Yale Law Journal* 100: 2403–83.

Weiler, J.H.H. (1994) 'A quiet revolution: the European Court of Justice and its interlocutors', *Comparative Political Studies* 26(4): 510–34.

Wincott, D. (2001) 'The Court of Justice and the European policy process', in J. Richardson (ed.), *European Union, Power and Policy-Making*, London: Routledge, pp. 179–97.

Zeitlin, J. (2011) 'Is the open method of coordination an alternative to the Community method', in R. Dehousse (ed.), *The 'Community Method': Obstinate or Obsolete?* Basingstoke: Palgrave Macmillan, pp. 135–47.

4

Battles on Working Time: Rejecting Court Influence

Our concern is that the SiMAP judgement, by interpreting 'working time' in a way which we believe was not intended, might have prejudiced the ability of many Member States to fulfil their obligations under the Directive. Under the national law of several Member States, time spent by doctors who are on call but resting is not characterised as working time. (...) The impact of the judgement on (all) health systems could be to significantly reduce the availability and productivity of doctors.

(Unofficial letter from the UK, Denmark, Sweden, and the Netherlands to the commissioner)

Of course there's room for disagreeing. There is always room for changing the case law of the Court, particularly if it's not based on the treaties—you know, if it's based on the legislation instead of the treaties itself .... I mean, working time is a good example of an issue where member states would be quite happy to overturn the case law of the ECJ.

(Interview, Council, 25 July 2012)

There 'wouldn't have been any need to negotiate anything if there hadn't been this ruling because the ruling created the practical problem ... [W]e negotiate because there is a problem in real life. And this problem was provoked by the Court. And that's why the purpose was to change the directive'.

(Interview, Social Partners, 4 July 2013)

EU working time regulation has long been a contested area of EU social policy. The Single European Act adopted in 1987 introduced a new article into the constitutional framework, article 118A (later article 137(1) EC; now article 153(1) TFEU), which stipulated that measures aiming to improve health and safety at work could be adopted by qualified majority voting. Based on article 118A, the Commission proposed a Working Time Directive (WTD) in 1990.[1] From the outset, the United Kingdom opposed the directive. In particular, it firmly opposed the choice of legal basis, arguing that working time is not a health and safety matter but rather an employment issue. Thus, according to the UK, the appropriate Treaty basis was either article 100 (now article 114 TFEU) or article 235 of the EEC Treaty (now article 352 TFEU), both of which require unanimity. If the unanimity rule applied, the UK could veto the proposal (Lewis [2003: 116]). The idea that the EU should regulate working time was thus disputed from the start.

Nevertheless, the Council of Ministers adopted a working time directive in 1993,[2] establishing SQ_{reg}^{1}. The WTD has proved to be one of the most controversial statutes in social Europe. The directive aims to improve the health and safety of workers by setting minimum standards for the organization of working time. In short, it establishes a maximum work-week of forty-eight hours on average within a reference period of four months, minimum daily and weekly rest periods, and a minimum of four weeks' paid leave per year. The CJEU played a key role in the interpretation of working time, at times directly ruling against the positions of powerful member states. EU regulation of working time is indeed an interesting case for examining the tensions and dynamics between law and politics in the European Community (Nowak [2008: 448]). The timeline of the process traced between T_1 and T_2 in the analysis below can be summarized as shown in figure 4.1.

Below, I first analyse the process through which the WTD was initially adopted and through which the regulatory status quo SQ_{reg}^{1} was thus established. The following section examines how the politically established status quo was seriously disrupted by subsequent legal interpretations, creating SQ_{Court}. The political responses to SQ_{Court} are then investigated by tracing why judicial influence on the policy output was ultimately rejected despite intense and prolonged interaction between political actors and social partners.

[1] Commission proposal *COM (1990) 317* for a directive concerning certain aspects of the organization of working time.

[2] Council Directive 93/104/EC of 23 November 1993 concerning certain aspects of the organization of working time.

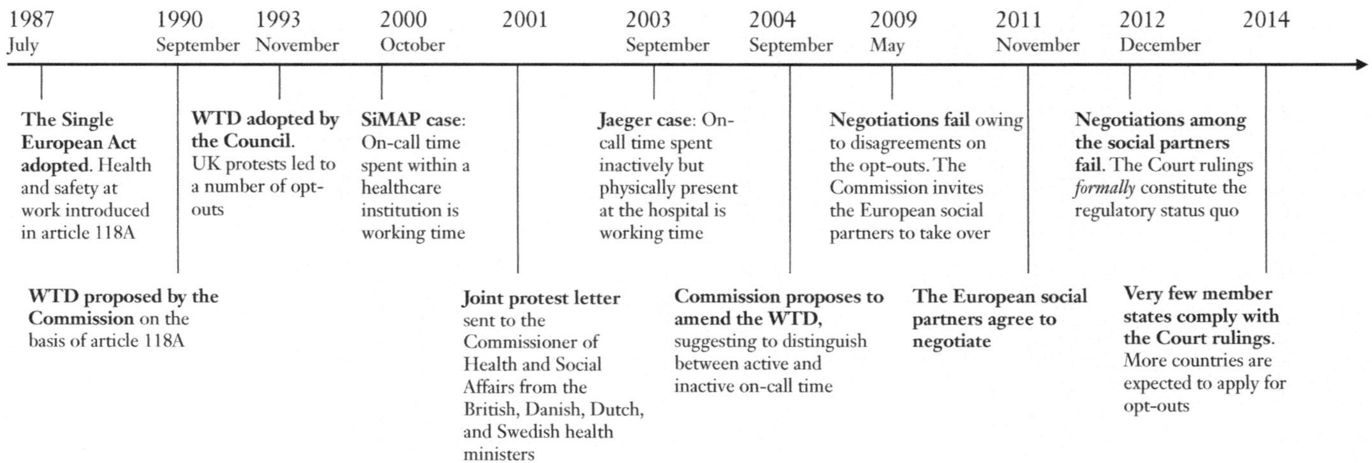

Fig. 4.1 Timeline of EU Working Time Regulation

Creating a Regulatory Status Quo: Adopting the Working Time Directive

The negotiations leading to the adoption of the WTD were difficult from the start. However, the UK's position regarding the directive's legal basis was not accepted, and Council negotiations on the proposal were initiated. Despite its constitutional opposition to the proposal, the UK participated in the Council negotiations, and many attempts were made to convince it to join the position of the majority. However, because the voting rule was merely a qualified majority, the other Council members were not required to consider the UK's position seriously. Negotiations nevertheless progressed, consistent with the consensus norm. In due course, the UK won some important concessions in the negotiations (Beach [2001: 156]). Moreover, the attempts to establish consensus in the Council led to variation and differentiation from the outset. Certain sectors were exempted from the directive, including air, rail, road, sea, inland waterway, and lake transport, sea fishing, other work at sea, and the activities of doctors in training (article 1(3) of the WTD).

The most important concession that the UK won was the ability to opt out of the forty-eight-hour maximum workweek. The opt-out facility established that workers could agree with their employer on an individual basis that the forty-eight-hour maximum did not apply to them (article 18(b)(i) of the WTD). However, this facility was made temporary. The last part of article 18(b)(i) states that, after seven years, the opt-out provision should be re-examined and its future status decided.

The Council could certainly have ignored the UK's requests. A sufficient qualified majority was established as early as 1991, but the Council continued the negotiations for another two years, seeking the UK's approval (Lewis [2003]). In the early history of EU working time regulation the Council's 'informal consensus-reflex' (Lewis [2003: 118]) was ultimately detrimental to the future development of the regulation of working time. The focus on a consensus norm by the European legislators pushed the policy output closer to the lowest common denominator than would have been the case if a vote had been held early in the EU negotiation on working time regulation:

> Working time illustrates how derogations and exemptions in the search for consensus can spiral into a pattern of lowest common denominatorism. (Lewis [2003: 119])

Because of the opt-out possibility and exemptions that were added to the text of the legislation from the outset, rules on working time became rather patchy and open to interpretation. The twelve Council members of that time were unable to agree but remained uneasy about outvoting one another. The attempts to accommodate the UK's position crucially characterized the text negotiated; however, they did not silence the British government. British opposition had not eased. The result was a contested directive with considerable variation.

Working time was defined as 'any period during which the worker is working, at the employer's disposal and carrying out his activity or duties', and rest periods were defined as 'any period which is not working time' (article 2(1) and (2) of Directive 93/104/EC). In the future course of integration, this *definition of working time* together with the *opt-out* possibility became the two main points of political conflict (Marks and Steenbergen [2002]). Political negotiations on EU working time thus proceeded in a two-dimensional political space. The disagreements on the definition of working time unfolded along a *left–right dimension*, whereas the opt-out involved a *more versus less integration dimension*.

During the early Council's negotiations, it was already clear that what constituted working time was open to debate. At that time, the European Parliament had no co-decision power because the cooperation procedure applied. Nevertheless, the EP intervened early in the debate on the definition. In 1991, the EP Committee of Women's Rights proposed that provisions concerning *on-call duty* for medical staff were included within the definition of working time (Nowak [2008: 450]). This extended view of what constituted working time was not considered, was not even referred to in the negotiations, and was indeed very far from the UK's position.

Despite the addition of the opt-out possibility and exemptions in the text of the legislation that were made to seek the British delegation's approval, the UK decided to abstain from the final vote in the Council of Ministers (Beach [2001: 156]). The UK's abstention from the vote became one manifestation of several against EU working time regulation by the British member state. The working time directive was nevertheless adopted by the Council in November 1993, and the regulatory status quo SQ_{reg}^{1} was created.

The Court of Justice and the Legal Integration of Working Time

Soon after the adoption of the directive, the UK brought an annulment procedure before the CJEU. The UK maintained its position that article 118A (now article 153(1) TFEU) was an improper legal basis for the directive. In

November 1996, the Court released its judgment. The European Court did not support the UK's position, concluding that article 118A *was* the correct legal basis for the directive.[3] However, the Court did acknowledge one of the UK's arguments, agreeing that the weekly rest period did not need to be on a Sunday, as established in article 5 of the Directive. The use of Sunday as the weekly rest period could not be connected to health and safety issues.

In 1998, the Commission presented a proposal to amend the WTD, primarily aiming to bring within the purview of the proposal all sectors, except for seafarers, that had been explicitly excluded by article 1(3).[4] At this point, the decision-making procedure had changed to co-decision, and the European Parliament was established as co-legislator. In 2000, the two legislators managed to agree and brought into the directive all the exempted sectors apart from seafarers.[5] The Commission's proposal made one reference to the case law of the Court, to the annulment case brought by the UK against the Council (see Annex 1 of this book on responses over time). The Commission justified the removal of article 5 by reference to the Court. The original directive's article 5 had set out that the weekly rest period should include Sunday. According to the Court, Sunday as a rest day could not be justified for health and safety reasons. The proposed amendment was approved by the two legislators, and thus, at this point, it codified the case law of the Court (see Annex 1).

The *SiMAP* Ruling: A New Court-generated Status Quo

While the Council and the European Parliament negotiated to revise the Directive, the Court prepared what came to be a controversial, landmark ruling: SiMAP. In SiMAP, the Spanish Trade Union of Doctors in Public

[3] C-84/94 *United Kingdom* of Great Britain and Northern Ireland v Council of the European Union [1996] ECR I-5755.

[4] *COM (1998) 662-2*, 18 November 1998, Proposal for a Council Directive amending Directive 93/104/EC of 23 November 1993 concerning certain aspects of the organization of working time to cover sectors and activities excluded from that directive.

[5] Directive 2000/34/EC of the European Parliament and of the Council of 22 June 2000, amending Council Directive 93/104/EC concerning certain aspects of the organization of working time to cover sectors and activities excluded from that directive.

Service requested the European Court to rule on whether on-call time for doctors was considered working time.[6] The SiMAP ruling established that doctors were not excluded from the directive, although article 2(2) of the directive allowed for the exemption of public service activities that maintain public order and security. Furthermore, the Court established that on-call *time* spent at a healthcare institution constituted working time within the meaning of the Directive, while on-call *duty* in which the doctor was not required to be at the healthcare centre did not constitute working time:

> Time spent on call by doctors in primary healthcare teams must be regarded in its entirety as working time and, where appropriate, as overtime within the meaning of Directive 93/104 if they are required to be at the health centre. If they must merely be contactable at all times when on call, only time linked to the actual provision of primary healthcare services must be regarded as working time. (CJEU conclusion in case C–303/98 *SiMAP*)

The conclusions of the ruling were fairly clear—but indeed controversial. The SiMAP ruling caused great political debate. The ruling went far beyond the Council's definition of working time. Based on the opinion stated by the European Parliament's Committee on Women's Rights, we know that on-call time had been addressed during early negotiations on the directive, but at that point on-call time did not even make it into the final report of the EMPL committee in the European Parliament, which was in charge of the proposal. In 1991, on-call time was set aside because it constituted a too-radical interpretation of working time. However, almost a decade later the issue was brought onto the agenda again, by the Court.

Initial Political Responses: Requests to Override the Court

The initial reactions to the SiMAP ruling simply refused to consider its implications, finding the decision too controversial to address. Only a few weeks after SiMAP, the Commission published a report evaluating the implementation of the WTD.[7] In this report, the Commission mentioned the SiMAP

[6] Case C–303/98 Sindicato de Medicos de Asistencia Publica (*SiMAP*) v Conselleria de Sanidad y Consumo de la Generalidad Valenciana [2000] ECR 1–7963.

[7] *COM (2000)* 787 final as of 1 December 2000.

case only briefly and did not substantially engage in the question of on-call time. The Commission's reluctance to address the new definition of working time indicates that, at this point, the Commission did not want to challenge the member states and did not want to use the Court's decision to push for strengthened social rights. In fact, the Commission shared the position of the member states that on-call time should not be considered working time. The Commission had followed the SiMAP case closely and had provided written observations to the Court, as had Spain, Finland, and the UK. It had submitted that, even when a doctor was at a health centre, on-call periods should not be considered part of working time as defined in article 2 of the directive. Thus essentially the Commission had argued that the Spanish practice was compatible with the directive.[8] The Court, however, ruled against the Commission's position. As is clear from the Commission's implementation report, the Commission deliberately decided to ignore a judgment that it did not agree with. In addition, the Commission knew that its position was in line with the political majority in the Council.

National reactions to the ruling were prompt. The German Federal Minister of Labour, Walter Riester, refused to acknowledge that the judgment had any general effect. He officially stated that because the ruling concerned the Spanish system, it did not apply to Germany, although Spanish and German regulations were quite similar (Nowak [2008: 456]). Political concerns regarding the judgment were also raised in a joint letter from the health ministers of the UK, Denmark, Sweden, and the Netherlands to the commissioner for Employment and Social Affairs, Anna Dimantpoulou. In the letter, the health ministers stated their concern as follows:

> Our concern is that the SiMAP judgement, *by interpreting 'working time' in a way which we believe was not intended*, might have prejudiced the ability of many Member States to fulfil their obligations under the Directive. Under the national law of several Member States, time spent by doctors who are on call but resting is not characterised as working time ... The impact of the judgment on (all) health systems could be to significantly reduce the availability and productivity of doctors. (Unofficial letter from the health ministers of the UK, Denmark, Sweden, and the Netherlands to the commissioner for Employment and Social Affairs, emphasis added)[9]

[8] See the opinion of Advocate-General Saggio in the SiMAP case, delivered on 16 December 1999, paragraph 33.

[9] The unofficial letter was acquired from one of the key respondents interviewed for this book. The letter is undated but signed by John Hutton, as minister of state for health from the UK; Lars Løkke Rasmussen, as minister for interior and health from Denmark; Lars Engquist, as minister of health and social affairs in Sweden; and Aart Jan de Geus, as health minister in the Netherlands.

The letter also stated that the health ministers found the definition of working time given by the Court 'departed from the definition of what constitutes "working time" contained in article 2(1) of the Directive' (unofficial letter from the health ministers of the UK, Denmark, Sweden, and the Netherlands to the commissioner for Employment and Social Affairs).

On 11 May 2001, the Commission and member state experts held a meeting to deliberate the implications of the SiMAP ruling. The member states called for the Commission to act and for legal certainty to be re-established. The member states raised concerns about the scope of the judgment. During the meeting, the member states questioned whether the judicial decision was restricted to the medical sector or applied generally, and thus to sectors such as the fire service, the fishing industry, boarding schools, the police, and defence. Germany was one of the member states noting that the judicial interpretation had unforeseen consequences and was out of line with the Directive:

> The SIMAP judgment took the German government and trade unions by surprise. At the time Directive 93/104 was adopted, things were not seen in the same light as the Court subsequently saw them in (the Commission too had been taken just as much by surprise as the Member States). The result was quite a good deal of uncertainty on this matter. (Unofficial minutes from the meeting of 11 May 2001 between the Commission and Member States' experts, emphasis added)[10]

The Commission's legal service also participated in the meeting. In contrast to the position of Germany, among other member states, the legal service found the SiMAP ruling to be 'exemplary' and to distinguish clearly two aspects of the WTD:

> Point 47 of the judgment highlights two aspects of the Directive: working time and rest time. *There is no third way: time is either working time or rest time.* Looking at the motives underlying points 49 and 50, the Court is referring to the essential objective of Directive 93/104, viz., protecting workers' health and safety. The decision is of an *exemplary* nature. (Unofficial minutes from the meeting of 11 May 2001 between the Commission and Member States' experts, emphasis added)

Thus, the Commission's legal service did not support the viewpoint that the judicial interpretations departed from the directive's meaning. However, the Commission DG on Employment and Social Affairs considered it too early to reach conclusions about the Court's interpretation of the direction

[10] The unofficial minutes were given to the author by one of the key respondents interviewed for this book.

from the meeting and wanted to examine the decision in more depth. Thus, no clear course of action emerged from this meeting. What was clear, however, was that the Court ruling was interpreted differently. Member states found it to depart clearly from the political aims of the directive, whereas the Commission's legal service found it to be exemplary. Conversely, the responsible Commission DG did not express its position.

Confirming Legal Interpretations: The Jaeger Case

While waiting for the Commission's response, further case law confirmed the conclusions of the SiMAP ruling. Moreover, a consolidated version of the WTD was passed through the legislators, who revised it to become Directive 2003/88.[11] However, this third version of the WTD did not make any substantial changes and only consolidated the previous text of the legislation. The directive made no reference to the case law of the Court.

The subsequent case of CIG repeated the conclusions of SiMAP,[12] and the later case of BECTU clarified that workers on short-term contracts also earned the right to paid annual leave.[13] In 2003, the Jaeger case followed.[14]

In this case, a higher German labour court asked the CJEU whether time spent on call, but spent inactively, was considered working time, even though the doctor was able to sleep during it. Denmark, France, Germany, the Netherlands, and the UK provided opinions in the case, sharing the viewpoint that time spent inactively on call was not working time. In this case, the Commission took a separate position. It held that on-call time was generally working time because the employee had to be at the disposal of the employer.[15] The Commission's position thus had changed and, at this point, been adapted to be consistent with the SiMAP ruling.

The member states that provided an opinion before the Court were indeed concerned. In the hearings before the Court, the German government

[11] Directive 2003/88/EC of the European Parliament and of the Council of 4 November 2003 concerning certain aspects of the organization of working time.

[12] C–241/99 Confederación Intersindical Galega (*CIG*) v Servicio Galega de Saúde (Sergas) [2001] ECR I–5139.

[13] C–173/99 Broadcasting, Entertainment, Cinematographic and Theatre Union (*BECTU*) v Secretary of State for Trade and Industry [2001] ECR I–4881.

[14] Case C–151/02 Landeshauptstadt Kiel v Norbert *Jaeger* [2003] ECR I–8389.

[15] See opinion of AG Ruiz-Jarabo in the Jaeger case, delivered on 8 April 2003, paragraph 18.

submitted a quite alarming economic impact assessment, stating that if the Court confirmed the precedent established in the SiMAP case, staffing requirements would increase by 24 per cent and between 15,000 and 27,000 additional doctors would have to be employed in Germany. The German government estimated that the additional costs would be approximately €1.75 billion.[16]

The submitted economic concerns did not make the Court change its line of reasoning. It did not adapt its ruling in consideration of these political-economic concerns. Instead, the CJEU's conclusions were largely a restatement of the SiMAP ruling, establishing that on-call time during which the doctor had to be physically present at the hospital, regardless of whether she or he could rest, constituted working time within the meaning of the directive. The Court found that whether the doctor had a bed in the hospital so that s/he could rest while on call was irrelevant (paragraph 60 of the judgment). Thus, the Court did not accept the member states' position that inactive on-call time did not constitute working time. After Jaeger, it was irrevocably clear that the inclusion of on-call time as working time applied generally and not specifically to the Spanish system, as had once been held by the German minister of labour. The new status quo SQ_{Court} that the Court's rulings had generated could no longer be ignored.

However, the new SQ_{Court} was not complied with. Despite the clarity of the case law and its confirmation through subsequent cases, many member states flouted the CJEU conclusions and did not implement them (*Financial Times*, 'UK seeks to keep working time opt-out', 2 December 2005).

Initial Political Responses

In January 2004, the Commission finally followed up on the SiMAP and Jaeger rulings, sending out a communication as an initial step to revise the WTD.[17] The Communication addressed the opt-out possibility in article 18(1)(b)(i), which allowed individual agreement between an employer and an employee to work beyond the forty-eight-hour workweek. The Communication also provided a dense impact analysis of the CJEU case

[16] See *COM (2003) 843*, 20 for this assessment.
[17] *COM (2003) 843*, 15 January 2004.

law. The Commission recognized that the judgments of the Court had to be considered but did not specify how to do this. In the Communication, the Commission made clear that the Court decisions had made more member states make use of the opt-out possibility. Before the SiMAP ruling, only the UK used it. However, because of the SiMAP ruling, France, Germany, the Netherlands, and Spain had adopted the opt-out for the hospital sector. Luxembourg had introduced it for hotels and catering. Furthermore, the Commission noted that, among the new member states, Malta, Cyprus, and Slovenia had already adopted the opt-out possibility in their national legislation and that Estonia, Hungary, Latvia, and Lithuania were expected to follow suit (*COM (2003) 843*, 15–16). The case law of the Court had thus expanded the use of the opt-out from one member state to thirteen, creating a considerable degree of differentiation in the application of the directive (Martinsen and Wessel [2014]).

The European Parliament promptly reacted to the Commission's communication through a resolution.[18] In this, the EP criticized the Commission for being vague about the way forward. The EP also called for the abolishment of the individual opt-out possibility. It noted that the use of the opt-out had grown considerably, extending from the UK to many other member states. It also noted that other member states had adopted the opt-out to overcome the problems raised by the SIMAP and Jaeger decisions:

> It can therefore be said that use of the opt-out has been general rather than specific, under subjective rather than objective conditions, and to an extent that it exceeds practical requirements. (*Resolution A5–0026/2004*, 13)

By this resolution, the co-legislator made it clear that it would enter negotiations to revise the directive with a strong position.

As a first attempt to revise the WTD, the Commission asked the social partners to enter negotiations and to work out an agreement. However, the social partners declined to do so (*COM (2004) 607*, 2), apparently on account of the refusal of the European employer organization UNICE (interview, social partners, August 2012).[19] It was therefore left to the Commission to initiate a legislative process to revise the WTD.

[18] *Resolution A5–0026/2004*, 29 January 2004.

[19] In 2007, the European employers' organization UNICE changed its name to Business Europe.

Commission Proposal: Overriding the Case Law of the Court

In September 2004, the Commission provided its official proposal for amending the WTD.[20] The proposal marked a departure from the course of legal integration, and the case law of the Court was only referred to once. This is remarkable because, as we have seen in the study over time, and as noted elsewhere, the Commission often refers to Court decisions in its proposals for justification (Nowak [2008: 467]). It is also remarkable because the January 2004 communication from the Commission had addressed the case law of the Court in detail. Among other aspects, the 2004 communication had pointed to the causal link between the judicial decisions and the extended use of the opt-out possibility. However, in the September 2004 proposal, the Jaeger and SiMAP decisions were mentioned only at one point (*COM (2004) 607*, 2). This deliberate disregard of the case law of the Court demonstrates the position and strategic behaviour of the Commission. Despite not stating so explicitly, the Commission in fact intended to override the course of legal integration.

What the Commission proposed was a fundamental breach with the established case law by distinguishing between '*on-call time*' and '*inactive on-call time*'. The new category 'inactive on-call time' was established as follows:

> The inactive part of on-call time *shall not be regarded as working time*, unless national law or, in accordance with national law and/or practice, a collective agreement or an agreement between the two sides of industry decides otherwise. The period during which the worker carries out his activity or duties during on-call time shall always be regarded as working time. (article 2a of *COM (2004) 607*, emphasis added)

In addition, the proposal maintained the *opt-out* of the forty-eight-hour work-week but introduced a requirement that the opt-out be established within a collective agreement between the social partners and that it could not be based on individual consent alone (*COM (2004) 607*, 4, paragraph 12). However, if no collective agreement was in place, individual consent would

[20] *COM (2004) 607* Proposal for a directive of the European Parliament and of the Council amending Directive 2003/88/EC concerning certain aspects of the organization of working time.

suffice. Furthermore, the Commission proposed to extend the *reference period* for the calculation of the maximum weekly working time from four months to one year (*COM (2004) 607*, 4, paragraph 14). In sum, the Commission's proposal not only departed from established case law but also gave companies and member states greater flexibility in organizing working time. Thus, the 2004 proposal was a setback for social rights and proposed to revert the course of legal integration. Without making explicit reference to the case law of the Court, the Commission in fact proposed to override judicial integration. Table 4.1 sets out the three provisions of the Commission's proposal that in fact responded to judicial decisions or that became major issues in subsequent political negotiations.

When placed on a two-dimensional matrix with *more integration versus less integration* as the vertical dimension and *left–right* horizontally, it can be seen that the Commission maintained less integration by means of the opt-out facility. In addition, its position towards social rights is to the right because it did not propose to strengthen workers' rights by treating inactive 'on-call time' as working time. In addition, the Commission proposed an extension of the reference period for the calculation of working time, which would grant the employer more flexibility when calculating working time. This position of the Commission in response to SQ_{Court} is summarized alongside the positions of the other political actors in the concluding figure 4.2.

Table 4.1 Provisions Responding to Judicial Decisions or that became Major Political Issues

	Commission proposal *COM (2004) 607* as of 22 September 2004
Working time	Article 2a inserted. Proposes a distinction between 'on-call time' and 'inactive on-call time'. Inactive on-call time shall not be considered working time. Proposes to override the case law of the Court
Reference period	Article 16(b): extension of the reference period for the calculation of maximum weekly working time from four months to one year
Opt-out possibility	Article 18(1)(b): maintains the opt-out possibility for the forty-eight-hour work-week

Political Positions in the Council and the European Parliament

The Council of Ministers welcomed the distinction between 'inactive on-call time' and 'on-call time', claiming that it would provide legal certainty. The Council also welcomed the extension of the reference period,[21] noting:

[t]he delegations generally welcomed the Commission's proposal on the grounds that it would improve legal certainty in this area, especially in the light of recent Court of Justice case law concerning time spent by doctors not working during on-call duty. (2606th Council Meeting, Employment, Social Policy, Health and Consumer Affairs, 4 October 2004, press release)

In political terms, the 'improvement of legal certainty' returned the course of integration to SQ_{reg}^{1}. Member state representatives emphasized the possibility of overturning the case law if necessary:

Of course there's room for disagreeing (on what constitutes legal certainty). There is always room for changing the case law of the Court, particularly if it's not based on the treaties—you know, if it's based on the legislation instead of the treaties itself. (...) I mean, working time is a good example of an issue where member states would be quite happy to overturn the case law of the ECJ. (interview, Council, 25 July 2012)

However, the member states disagreed about the opt-out possibility. France and Sweden were the most active advocates for removing it, while Poland backed the UK on maintaining the right to opt out (*Financial Times*, 'UK seeks to keep working time opt-out', 2 December 2005).

The position of the co-legislator was indeed different. Within the European Parliament, the EMPL Committee was responsible for the proposal, and the rapporteurship was held by a Spanish MEP from the S&D group, Alejandro Cercas.[22] From the first reading of the proposal, the EP took a firm stand against the Commission's proposal, finding, among other aspects, that it unacceptably overturned the Court's case law:

However, the solution being sought by the Commission is not the best one. *We cannot lightly alter the acquis communautaire and legislate against the case law of the Court of*

[21] On the early positions of the Council, see press releases from 2606th meeting, 4 October 2004 and 2624th meeting, 6–7 December 2004, Council for Employment, Social Policy, Health, and Consumer Affairs.

[22] See report on the proposal from the EP Committee on Employment and Social Affairs *A6–0105/2005 final* (Rapporteur: Alejandro Cercas), 25 April 2005.

> *Justice*, which has been repeatedly and supremely well-argued and established that on-call duty is working time. It is essential that the European institutions respect the inviolability of the acts that they have adopted and which affect the legal situation of legal persons ... (EP report *A6–0105/2005*, 19, emphasis added)

Furthermore, the EP strongly opposed maintaining the opt-out possibility and extending the reference period. It found that the Commission had disregarded the EP's early opinion and that the entire proposal directly opposed what the EP had clearly stated as its position (EP report *A6–0105/2005*, 16–17).

In May 2005, the European Parliament accepted all of the amendments that were proposed by the rapporteur. Beginning with early negotiations, the European Parliament thus had maintained a unified position across the political groups (interview, Commission, 3 March 2012). The EP's amendments proposed including a general reference to the case law of the Court and inserting the Court's definition of working time in the recitals. Furthermore, the EP's position was to amend the Commission's proposal so that it codified the case law of the Court, thus defining all on-call time, including inactive on-call time, as working time (EP report *A6–0105/2005*).

Despite the clearly stated position of the EP, the Commission did not consider the EP's primary amendments when amending its proposal (*COM (2005) 246* as of 31 May 2005). The Commission maintained the new concept of 'inactive on-call time' and did not propose to phase out the opt-out, as advanced by the EP. The positions of the Commission, the Council, and the Parliament regarding how to respond to the case law of the Court thus differed starkly. The Commission proposed to override the judicial decisions. The Council supported such an override. Conversely, a unified EP wanted to codify the case law and remove the opt-out facility. Meanwhile, the extended use of that possibility meant that increasingly more member states were departing de facto from complying with the Court's jurisprudence (interview, Council, 10 October 2011).

Political Interaction in the Council and the European Parliament

For the next three years, the member states negotiated the proposal in the Council. In negotiations on the amended proposal, the Council faced severe difficulties in establishing a compromise over the opt-out possibility, with member states remaining divided between those that wanted to abolish it and those that wanted to maintain it (*Financial Times*, 'UK to try for deal on working hours', 3 December 2005; Council press release *PRES/2005/117*). Concerning the responses to the case law of the Court and the definition of working time, the Council had a much more unified position and was clear about the aim of the proposal:

> … to *improve legal certainty* with regard to regulating working time, particularly in the light of the case law of the Court of Justice relating to inactive periods of on-call time in certain professions, particularly the medical profession. (Council press release *PRES/2005/117*, emphasis added)

In the later Council negotiations of November 2006, the objective to overturn jurisprudence was made more explicit:

> … to *avoid any consequences of the European Court of Justice's case law*, in particular rulings in the SiMAP and Jaeger cases, which held that on-call duty performed by health professionals and other workers, when they are required to be physically present at their places of work, must be regarded as working time. (Council press release, *PRES/2006/298*, emphasis added)

The Council took a common position on the need to avoid the 'negative effects' of the case law (Council press release *PRES/2007/284*). Its clear priority was thus to override the course of legal integration (interview, Commission, 3 March 2012). Nevertheless, Council negotiations stalled because of the different positions on the opt-out. In the first half of 2007, the Portuguese presidency therefore decided to present a compromise proposal, joining the proposal on working time to the proposal on working conditions for temporary workers (Council press release *PRES/2007/284*).[23] The strategy was to present the two proposals as a package deal to enable a compromise. A package deal would make it possible to find a common position in the Council on two problematic directives because the member states that won concessions on working time might then be willing to compromise on temporary agency workers (interview, EP, 7 October 2011). In essence, the UK agreed to back the temporary agency workers directive in return for being allowed to retain its opt-out (*Financial Times*, 'Agency workers set to win new rights', 22 October 2008).

[23] *COM (2002) 149*, Proposal for a Directive of the European Parliament and the Council on working conditions for temporary workers.

Against this background, a compromise was finally reached in the Council by the Slovenian presidency. In June 2008, an agreement was established in the Council by QMV (Council press release, *PRES 2008/116*). The Council's common position maintained the concept of 'inactive on-call time'. The joint position of the Council throughout the negotiations supported this overturn of the case law of the Court. The compromise was achieved through the package deal, simultaneously negotiation of the proposal on the temporary agency workers directive and the WTD. The package deal made it possible to establish a compromise on the opt-out possibility (interview, EP, 7 October 2011; interview, European Commission, 3 March 2012). Within the Council's common position, when using the opt-out workers working more than forty-eight hours should reaffirm consent to their employers once a year (Council press release, *PRES 2008/116; Financial Times*, 'Britain fights for working hours opt-out', 16 March 2009). However, essentially the opt-out possibility was maintained. In return, the UK made what it felt were significant concessions on the temporary agency workers directive (*Financial Times*, 16 March 2009). To protect the opt-out on working time, the UK left the blocking minority on the temporary workers directive, and the Council was now ready to adopt this directive, assuming that the European Parliament would concede on working time in return (interview, social partners, 14 August 2012).

Inter-institutional Interactions: Failed Political Negotiations

Because the two legislators had not been able to agree thus far, representatives from the two institutions and the Commission entered the third reading in the conciliation committee. The Council was surprised to learn that the European Parliament was not persuaded by the package deal strategy. By the end of April 2009, the EP had vetoed the Council compromise (Conciliation committee decision, 29 April 2009). For the first time, a third reading in the conciliation procedure between the European Parliament and the Council did not manage to reach an agreement (interview, social partners, August 2012). The EP accepted the amended proposal on temporary agency workers but rejected the WTD:

> ... We teased the Council a little, since they (the Council) wanted to link this to the Working Time Directive in the way that if the Parliament could get the Temporary

Workers Directive the way they wanted, then in return we would solve that thing about the on call, so that the British could keep their opt-out. But we would not. (interview, European Parliament, 7 October 2011)

The strategy to present the two controversial proposals together failed (interview, social partners, 14 August 2012; interview, Commission, 3 March 2012). The Council had expected the European Parliament to accept the package but had miscalculated the co-legislator's willingness to actually use its veto power (interview, Council, 22 February 2012). Headed by its rapporteur Alejandro Cercas, the European Parliament instead stood firm on its call to remove the opt-out possibility (*Financial Times*, 'Call to reject revisions on work hours', 16 December 2008). Essentially, the opt-out made an inter-institutional compromise between the European Parliament and the Council impossible. The parliament's position was that the opt-out possibility was temporary and that it had originally been adopted as a temporary concession to one member state during difficult negotiations. According to the EP, it was never intended to become permanent (interview, Commission, 3 March 2012; interview, European Parliament, 29 March 2012). Conversely, the Council was internally divided on the issue. Some member states were willing to remove the opt-out, while others were willing to phase it out. However, for an increasing number of Council members, the opt-out possibility had become a fundamental issue 'that they never intended would be other than permanent' (interview, Commission, 3 March 2012). The Council alliance insisting on maintaining the opt-out had been further strengthened by enlargement. A considerable number of the new member states took the same approach as the UK and adopted an opt-out that applied across all sectors: Cyprus, Estonia, Malta, and Bulgaria. Other new member states had demanded a more limited opt-out that was restricted to specific sectors, particularly healthcare: the Czech Republic, Hungary, Latvia, Poland, Slovakia, and Slovenia. Moreover, Germany, Belgium, France, the Netherlands, and Spain had opt-outs for certain sectors (*COM (2010) 802; COM (2010) 1611*, 84–99). Thus, the opt-out had developed from being a concession granted to *one* member state into a derogation for the *majority* of the member states (Martinsen and Wessel [2014]). This majority saw no reason to compromise on the opt-out possibility, which allowed them to avoid what they considered the negative consequences of the case law of the Court. The opt-out became the main reason why the European Parliament and the Council were unable to reach a compromise in the conciliation committee.

The European Parliament decided to reach a compromise over the case law of the Court with the Council and the Commission. During the second reading of the directive, the European Parliament now accepted that the 'inactive part of on-call time' could be calculated in a specific way to comply with the maximum forty-eight-hour work-week.[24] Inactive on-call time would continue to be defined as working time, but it could be calculated differently (interviews, European Parliament, 29 March 2012; social partners 28 January 2013). Thus, the European Parliament made a considerable step toward compromising with the Council and the Commission. It provided some leeway to compromise on the case law of the Court by treating 'inactive on-call time' in a more flexible manner. In essence, it allowed for modification of legal integration. However, fixed positions on the opt-out possibility blocked a final compromise.

The long-lasting political negotiations had failed, and despite five years of dialogue, bargains, and concessions, no solution was found to the 'case law problem' and the extended use of the opt-out. The conciliation committee failed to reach a compromise, leaving an unviable institutional situation with considerable discrepancies between $SQ_{reg}{}^{1}$ and SQ_{Court}. The Court's interpretation had extended the definition of working time beyond what the majority of member states were willing to accept. The Council's common position would have overridden the course of legal integration, if the decision regarding the legislation had been made by the Council alone.

The European Parliament as co-legislator was unwilling to change its position on the opt-out possibility. However, note that the EP was actually willing to modify judicial influence on the definition of working time by compromising on how to calculate 'inactive on-call time'. However, in the end, it decided to veto the compromise proposal because it could not accept the permanency of the opt-out.

Political inability to override the case law of the Court did not make the member states abide by judicial decisions. Although EU legislators failed to respond, member states increasingly used the opt-out to safeguard themselves from the impact of the Court. Thus, the unwanted course of legal integration extended the opt-out:

> And the problem with the opt-out is that of course the ruling has created a situation where countries in order to be able to cope had to introduce the opt-out, although

[24] See the amendments proposed by the EP in the second reading of article 2a; *P6_TA(2008)0615*.

they hadn't introduced the opt-out before, like Germany, for instance, or many other countries ... The opt-out was not a subject matter for the case law, because the ruling was only about on call, but the increasing recourse to the introduction [of] the opt-out was the direct consequence of the ruling of on-call time. (interview, social partners, 4 July 2013)

Furthermore, according to the Commission, 'a significant number of member states' did not treat 'on-call time' at the work place in accordance with the case law of the Court (*COM (2010) 802*, 4). The majority of member states did not comply with the SQ_{Court} (interview, social partners, 14 February 2012). Implementation of the directive varied considerably, creating an uneven and uncertain situation with respect to EU working time regulation (*SEC (2010) 1611*, for EU15 see Falkner et. al. [2005: 94–118]).

Bringing in the Social Partners

Despite failed negotiations, a solution to the 'on-call *problématique*' still sounded loud (*Financial Times*, 'Britain fights for working hours opt-out', 16 March 2009). In March 2010, the Commission restarted the process of revising the WTD by consulting with the European social partners.

It took a long time for the social partners to agree on whether to participate in the negotiations (interview, Commission, 3 March 2012). However, their acceptance of the invitation demonstrated a certain commitment from the different organizations:

So they knew what they were going into, and I presume that they had good reasons for opening the negotiations and investing the ... fairly substantial amount of effort and political capital there is involved. I do not think that they would have done it if it were just an exercise for show. Secondly, I think that they are both conscious that it is [a] terribly difficult time for Social Europe, especially at the moment. (interview, Commission, 3 March 2012)

After eighteen months of careful consideration, the European social partners declared that they were willing to negotiate in accordance with the social consultation procedure established in articles 154 and 155 TFEU. Business Europe had thus changed its position and now accepted the Commission's invitation—in part because its members broadly requested legal clarification and in part because the public employers' organization CEEP pressured Business Europe to enter negotiations (interview, social partners,

14 February 2012). Public employers in particular placed their employees 'on-call' and accordingly called for a solution. In addition, European employers' and employees' organizations all had an interest in revitalizing the 'corporatist policy community' from the 1990s, which had successfully concluded European collective agreements on labour law issues (interviews, social partners, 30 March 2012, 14 August 2012; Commission, 3 March 2012; Falkner [1998]; Martinsen and Falkner [2011]).[25] The ETUC represented European employees,[26] while the employer side was represented by three organizations: Business Europe, CEEP,[27] representing public sector employers, and UEAPME,[28] representing employers from small and medium-sized enterprises. For the ETUC, revising the WTD was an absolute priority in the social dialogue and was considered of utmost importance to social Europe (interview, social partners, 30 March 2012).

With the prospect of working time being negotiated by the European social partners, the UK made the opt-out high politics. In November 2011, Prime Minister David Cameron and German Chancellor Angela Merkel agreed to consider the continuation of the British opt-out if the UK in return was willing to support swift and limited Treaty change to reinforce budgetary discipline in the Eurozone (*Financial Times*, 'Cameron and Merkel edge closer on EU reform', 20 November 2011; interview, Council, 25 July 2012). However, this attempt to save the British opt-out facility failed when the UK vetoed the Treaty change option one month later (*Financial Times*, 'Cameron triggers two-speed Europe', 9 December 2011). Despite failure, this attempt to link high politics with social affairs demonstrates that the matter had remained of considerable importance to the UK since the initial negotiations on the Directive (Falkner et al. [2005: 97–8]).

Social Partners' Positions and Interactions

The first meeting of the social partners was held on 8 December 2011. Negotiations were slow from the outset. The first six months primarily

[25] During the 1990s three legally binding collective agreements, which were implemented in directives, were concluded: parental leave in December 1995, part-time work in June 1997, and fixed-term work in March 1999 (Martinsen and Falkner [2011: 133]).

[26] European Trade Union Confederation.

[27] European Centre of Employers and Enterprises providing Public services.

[28] The European Association of Craft, Small and Medium-sized Enterprises.

involved agreeing on which issues could be negotiated (interviews, social partners, 30 March 2012, 1 November 2012). Reaching an agreement and a unified position between the employers proved difficult throughout negotiations. Business Europe wanted to concentrate on solving the 'case law problem', the main purpose being to override the case law, while it insisted on maintaining the opt-out (interviews, social partners, 14 February 2012, 14 August 2012, 1 November 2012, 4 July 2013).

As one social partner stated:

> There 'wouldn't have been any need to negotiate anything if there hadn't been this ruling, because the ruling created the practical problem ... [W]e negotiate because there is a problem in real life. And this problem was provoked by the Court. And that's why the purpose was to change the directive'. (interview, social partners, 4 July 2013)

As an organization of public employers, CEEP's main interest was to come to an agreement on working time. CEEP was more accommodating towards the position of employees and was willing to consider some limitations to the opt-out possibility (interviews, social partners, 30 March 2012, 1 November 2012). On the employees' side, the ETUC insisted on negotiating the opt-out (interviews, social partners, 30 March 2012, 14 August 2012). The employees took the same position as the European Parliament, viewing the opt-out and its 'spread like ripples in a pond' as the primary problem in EU working time regulation (interview, social partners, 1 November 2012). At the same time, the ETUC wanted to codify the case law of the Court (interviews, social partners, 30 March 2012, 13 June 2013).

The Commission agreed to extend the nine months initially granted for negotiations to 31 December 2012, 'given that their negotiations are making progress' (Commission press release, *IP/12/903*, 16 August 2012). However, the timeframe was tight, and disagreements considerable. Although the employers formally agreed to negotiate on the opt-out possibility, they disagreed among themselves on whether the issue should be negotiated. Business Europe had not been willing to negotiate the opt-out at first but had reluctantly been forced to bring it into the negotiations. Its willingness to negotiate it seriously was limited, however. CEEP took the position that it was willing to limit the opt-out by adding measures to control when it could be used. Conversely, the ETUC asked the employers to agree on gradually phasing out the opt-out (interview, social partner, 13 June 2013). Throughout the negotiations, the ETUC and the CEEP were more consistent and willing to compromise. However, CEEP was held back by Business Europe; meanwhile, national trade unions had given a limited mandate to the ETUC (interviews, social partners, 28 January 2013, 13 June 2013).

As with the negotiations between the EP and the Council, the negotiations were characterized by conflicts along two dimensions. The main disagreements concerned the definition of working time and the opt-out possibility (interviews, social partners, 13 June 2013, 4 July 2013). Business Europe's position was ultimately inflexible, demanding an override of the case law of the Court (interviews, social partners, 28 January 2013, 13 June 2013). In November 2012, the employers advanced what they saw as a compromise (interview, social partners, 4 July 2013). The ETUC announced that they needed a new mandate to negotiate further. After a meeting of the ETUC executive committee on 5–6 December 2012, the ETUC decided not to respond to the proposed compromise. This non-response communicated that the ETUC did not wish to continue the negotiations. In a short press release it declared that negotiations could not continue:

> Convened on 5 and 6 December, the Executive Committee of the European Trade Union Confederation (ETUC) extensively discussed the submitted interim report on the progress of the negotiations to revise the European directive on working time. The Committee regretted to note that the 'final offer' from the employers was not sufficiently balanced and consequently did not make it possible to continue the negotiations as such. (ETUC press release, 14 December 2012)

Although the employers did not consider the ETUC's non-response as officially ending the negotiations, they must have known that they had ended in reality. The previous openings had closed:

> When we informed the employers that we were opening the door (i.e., willing to establish compromises) and the employers wanted to use that opening to … have everything for all sectors, etc., then it's like an oyster. Then, it clapped. Finished … We said to the employers, it's not acceptable. It's not balanced any more. (interview, social partners, 13 June 2013)

The social dialogue on working time had failed, and the latest attempt to revise EU regulation of working time had not been able to overcome the policy deadlock. In the press release after the end of the negotiations, the general secretary of CEEP, Valeria Ronzitti, urged the ETUC to come back to the negotiation table, warning of the consequences of the failed negotiations for the social dialogue:

> We urge ETUC to answer to the latest employers' proposal at the negotiating table. Negotiations are based on the principle that 'nothing is agreed until everything is agreed', and a non-answer is the worst possible signal in this context. A negotiated

solution of the issue of on-call time and its link with the spreading of the opt-out is the highest priority for public services employers and is primarily in the interest of their employees. Moreover, the end of these negotiations will represent a major defeat for European Social Dialogue, which should on the contrary be the best tool to restore the credibility of European law. (individual statement of CEEP in the joint press release of Business Europe, CEEP, and UEAPME, 14 December 2012)

No compromise was reached on the opt-out or the case law of the Court. Neither the political organizations nor the social partners managed to override, modify, or codify the precedent that the Court had established. In its individual statement, the director general of Business Europe, Markus Beyrer, emphasized that the legal situation created by the Court was unsustainable:

A solution is urgently needed to restore legal certainty and the credibility of EU law. In particular, in the current economic climate, this should be the aim of any revision of the directive, rather than creating new social rights. Also important is to maintain the opt-out as a permanent provision of the directive. (individual statement of Business Europe in the joint press release of Business Europe, CEEP, and UEAPME, 14 December 2012)

After Non-adoption Comes ...?

The judicial decisions from 2000 onwards did not result in subsequent legislation. They were neither codified, modified, nor overturned. Instead, the Commission's proposal on how to respond to the case law of the Court was not adopted. Inter-institutional interaction was unable to change the positions of the involved parties. Despite almost ten years of negotiations, the European legislators and the social partners did not manage to establish a solution. The parties came close to a compromise modifying the course of legal integration. However, divergent positions on the opt-out possibility blocked further progress.

The regulatory status quo after the rejection of the Court influence is a suboptimal one, with a considerable discrepancy between SQ_{reg}[1] and SQ_{Court} and with few member states complying with the case law (interviews, social partners, 1 November 2012, 28 January 2013, 13 June 2013, 4 July 2013). Judicial decisions have 'established rules nobody follows' (interview, social partners, 1 November 2012). It is also expected that more member states will adopt the opt-out in the future to avoid the case law of the Court (interviews, social partners, 1 November 2012, 28 January 2013, 4 July 2013).

Accordingly, EU working time regulation resembles 'an emmentaler with more holes in [it] than [cheese]' (interview, social partners, 30 March 2012). The directive is thus rather meaningless 'because everybody is doing what they want' (interview, social partners, 30 March 2012). In such a situation, the Commission's enforcement capacity is low because it cannot charge all member states with non-compliance with the directive. In addition, the position of the Commission throughout the negotiations suggests that it has deliberately avoided systematically taking member states to Court. Although neither the member states nor the employers' side of the social partners managed to override the case law of the Court, judicial influence on EU working time regulation in practice remains minimal. The influence of the Court is deeply dependent on how its judgments are perceived and received:

> ... the Court needs help to carry out its rulings. And if implementation does not take place, if the implementers are not supportive, there is very little the Court can do. (interview, social partners, 28 January 2013)

A general state of disobedience among the member states harms the legitimacy of the CJEU, compromising its authority. A mere rejection of SQ_{Court} is not a viable situation. Either the Commission must come forward with a new proposal in which it changes its position from suggesting an override of the Court precedent to suggesting a modification of it; or the Court must adapt its position in future case law by considering political positions and allowing for a more flexible calculation of on-call time.

Judicial Influence on EU Working Time Regulation

The envisioned reform of the WTD demonstrates the intense battles that may occur between law and politics in the EU. It demonstrates how political actors and institutions interpret and use the case law of the Court differently and how this diverse interpretation of 'the state of legal affairs' influences their interaction. Ultimately, the different interpretations and uses of case law and the different positions on the opt-out possibility blocked a political compromise and created an uncertain regulatory situation.

The original regulatory status quo, SQ_{reg}^{1}, created when the directive was adopted in 1993, proved fragile because of subsequent legal interpretations of the directive. The Court rulings produced a new status quo: $SQ_{Court.}$ The discrepancy between political and legal integration demanded a political response. The Commission took a firm position against the course of legal integration and proposed to override the case law of the Court. A sufficient majority of member states supported the Commission's proposal. A common position to override the case law of the Court was established in the Council. However, the Commission had not foreseen the unified position of the European Parliament, wanting to codify the case law of the Court and thus to strengthen social rights. After prolonged inter-institutional interaction, the EP was ready to modify its position on how to calculate on-call time. A compromise was within reach, but fixed positions for or against maintaining the opt-out definitely ended the negotiations between the Council and the European Parliament.

The Commission attempted to employ an arena-shifting strategy (Falkner [1998]) by bringing the European social partners into negotiations. However, disagreements on the opt-out possibility and the case law of the Court were even more pronounced among the social partners. Negotiations among these parties also failed, and SQ_{Court} was neither adopted, overridden, nor modified.

Thus, political contestation occurred along two different dimensions (Marks and Steenbergen [2002]). Political positions diverged along a *left–right* dimension, with positions for or against the case law of the Court (*left* = strengthen social rights by including on-call time within the EU working time definition; *right* = exclude on-call time from the EU working time definition). Furthermore, positions diverged along a *more integration versus less integration* dimension (*more integration* = remove the opt-out possibility; *less integration* = maintain the opt-out possibility). Despite the substantial interaction between T_1 and T_2, the parties' positions concerning the opt-out remained largely fixed, and rejection of judicial influence on the definition of working time became the result. The different positions can be visualized on the two-dimensional matrix as shown in figure 4.2 below.

The current regulatory situation is characterized by uncertainty, in which SQ_{reg}^1 has been challenged by the Court while the member states respond to SQ_{Court} with disobedience. Non-adoption of the Court's rulings is an insufficient policy response, in which the maintained discrepancy between SQ_{reg}^1 and SQ_{Court} leaves a state of high legal uncertainty. Moreover, the state of uncertainty and the disobedience of member states ultimately damages the legitimacy of the Court. Its authority is tested when it has created rules that 'nobody follows' (interview, social partners, 1 November 2012).

The analysis carried out in the 'legal-politics game' supported the expectation that the EU decision-making rules are likely to hinder both override and codification of the case law of the Court. Although the Commission's

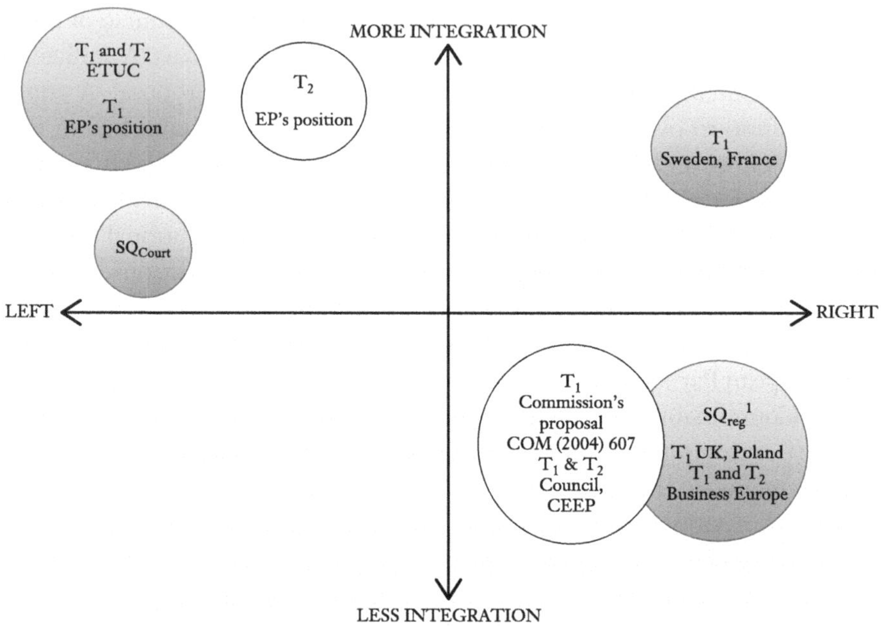

Fig. 4.2 Political Positions in EU Working Time Regulation

proposal to override legal integration found a sufficient majority in the Council, it was vetoed by the European Parliament. Shifting the negotiating arena to the social partners offered the next possibility for an agreement. Here, the European trade unions blocked such an override. Nor was codification of the case law possible, despite the fact that a unified EP wanted a full adoption of the Court's ruling in the directive. Codification faced two veto points: the Commission proposed the opposite, namely an override, and the Council majority supported the Commission on this point.

Conversely, the findings did not support the expectation that judicial decisions will be adopted into policy outputs as the Commission proposes. From the outset, the Commission acted strategically, siding with the majority of Council members. However, its attention span proved insufficient because it clearly miscalculated the unified and fixed position of the European Parliament. Its strategy to shift arenas was also unsuccessful. The analysis shows that the Commission does not simply support the course of legal integration; it has a position of its own regarding the way forward for European integration. This also shows that the Commission did not act in possession of complete information. The process formed in a chaotic and unsteerable manner. 'Bounded rationality' showed through in a process in which the Commission initially offered a vague response to the considerable discrepancy between SQ_{reg}^{1} and SQ_{Court} and subsequently miscalculated the positions of the involved political parties and member states (Jones [1999]; Simon [1985]). Once the Commission finally established its own position, proposing to overturn the legal rulings, its main failure was clearly to disregard the position of the co-legislator—the European Parliament.

These findings support the last expectation, that when political actors disagree along key conflict lines and their positions remain fixed, override, modification, and codification of legal integration are unlikely policy outputs. While dynamic positions could have enabled compromise (modification) on the definition of working time, political gridlock on the opt-out resulted in non-adoption. Political actors maintained their positions despite prolonged negotiations and much deliberation, and do not appear to have been limited by a short time horizon (Alter [1998]), but instead considered the larger implications of the course of legal integration.

Non-adoption is not a viable situation in a rule-of-law system. It has a number of consequences. It produces a state of legal uncertainty and severe non-compliance. Furthermore, it questions the authority and legitimacy of both the Commission and the Court of Justice. Rules that 'nobody follows' fundamentally challenge and question the Union's rule of law system and its effectiveness.

The considerable discrepancy created between SQ_{reg}^{1} and SQ_{Court} has created an unsustainable state of legal uncertainty. A solution to the 'case law problem' remains a requirement. The new Commission in office since autumn 2014 will be expected to offer a new proposal on how to respond to the case law of the Court. This time, it is likely to come forward with a proposal that modifies judicial influence.

References

Alter, K. (1998) 'Who are the 'Masters of the Treaty'? European governments and the European Court of Justice', *International Organization* 52(01): 121–47.

Beach, D. (2001) *Between Law and Politics: The Relationship Between the European Court of Justice and EU Member States*, Copenhagen: DJØF Publishing.

Falkner, G. (1998) *EU Social Policy in the 1990s: Towards a Corporatist Policy Community*, London: Routledge.

Falkner, G., Treib, O., Hartlapp, M., and Leiber, S. (2005) *Complying with Europe. EU Harmonisation and Soft Law in the Member States*, Cambridge: Cambridge University Press.

Jones, B.D. (1999) 'Bounded rationality', *Annual Review of Political Science* 2(1): 297–321.

Lewis, J. (2003) 'Institutional environments and everyday EU decision making: rationalist or constructivist?', *Comparative Political Studies* 36(1/2): 97–124.

Marks, G. and Steenbergen, M. (2002) 'Understanding political contestation in the European Union', *Comparative Political Studies* 35(8): 879–92.

Martinsen, D.S. and Falkner, G. (2011) 'Social policy: problem-solving gaps, partial exits, and court-decision traps', in G. Falkner (ed.), *The EU's Decision Traps. Comparing Policies*, Oxford: Oxford University Press, pp. 128–45.

Martinsen, D.S. and Wessel, A.U. (2014) 'On the path to differentiation: upward transfer, logic of variation and sub-optimality in EU social policy', *Journal of European Public Policy* 21(9): 1255–72.

Nowak, T. (2008) 'The Working Time Directive and the European Court of Justice', *Maastricht Journal of European and Comparative Law* 15(4): 447–71.

Simon, H.A. (1985) 'Human nature in politics: the dialogue of psychology with political science', *American Political Science Review* 79(02): 293–304.

5

Patients' Rights in Cross-border Healthcare: Modifying Judicial Influence

> It is equally clear we are not starting with a clean sheet of paper; this is not a time for 'blue sky' drafting. The Treaties have provided the ECJ with the legal basis for its judgments and the Court has written its draft of consequent policy. They have set in motion a process which has the potential to empower patients and enhance the health of Europe's citizens
>
> (European Parliament rapporteur John Bowis, 20 November 2008)[1]

> Because the worst that could happen—and that goes for all policy areas—would be just to leave it to the European Court to decide. You don't find many politicians who think that would be great
>
> (Interview, European Parliament, 17 February 2009)

> And the Court ruling—and that was a golden moment—said that OK, in order to ensure continuity of care, in order to ensure proper use of equipment, governments have the competence to do some kind of reassuring and intervening and controlling equal access, etc. So that was … It came at a very significant moment. The Commission lost the case
>
> (Interview, Council, 20 June 2011)

[1] As stated in his draft report, PE 415.355, 20 November 2008.

European integration of healthcare has been greatly disputed. Member states have generally sought to maintain the competence to organize, design, and plan their care for sick people and preventative health actions. Member states have also sought to exclusively decide on the quality and financing of healthcare. Furthermore, healthcare has been a core theme within national electoral campaigns and a key element in the social contract between the state and its citizens. Free movement of healthcare services and patients has not, however, been part of visionary strategies for European integration as collectively formulated between heads of states and healthcare ministers. Nevertheless, the right to cross-border healthcare is today part of the Union's regulatory portfolio.

The regulatory status quo SQ_{reg}^1 long consisted of regulation 1408/71 on the coordination of social security for migrant workers, which gave limited access to planned, reimbursable healthcare in another member state. As demonstrated below, early jurisprudence challenged this status quo but was overturned by the Council of Ministers. Furthermore, in 1992, the Treaty of Maastricht inserted a sector-specific emphasis on the principle of subsidiarity concerning healthcare. SQ_{reg}^1 was thus a position of considerable national control, with almost no free movement for planned healthcare services and very limited flow of patients across borders. However, this high degree of national control was challenged anew by a line of CJEU case law specifying that healthcare was not exempted from single market principles. Politics clearly did not like this new turn in legal integration but took its time to respond. The process unfolding between law and politics, as traced in the analysis below, can be summarized as in figure 5.1. The timeline sets out EU cross-border healthcare between T_1 and T_2.

This chapter first presents the original regulatory status quo SQ_{reg}^1 and how it was challenged by early Court rulings but re-established by political override. It then turns to the next sequence of Court interpretations SQ_{Court}, applying internal market principles to the healthcare sector and severely disturbing SQ_{reg}^1. The subsequent sections examine how politics responded to this SQ_{Court}, with extensive inter- and intra-institutional disputes but finally adopted the patients' rights directive in cross-border healthcare. The political actors thus managed to adopt a new regulatory status quo SQ_{reg}^2 whereby a considerable degree of national control was regained and the impact of SQ_{Court} modified.

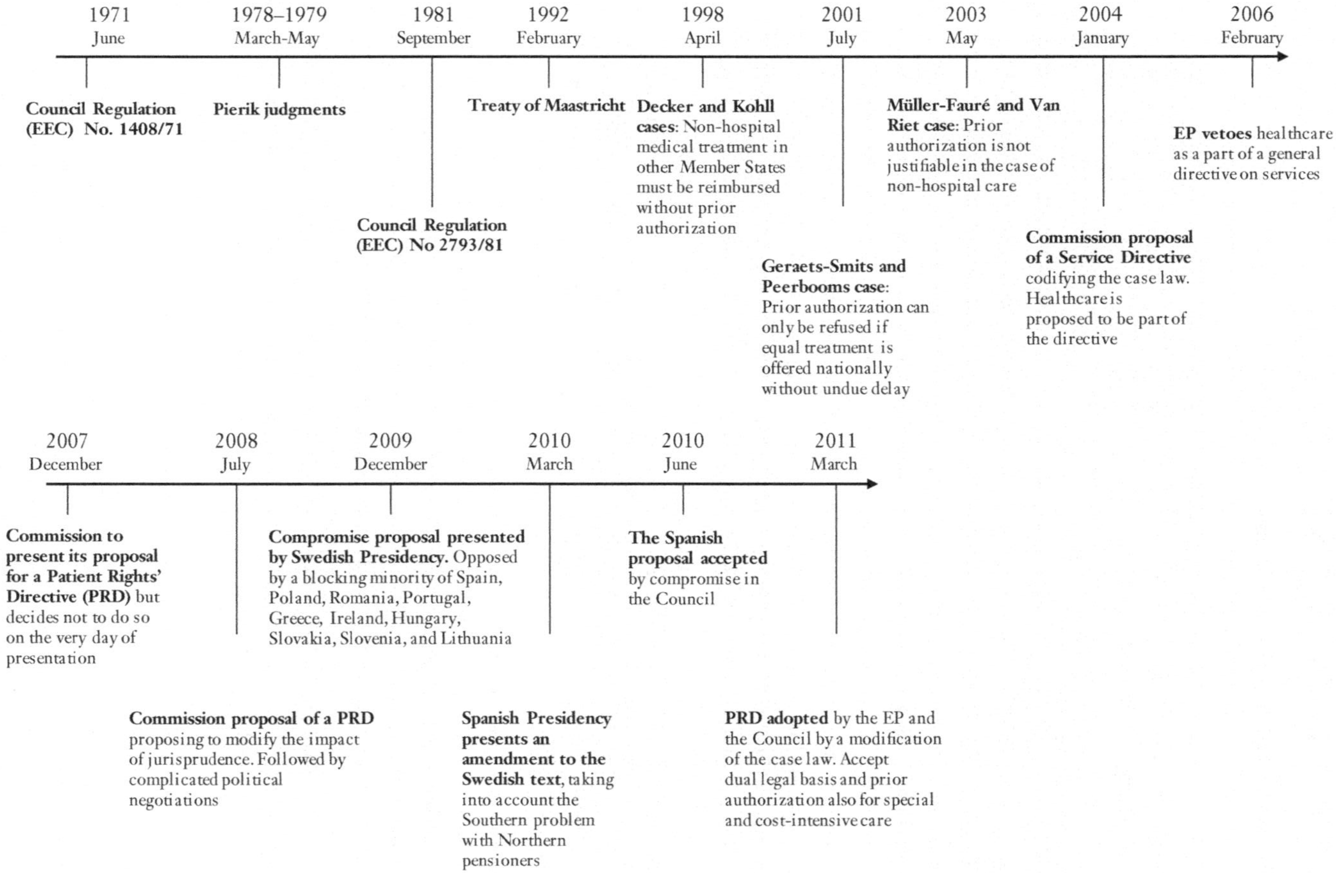

Fig. 5.1 Timeline of EU Cross-border Healthcare

Prior Authorization and National Control of Cross-border Healthcare

To access the healthcare systems of other member states and have the cost reimbursed by one's member state of affiliation was for a long time a right granted exclusively to the worker,[2] the self-employed, and their family members by means of regulation 1408/71.[3] In 2004, the regulation was extended to cover EU citizens in general. The regulation grants rights to benefit in kind in the member state of residence, to emergency healthcare during a temporary stay in another member state, and to planned healthcare treatment in another member state under a set of conditions (Hervey and McHale [2004: 115–19]). Receiving planned treatment in another member state was firmly controlled by one's member state of affiliation. The member state of affiliation would issue a 'prior authorization' to the patient planning care in another member state and thereby govern the scope of cross-border care (Martinsen [2009: 794–5]; Palm and Glinos [2010: 514–15]). 'Prior authorization' thus provided an effective means of national control. Upon authorization, the member state of affiliation would pay the full costs of care and reimburse the member state of treatment directly, so that the patient would not need to pay up front. Thus, in many ways, this system institutionalized on the basis of the regulation is unique internationally, allowing for cross-border access to healthcare without burdening the patient with the cost of care:

> The most comprehensive system of access to cross-border care in the field of international social law is, without contest, the social security co-ordination system in place within the European Union. It is the culmination of an historic process of agreements between States and of the construction of the 'Common Market', the first stage in the construction of Europe. (Palm et al. [2000: 28])

However, prior authorization for planned cross-border treatment has only seldom been granted. In 2001, for example, Finland granted 9 authorizations, Denmark 75, Portugal 246, and Spain 651 (Martinsen [2007: 14];

[2] The patient's member state of affiliation is defined as the home member state, in which the patient is covered for national healthcare provision (Hervey and McHale [2015: 86]). The member state of affiliation thus has the financial responsibility for the cost of care.

[3] Regulation (EEC) No. 1408/71 of the Council of 14 June 1971 on the application of social security schemes to employed persons, to self-employed persons, and to members of their families moving within the Community. The regulation was substantially reformed with the adoption of Regulation 883/2004, adopted 29 April 2004.

Mossialos et al. [2002: 85]). Luxembourg authorized its citizens to obtain cross-border medical treatment more frequently; however, in general, the number of patients receiving planned cross-border treatment paid for by their member states of affiliation appears to have remained extremely low. For example, in 2013 the Danish government estimated that the regions received a total of approximately sixty applications for prior authorization annually, of which approximately ten authorizations were granted (interviews, November 2012, August 2013).[4] However, to date, no comparative, exhaustive figures exist on cross-border movement within healthcare.

The limited number of authorizations for cross-border treatment demonstrates that the principle of territoriality continues to be a strong governing principle in national healthcare policies (Cornelissen [1996]; Ferrera [2005]; Rosa [2012: 16]; Van der Mei [2003: 226]). Using territorial conditions for entitlement, member states have aimed to control the quality of care, financial sustainability, and planning of healthcare infrastructure and capacity (Glinos et al. [2010: 104]). A European citizen planning to obtain healthcare treatment abroad has thus had to act mainly on private initiative and finance this treatment by private means. However, CJEU judgments came to seriously upset the established status quo SQ_{reg}^{1} between Community law and national legislation.

First Court Challenge: Creating an Independent Social Security Law?

Regulation 1408/71 has led to its own confrontations between the judiciary and the EU legislature. Article 22(1)(c) of the Regulation established prior authorization as a means of national control.[5] Additionally, article 22(2) clarified when authorization could not be refused, originally reading 'The authorisation required under paragraph [22] 1 (c) may not be refused where the treatment in question cannot be provided for the person concerned within the territory of the Member State in which he resides'. In the late 1970s, article 22(2) became a matter of contestation when judicial interpretations in

[4] See also the Danish law proposal to implement the Patients' Rights Directive L 33 'Forslag til lov om ændring af sundhedsloven og lov om klage- og erstatningsadgang inden for sundhedsvæsenet', p. 20; presented 3 October, 2013.

[5] Now article 20(1) of Regulation 883/2004.

the *Pierik* cases came to contradict the political intentions behind this specific provision.[6] In the cases, the Court was requested to rule on the situation of Mrs Pierik. She resided in the Netherlands, where she received a disability pension. The Dutch competent health insurance refused to reimburse the costs of a hydrotherapy treatment that Mrs Pierik had received in Germany. Prior authorization had not been granted because hydrotherapy was not a treatment offered by the Dutch health system. The cases addressed whether authorization could be refused on the basis of article 22(2) when the specific treatment was not part of the healthcare package of the competent state.

The Pierik judgments became controversial indeed. The Court disregarded the far-reaching consequences that were depicted in the submitted member states' opinions. In Pierik I, the British government argued that if article 22(2) of the Regulation meant that the competent institution was obliged to pay for the costs of a treatment abroad that was not provided by its own law, then the

> scope of those provisions would be distorted since they would have the effect of creating an independent social security law of the Community instead of merely co-ordinating the social security law of the member states. (Case C–117/77, Pierik, 831)

Despite these political warnings on harmonization effects, the Court ruled that, independently of whether the treatment was part of national policy, a competent institution was obliged to authorize a treatment in another member state if the foreign treatment had been recognized as necessary and effective:

> The duty laid down in the second subparagraph of Article 22(2) to grant the authorisation required under Article 22(1)(c) covers both cases where the treatment provided in another Member State is *more effective* than that which the person concerned can receive in the Member State where he resides and those in which the treatment in question *cannot be provided* on the territory of the latter State. (Case C–117/77, Pierik, paragraph 22, emphasis added)

Dissatisfied with the answer from the supranational Court, the Dutch court decided to ask again. However, the CJEU did not change its position in its second Pierik judgment.[7] With the judicial decisions in Pierik, the Court

[6] Case 117/77, Bestuur van het Algemeen Ziekenfonds Drenthe-Platteland v G. *Pierik* [1978] ECR‡825 (Pierik I) and Case 182/78, Bestuur van het Algemeen Ziekenfonds Drenthe-Platteland v G. *Pierik* [1979] ECR–1977 (Pierik II).

[7] The Dutch national court was not convinced by all aspects of the first Pierik judgment and accordingly requested the CJEU for another preliminary ruling in the second Pierik case. The Court did not modify its previous conclusions, but simply restated that the competent institution

established that the deciding factor in the right to cross-border treatment was a person's state of health and not whether the relevant treatment was part of the healthcare scheme in the member state of affiliation. The decisions thus opened up the possibility of 'regime shopping' (Ferrera [2003: 634]). However, this time, the judicial decisions were met with a swift political response.

Political Response: Overriding the Court

The Court's decisions in the Pierik cases went far beyond political intentions. By obliging national health insurance institutions to send patients abroad—at their expense—even if the necessary treatment was not part of the national basket of healthcare, the Court considerably limited national control and the autonomy to define which healthcare treatments to provide.

However, this time, collective political response was able to override the Court. One year after the second Pierik ruling, the Commission proposed overturning the prevailing legal interpretation.[8] To meet political concerns the Commission thereby initiated a political correction of jurisprudence. However, notably, the Commission in its proposal did not justify its initiative with reference to the Pierik cases or to the Court. This omission suggests that, when departing from a line of legal reasoning, the Commission deliberately omits references to the Court.

The Council was in full accord with the Commission and acted promptly.[9] Only two years after the second Pierik ruling, the member governments unanimously adopted Regulation 2793/81.[10] The Community legislator

had a duty to authorize treatment abroad where such was recognized as more effective than the ones provided within its own borders, as well as when a treatment could not be provided by the competent state itself (C–182/78, Pierik, paragraphs 9 and 10).

[8] *COM (1980) 580* of 21 October 1980, Proposal for a Council Regulation amending Regulation (EEC) No. 1408/71 on the application of social security schemes to employed persons and their families moving within the Community and Regulation (EEC) No. 574/72 fixing the procedure for implementing Regulation (EEC) No 1408/71.

[9] The Commission's proposed article 22(2) was almost identical to the article 22(2) adopted by the Council. Article 22(2) as proposed in *COM (1980) 580* reads as follows: 'The authorization required under paragraph 1(c) cannot be refused if the treatment in question is among the benefits provided for by the legislation of the Member State on whose territory the person concerned resides and if he cannot be given such treatment in time, taking account of his state of health'.

[10] Council Regulation (EEC) No 2793/81 of 17 September 1981 amending Regulation (EEC) No 1408/71 on the application of social security schemes to employed persons and their families

adopted a new article 22(2) as a response to the jurisprudence (Van der Mei [2003: 254]). The new article directly corrected the Court's interpretations and granted wide discretion for the member states in defining their authorization policies (Mossialos et al. [2001: 44]). National control was reasserted (Hervey and McHale [2004: 116; 2015: 193]). The article thus reformulated is similar to the ruling provision today,[11] specifying that the competent institution is obliged to authorize treatment abroad only when this is considered administratively and medically necessary and when the treatment is part of the healthcare package provided nationally. Article 22(2)2 came to read as follows:

> The authorization required under paragraph 1(c) may not be refused where the treatment in question is among the benefits provided for by the legislation of the Member State on whose territory the person concerned resides and where he cannot be given such treatment within the time normally necessary for obtaining the treatment in question in the Member State of residence, taking account of his current state of health and the probable course of the disease.

In 1981, the member states were able to act in consensus and override the Court. The member states responded against what they feared to be considerable socio-economic implications of the Pierik decisions—financial implications, inability to plan and prioritize healthcare, and scope for patients to circumvent waiting lists by exiting from domestic supplies. Thus, national control was then re-established, and the legislature had proven its ability to contradict the Court by a legislative override. However, the collective decision was taken within a different institutional setting than later confrontations between law and politics. On one hand, unanimity implied a higher threshold than qualified majority voting. On the other hand, the decision had to be taken among only ten member states. Additionally, the European Parliament was not co-legislating. On balance, institutional thresholds were lower and member states proved able to unify on overriding judicial decisions.

For almost two decades, the balance between national and Community competencies concerning cross-border healthcare appeared settled; that, however, was before the Decker and Kohll rulings of 1998.

moving within the Community and Regulation (EEC) No 574/72 fixing the procedure for implementing Regulation (EEC) No 1408/71.

[11] Now article 20(2) of Regulation 883/2004.

A New Court-generated Status Quo: Free Movement of Healthcare Services

With the legislative correction of the Pierik decisions, politics had made its voice heard and returned to the 'driver's seat' (Pollack [2003]). Furthermore, in 1992 the Maastricht Treaty introduced article 152 EC (now article 168 TFEU) on public health, in which article 152(5) EC (now article 168(7) TFEU) established that Union action within the healthcare arena would respect the responsibilities of the member states for the organization and delivery of healthcare services and medical care. Thus, article 152(5) implied a sector-specific emphasis on the subsidiarity principle, with which the member states sought to clarify that they had the main competence within the healthcare area (Hancher and Sauter [2012: 13–14]; Ruijter [2015: 223]).

Nevertheless, in the late 1990s, once again the CJEU disturbed the balance politics was thought to have achieved. In a series of judgments, the Court addressed the status of healthcare in relation to the Treaty and examined the justification of 'prior authorization' in the light of the internal market. The Court came to gradually establish that the principles of the internal market—and especially article 49 EC (now article 56 TFEU)—also apply to national health policies. The judicial change of status quo was thus based on interpretations of primary law and could be fully overridden only by a Treaty amendment.

The Court's application of internal market principles to the healthcare sector unfolded through a decade of step-wise interpretations. The first cases in which Treaty provisions were applied to the healthcare sector were barely noticed (Hatzopoulos and Hervey [2013: 2]).[12] However, with the Decker and Kohll cases of 1998,[13] it became irrevocably clear that the healthcare sector was not exempted from the internal market. The Court established that healthcare was a service within the meaning of the Treaty and therefore in principle subject to the free movement principles. The requirement of

[12] As noted by Hatzopoulos and Hervey among others, the joined cases 286/82 and 26/83 Graziana *Luisi* and Giuseppe *Carbone* v Ministero del Tesoro [1984] ECR 377 were the first cases in which the Court explicitly stated that the principle of freedom to provide services applies to privately paid medical services (Hatzopoulos and Hervey [2013]; Hervey and McHale [2004]; Van der Mei [2003]).

[13] In the cases C–120/95 Nicolas *Decker* v Caisse de maladie des employés privés [1998] ECR I–1831 and C–158/96 Raymond *Kohll* v Union des caisses de maladie [1998] ECR I–1931.

prior authorization was found to be a barrier to the exercise of free movement that could nevertheless be justified under certain circumstances. Court decisions thus had to reach a delicate balance of, on one hand, cross-border freedom to provide services and, on the other hand, justifiable grounds upon which to deviate therefrom. Certain deviations from the general rule of free movement were acknowledged by the Court: the risk of seriously undermining the financial balance of the social security system, the need to maintain a balanced medical and hospital service open to all, and the need for capacity planning within the healthcare sector.[14] In this way, the Court entered a conflict-ridden terrain between the market freedoms of the European Union and the redistributive competences of the member states.

The scope of the 1998 judgments could, however, be viewed as limited. The Decker and Kohll decisions concerned goods and services outside the hospital sector, namely a pair of spectacles and dental treatment. Furthermore, the early judicial decisions concerned the reimbursement-based Luxembourg healthcare system. Although at first upset, politicians found themselves reassured that the impact was limited to specific goods and services and to particular healthcare systems, such as the Luxembourg reimbursement system (Palm et al. [2000: 78–87]). When the Decker and Kohll cases were adjudicated, only Belgium and Luxembourg had reimbursement social health insurance systems in which patients had to pay up front for treatment and the costs were subsequently reimbursed by their sickness fund upon presentation of a receipt (Van der Mei [2003: 224]).

On a Legal Course of Integration

However, in subsequent rulings the CJEU extended its line of reasoning to the full range of EU healthcare systems. The Geraets-Smits and Peerbooms judgments of 2001 repeated—this time with regard to the Dutch 'benefit in

[14] See Kohll, paragraphs 41, 50, 51; Case C–157/99, B.S.M. *Geraets-Smits* v Stichting Ziekenfonds VGZ and H.T.M. *Peerbooms* v Stichting CZ Groep Zorgverzekeringen [2001] ECR I–5473, paragraphs 72, 73, 74; Case C–385/99, V.G. *Müller-Fauré* v Onderlinge Waarborgmaatschappij OZ Zorgverzekeringen UA and E.E.M. *van Riet* v Onderlinge Waarborgmaatschappij ZAO Zorgverzekeringen [2003] ECR I–4509, paragraphs 67, 73; Case C–372/04, The Queen, on the application of Yvonne *Watts* v Bedford Primary Care Trust and Secretary of State for Health [2006] ECR I–4325, paragraphs 103–5.

kind' health insurance system—that prior authorization constituted a barrier to the free movement of services.[15] This barrier could, however, be justified provided that (1) the decision whether to grant treatment abroad was based on 'international medical science' and (2) an equivalent course of treatment could be provided in the competent member state without 'undue delay', taking into consideration the medical condition of the patient, broadly defined. In the case of Peerbooms, the Court considered the right of the applicant to access a treatment that was not provided as part of the national healthcare package but rather considered experimental by the Dutch system. The CJEU ruled that the decision on what was regarded as 'normal' or a standard treatment had to be based on international medical science and not on national considerations alone. In this way, the Court confirmed as a general rule that citizens could not claim reimbursement for a service that was not included in their home states' healthcare packages but at the same time stated that the list of provided benefits had to be based on objective criteria and sufficiently supported by *international* medical science (Palm and Glinos [2010: 519]). Additionally, the Smits and Peerbooms cases addressed another delicate question: what constitutes a reasonable waiting time for healthcare treatment? The Court established that the patient should not suffer '*undue delay*'. If a patient could not be treated within a reasonable time, the competent authority was obliged to authorize cross-border care. Waiting lists as a planning instrument in national health care organizations were thereby challenged by legal interpretations.

In the cases of Smits and Peerbooms, the Court further restricted national authorities' discretion in granting prior authorization by emphasizing that it could be a justifiable barrier to the principle of free provision of services only when based on

> '*objective, non-discriminatory criteria known in advance*' so that national authorities *cannot control* the procedure *arbitrarily*. Requests for authorisation must furthermore be dealt with within a reasonable time, and refusals to grant authorisation *must be open to appeal.* (Case C–157/99, Smits and Peerbooms, paragraph 90, emphasis added)

A further significant step in the construction of EU cross-border healthcare took place two years later with the case of Müller-Fauré and van Riet.[16] In this case, the Court introduced a distinction between hospital and non-hospital care. As regards *hospital care*, the Court restated its view that the requirement

[15] See note 14 above. [16] See note 14 above.

for prior authorization was justified on the condition that it was exercised proportionately and that the national authority did not act in an arbitrary manner. The requirements for *non-hospital care*, however, differed considerably. The Court ruled that national authorization constituted a barrier to the freedom to provide services for non-hospital care and that persuasive justification for maintaining this barrier had not been presented to the Court.

The Court proceeded further in the case of Watts,[17] where it ruled against the UK. The Watts case considered for the first time the implications of internal market principles for national health service systems, in which healthcare is generally publicly provided as benefits in kind and tax-financed, such as in the UK, Ireland, the Scandinavian countries, and the Southern member states. In relation to the earlier line of case law, member states with national health service systems had previously argued that this organization generally shielded them from the application of the free movement principles. After being refused treatment in the UK, Mrs Watts underwent a hip replacement operation in France for which she herself paid £3,900. The operation was carried out by a private provider in France, since the UK NHS did not entitle patients to be treated within the private sector established in the UK. Mrs Watts had waited for more than a year for her hip replacement in the UK, and the case thus concerned what constituted 'undue delay'. In the Watts case, the Court specified reviewable criteria for determining whether a period of waiting time was acceptable in the context of Community law. It concluded that waiting time must not:

> exceed the period which is acceptable on the basis of an *objective medical assessment* of the clinical needs of the person concerned in the light of all of the factors characterising his medical condition at the time when the request for authorisation is made or renewed, as the case may be. (Case C–372/04, Watts, paragraph 79, emphasis added)

Furthermore, the decision whether the length of waiting time is undue must be based on

> an *objective medical assessment* of the patient's medical condition, the history and *probable course of his illness*, the *degree of pain* he is in and/or *the nature of his disability* at the time when the request for authorisation was made or renewed. (Case C–372/04, Watts, paragraph 119, emphasis added)

This line of reasoning opened up the possibility of new opportunities and rights that many EU patients did not have in their member states because it

[17] See note 14 above.

established demanding criteria for a waiting period to be justified (Palm and Glinos [2010: 533]). Repeating the conclusions from Smits and Peerbooms and Müller-Fauré and van Riet, the Court stated that the prior authorization procedures in member states cannot be discretionary but rather must be based on objective, non-discriminatory criteria and allow for decisions on authorization to be challenged in judicial or quasi-judicial proceedings (Case C–372/04, Watts, paragraphs 115–16). Furthermore,

> [t]o that end, refusals to grant authorisation, or the advice on which such refusals may be based, must refer to the *specific provisions* on which they are *based* and *be properly reasoned* in accordance with them. Likewise, courts or tribunals hearing actions against such refusals must be able, if they consider it necessary for the purpose of carrying out the review which it is incumbent on them to make, to seek the advice of *wholly objective and impartial independent experts*. (Case C–372/04, Watts, paragraph 117, emphasis added)

One year later, the Court proceeded to consider Greek administration of cross-border treatment. In the 2007 case of Stamatelaki,[18] the Court ruled that a member state could not refuse to reimburse treatment in another member state on the grounds that it was provided in a private hospital. In the case, the Greek government submitted that the balance of the system was at risk if citizens could travel to private hospitals in other EU countries without Greece having established agreements with those hospitals. However, these concerns were dismissed by the Court, which instead clarified that the Greek ban on reimbursement for private healthcare abroad was against Community law.

Fine-tuning Legal Integration of Cross-border Healthcare

The line of case law from Decker and Kohll onwards to Stamatelaki implied progressive intervention of internal market principles in the healthcare sector. Step by step, jurisprudence came to include all healthcare systems, public and private provision, and gradually limited the justified scope of national conditions. However, the Court may have had little awareness of the implications of its initial rulings. As noted by Greer and Jarman, the Court probably

[18] Case C–444/05 Aikaterini *Stamatelaki* v NPDD Organismos Asfaliseos Eleftheron Epangelmation (OAEE) [2007] ECR I–3185.

had not realized the difficulty of the terrain to which it applied the internal market principles when it first began doing so:

> It is hard to find any evidence in its early healthcare decisions that it (the CJEU) knew much about the substance of healthcare—even that it knew enough to realize that it was entering a complex, politically difficult and very expensive area that has a record of creating serious policy headaches. (Greer and Jarman [2012: 267])

As the rulings developed, their scope was gradually clarified. On one hand, the Court applied its reasoning to all healthcare systems. On the other hand, it also established that deviations from the free movement principles were justifiable under certain conditions (Ruijter [2015: 228]). As Obermaier has noted, it gradually came to 'fine-tune' its jurisprudence, which by permitting certain deviations from internal market principles became less confrontational and more acceptable to the member states (Obermaier [2009]).

However, the application of internal market principles was clearly neither initiated nor envisioned by politics but instead conceived by judicial interpretations. It is also clear that, for a decade, regulating the scope of a European healthcare system was indeed left to courts, litigants, and lawyers (Leibfried [2005]). The CJEU progressed considerably in its interpretations without any political guidelines, formal approvals, or corrections. In this way, the scope of the legal interpretations was established entirely in the courtroom. It was thus no longer disputable that internal market principles applied to the healthcare sector, disregarding how healthcare was financed or organized. Where was the 'messy world of politics' in these processes (Weiler [1991: 2411])? A political response came late but did in fact manage to rein in the course of legal integration, as the following analysis will demonstrate.

Initial Political Responses: Outcry, Silence, and Non-adoption

The Court's intervention in the healthcare field was by no means welcomed by the national health ministers. Indeed, the Decker and Kohll jurisprudence sent shockwaves through the healthcare ministries of the EU member states (Lamping [2005: 30]). As two respondents described it, 'that night of the Decker and Kohll rulings was the night where lights were on in all the EU healthcare ministries ... where we turned to one another, read the rulings over and over again and asked "what the hell are they up to?"'[19]

The former German minister of health, Horst Seehofer, argued impetuously in the wake of the judgments that the member states had to overturn the rulings through a Treaty amendment and that Germany would not comply with the premises of the judgments (Langer [1999: 54]). The former health minister found the Decker and Kohll decisions 'revolutionary' and argued that adopting their premises would threaten the long-term sustainability of the German health system (*Der Spiegel* [1998] 17/98, Fokus from May 1998; Eichenhofer [1999: 114]). A Treaty amendment was called for that would clarify that internal market principles did not apply to healthcare (Martinsen and Falkner [2011: 134]; Obermaier [2009: 77]). As we now know, these Treaty amendments were never adopted. In the end, member states did not prioritize the matter sufficiently when negotiating the Treaty of Nice, and a Treaty clarification exempting healthcare from the internal market was not inserted.

This initial outburst was later met with a long period without any EU initiatives:

even though the Member States consulted each other, formally and informally, on the measures or stance to be taken following the rulings, in terms of public opinion the strategy taken was very much a conspiracy of silence and rejection. (Palm et al. [2000: 78])

What followed was a long period of legal uncertainty. The member states waited for the Commission to take the initiative. The Commission met the political call with 'deafening silence' (Palm et al. [2000: 78]). Apparently, the European executive was already crippled by internal disagreement over how to draft a satisfying proposal (Rosa [2012: 25]). In the meantime, the European Court continued to develop its interpretations on cross-border healthcare.

The first Commission attempt to respond to the Court's rulings came in March 2004. The Commission proposed to integrate the healthcare area into the proposal for a Directive on Services in the Internal Market, commonly referred to as the Bolkestein Directive, named after the initiating commissioner.[20] The DG Internal Market and Services (MARKT) was assigned as the responsible Directorate General, which gave the initial proposal a

[19] Quote from informal conversation with two key respondents about the day of the Decker and Kohll ruling, 28 April 1998.

[20] Proposal for a Directive of the European Parliament and of the Council on services in the internal market, *COM (2004) 2*, 3 March 2004.

strong attachment to the market, suggesting placing healthcare into an 'undiluted economic logic' (Sauter [2011: 7]). The Commission proposed to codify the case law of the Court, and the main justification for including healthcare in a service directive was made on the basis of jurisprudence:

> Article 23 of the proposal incorporates the distinction between hospital and non-hospital care that has been clearly established by the consolidated case-law of the Court of Justice. As regards the circumstances in which such prior authorisation is justified, the proposal clarifies the specific conditions for authorisation, in accordance with the case-law of the Court of Justice. (*COM (2004) 2*, 14)

In essence, article 23 proposed a codification of the case law of the Court as follows:

(1) An internal market for non-hospital care, in which the patient has a right to seek treatment in another member state without prior authorization and subsequently have the costs reimbursed by the competent national institution.

(2) A right to hospitalization in another member state, provided that the state of affiliation offers the same treatment and that authorization has been granted beforehand.

It was indeed a daring move from the Commission to include healthcare in the de-regulation agenda of the Bolkestein Directive (Szyszczak [2011: 116]). That move was legitimized with reference to the Court. The main justification put forward by DG MARKT was judicial decisions. 'In the light of the case-law of the Court', the requirement of prior authorization had to be abolished for all types of non-hospital care (*COM (2004) 2*, 39, recital 54). The clear-cut distinction between hospital and non-hospital care was again justified on the basis of 'the consolidated case-law of the ECJ' (*COM (2004) 2*, 14).

The Commission's attempt to codify the case law of the Court within a directive aiming to improve market efficiency underestimated the political reactions. The responses at the national level were fierce and hostile (Ruijter [2015: 234–5]; Szyszczak [2011: 116–17]). Furthermore, DG MARKT had underestimated the response from the European Parliament. The co-legislator emphasized the special nature of healthcare. In April 2005, with John Bowis from the European People's Party (EPP) as rapporteur, the Parliament brought forward a motion for an EP resolution in which it disapproved of healthcare being regulated as part of the Service Directive and instead called for a separate Commission proposal on patients' rights.[21] In the motion, the EP explicitly called for politics to play a role in the process and for the matter not to be left to the European Court to decide:

> The new rights for patients conferred by the European Court of Justice in its sequence of judgments are potentially good news for patients but a substantial headache for health service budget holders and insurers. So far the pace has been set by the courts and patient pressure. If we are happy to leave it to the courts to decide policy and spending priorities, the European Union need do nothing, except to prepare to pay heavy and unpredictable bills, whenever patient probing and legal opinions are delivered. That is no way to run a Country, much less the venture that is New Europe. (EP motion, A6-0129/2005, 11)

On 16 February 2006, the EP vetoed the inclusion of healthcare in the Service Directive, demanding a separate cross-border directive to establish legal certainty and clarity:

> This Directive does not affect the reimbursement of healthcare provided in a Member State other than that in which the recipient of the care is resident. That has been addressed by the Court of Justice on numerous occasions, and the Court has recognised patients' rights. It is important to address this issue in another Community legal instrument in order to achieve greater legal certainty and clarity. (EP's first reading, P6_TA (2006)0061, 11, recital 28, 16 February 2006)

Additionally, the Council refused to have the policy area regulated as part of a general directive on services, placed under the responsibility of DG MARKT with healthcare treated as simply another public service (Baeten and Palm [2013: 390]). Article 23 and thus the healthcare area was removed from the directive (Jensen and Nedergaard [2011]), and the Commission had to restart from scratch its deliberations on how to address the patients' rights case law and increase legal certainty.

Drafting a Separate Healthcare Proposal

With the veto of the European Parliament, it was clear that European healthcare could not be regulated from an overall internal market perspective. However, a political response was still called for, not least in light of the Watts case, making it irrevocably clear that free movement principles

[21] European Parliament 'Report on patient mobility and healthcare developments in the European Union', *A6-0129/2005* (Rapporteur: John Bowis), 29 April 2005.

applied to all healthcare systems, whatever their financing or organization (Greer [2009: 41]). The College of Commissioners therefore decided that DG Health (SANCO) should take over primary responsibility from DG MARKT to draft a new proposal.

In September 2006, DG SANCO communicated a consultation procedure for health services.[22] It received a total of 266 contributions from member states and EEA states, regional authorities, national parliaments, national organizations, international organizations, citizens, universities, and commercial organizations and companies. France, Bulgaria, and Portugal were the only member states that did not submit contributions. In the submitted contributions, member states expressed concerns about the distinction between hospital and non-hospital care, undue delay, equal possibilities to use cross-border healthcare, and the financial implications of cross-border care (Martinsen [2007: 38–44]). The Commission should thus have been well aware of the many political concerns aroused by EU intervention in healthcare.

One year later, it made its first attempt to present a proposal. DG SANCO announced that the proposal would be presented on 19 December 2007. However, in a surprise to many, on that day the Commission decided not to present its proposal (Martinsen [2009: 801])). Political tensions and concerns about the proposal ran high.

Many different actors and organizations worked behind the scenes in the run-up to the presentation of the initiative (Martinsen [2009]). Furthermore, the Commission was split internally on the proposal (Greer and Martín de Almagro Iniesta [2014: 369]). The College of Commissioners disagreed strongly on the proposal and its principles. Some commissioners intervened against the proposal just before it was presented, expressing concerns about its impact on national health systems (Martinsen [2009]). Other commissioners were concerned about how the proposal would be received by the public, fearing that it could cause protests similar to those over the Bolkestein Directive. These new public protests were again feared to potentially influence the ongoing national ratifications of the Treaty of Lisbon and ultimately lead to rejection of the new Treaty (Martinsen [2009]; Peeters [2012: 31]).

Members of the EP also intervened in the process, arguing along the same lines as the sceptical commissioners. Key members of the EP Socialists and

[22] See *SEC (2006) 1195/4*, Consultation regarding Community action on health services, 26 September 2006.

Democrats (S&D) group urged the Commission to withdraw the proposal, arguing that it would have considerable negative consequences for national healthcare systems (Martinsen [2009]; interview, European Parliament, 16 November 2009). Additionally, S&D members linked the proposal with the ratification of the Lisbon Treaty, arguing that the timing was poorly chosen because the Lisbon Treaty remained to be ratified in several member states (Politiken, Nyrup advarer mod nyt EU-kaos, 10 January, 2008). In the end, the Commission decided not to present the December version of the proposal.

The Commission's Final Proposal: Departing from the Case Law of the Court

The December 2007 attempt to present a proposal for cross-border healthcare had failed, despite many years of careful preparation. However, the Commissioner for Health, Markos Kyprianou, continued to argue for the need to regulate the field of cross-border healthcare, given the decisions of the CJEU. According to Kyprianou, the Commission had no other option but to regulate, being prompted by the judicial decisions. With reference to judicial activism, the commissioner argued that a directive was a sheer necessity:

> 'I don't think [we] have a choice .... It's not an initiative of the Commission to create any new right, [but] offering legal certainty' (Markos Kyprianou, quoted in *EU Observer*, 'EU health bill faces indefinite delay', 7 February 2008).

On 2 July 2008, the Commission finally came forward with its proposal for a Directive on Patients' Rights.[23] The long drafting and preparation time substantiates the difficulties and conflicts that characterized the dossier.

Reference to judicial decisions runs through the proposal as a recurrent point of justification. The Commission thus justified the need to regulate on the basis of the Court's interpretations, which according to the Commission had created a need to establish legal certainty. The proposal began with reference to the Court's rulings, and jurisprudence continued to serve as the main justification for the necessity of the initiative. The reasoning presented

[23] Proposal for a Directive of the European Parliament and of the Council on the application of patient rights in cross-border healthcare, *COM (2008) 414*.

included 'as the Court has held', 'as confirmed by the Court', 'as was recognized by the Court', 'as established by the Court', 'as already addressed by the Court', 'in the light of the case law', and 'in order to achieve a more general and effective application of principles developed by the Court'. In the explanatory memorandum and the recitals of the proposal, the 'Court' was mentioned thirty-seven times, 'case law' seven times, 'legal certainty' four times, 'judgment' four times, and 'jurisprudence' twice. Ten footnotes referred specifically to the case law of the Court.

Two of the most controversial parts of the proposal were directly justified on the basis of the previous judicial decisions—a Treaty base for the Directive and the issue of prior authorization.

The first justification based on judicial decisions concerned the legal basis of the proposal. The Commission proposed the legal basis as *article 95 EC of the Treaty* (now article 114 TFEU), i.e. the article *regulating the internal market*. The objective of the proposal was stated as improving the internal market. In the Commission's view, the internal market could be improved while fully respecting member states' competences to deliver and organize health services. The Commission proposed a need to ensure 'a more general and effective application of these internal market rights in practice', as 'recognized by the Court' (*COM (2008) 414*, 6–7).

> The *Court has held* that the freedom to provide services includes the freedom for the recipients of services, including persons in need of medical treatment, to go to another Member State in order to receive those services there. *As the Court has also held*, the fact that the legislation of the Member State of affiliation does not guarantee a patient covered by that legislation a level of reimbursement equivalent to that to which he would have been entitled if he had received healthcare in the Member State of affiliation is a restriction of the freedom to provide services within the meaning of Article 49 EC. (*COM (2008) 414*: 6–7, emphasis added)

The second judicial justification considered the scope and limits of *prior authorization*, as presented in articles 7 and 8 of the proposal. The Commission asserted that, according to the case law of the Court, prior authorization should be as limited as possible. Having learned from the political response to the proposal for a service directive, the Commission this time proposed to modify instead of codify the impact of legal interpretations. It thus departed from the clear-cut distinction between non-hospital care and hospital care that was presented in article 23 of the original service directive proposal. The Commission maintained a Community definition of hospital care as inpatient care and defined hospital care as treatment that requires at least one night of stay in a hospital or clinic (*COM (2008) 414*, 15; article 8.1.a of the proposal). In article 7, the Commission maintained that non-hospital care should circulate freely and that here, prior authorization was not justifiable. However, this time, the Commission tried to accommodate the political concerns by extending the scope of prior authorization to include not only hospital care but also highly specialized and cost-intensive healthcare (articles 7 and 8.1.a and 8.1.b of *COM (2008) 414*).

On one hand, this example demonstrates the Commission's adaptive behaviour. Owing to the rejection of the original proposal for a service directive and the December 2007 version of the patients' rights proposal, the Commission put forward a proposal modifying judicial impact. On the other hand, it should be noted that the Commission attached considerable conditions to the extended use of prior authorization, proposing important limitations on its use.

Again, this need to limit the use of prior authorization was justified by a lengthy recourse to the case law of the Court (see explanatory memorandum of *COM (2008) 414*, 13–16). First, what could be defined as highly specialized and cost-intensive care would be included on a specific list, created and regularly updated by the Commission and regulated using the Comitology procedure (interview, European Commission, 23 June 2011; *COM (2008) 414*, 15–16, recital 30 and article 8.2). In this way, the Commission would gain considerable control of what could be classified as such. Second, an important condition for the prior authorization procedure to be justifiable was that member states provide evidence that outflow of patients would 'seriously undermine or [was] likely to seriously undermine' the financial balance, planning, or rationalization of the hospital sector (*COM (2008) 414*, 14, recital 31, and article 8.3.b). The Commission thus laid a considerable burden of proof upon the member states, assuring itself significant governing capacity in deciding whether prior authorization was a necessary means of national control (Hancher and Sauter [2012: 206–7]).

Thus, although the Commission had extended the use of prior authorization, it still emphasized that it should be used as an exception and not as the general rule:

> ... according to the relevant jurisprudence, the introduction of a prior authorisation scheme, which will limit the exercise of rights conferred upon the citizens directly by the EC Treaty, must be proportionate and justified by imperative reasons as those mentioned in the same case law. (*COM (2008) 414 final*, 14)

The proposal also justified its article 9 by reference to procedural guarantees on the basis of the case law of the Court.

The scope of the directive was specified as covering only the healthcare package from the member state of affiliation. The scope of the proposal was thus a direct leftover from the political responses to the Pierik judgments. Political override of early jurisprudence was carried into the text. Concerning providers, the proposal simply stated that '"healthcare provider" means any natural or legal person legally providing healthcare on the territory of a Member State' (article 4.e of the proposal), meaning that providers not publicly contracted in the member state of treatment could also provide cross-border healthcare. This inclusion of non-contracted providers, however, was not justified further in the proposal. Nevertheless, it was subsequently contested in Council negotiations.

Additionally, the proposal contained provisions on contact points to be established to allow patients to make informed choices, enhanced cooperation between member states, mutual recognition of prescriptions, and e-health as important parts of the proposal, which, however, came to be less controversial in the negotiation process. Table 5.1 sets out the provisions of the Commission's proposal that responded to judicial decisions or became major issues in subsequent political negotiations.

Viewed along the conflict lines of the two dimensions *more integration versus less integration* and *left–right*, the Commission proposed less integration than originally proposed in the Service directive by allowing more national control. However, it also assigned itself an important monitoring role in overseeing how member states would establish and apply their prior authorization policies. Additionally, the Commission did not propose a dual legal basis, including article 168(7) with the principle of subsidiarity. The left–right dimension here concerned the extent to which the proposal focused on equality of patients' rights. Equality was not a major consideration in the Commission's proposal. Patients would be reimbursed only up to the level of costs in their member states of affiliation and would have to pay up front for treatment themselves, making it more difficult for less-well-off patients to make use of the directive. However, compared with the original proposal for a service directive, the new proposal placed more emphasis on patients' ability to make an informed choice and their procedural guarantees and was thus somewhat less to the right than the former. The position of the Commission in relation to SQ_{Court} is summarized alongside the other political positions on the two dimensions in this chapter's concluding figure 5.2.

Table 5.1 Key Provisions in Commission's Proposal

	Commission proposal *COM (2004) 414* as of 2 July 2008
Legal basis	Proposed as article 95 EC (now article 114 TFEU) of the Treaty. Justified on the basis of the Court. Proposing to codify.
Prior authorization	Article 7: Non-hospital care not subject to prior authorization. Article 8: • Article 8.1.a: Prior authorization justifiable for hospital care. • Article 8.1.b: Prior authorization justifiable for highly specialized and cost-intensive care included on a specific list. • Article 8.2: What qualifies as highly specialized and cost-intensive to be determined by Commission. • Article 8.3.b: Member state may have a system of prior authorization, provided outflow of patients is 'seriously undermining' or likely to 'seriously undermine' financial balance of social security system or its planning or rationalization. Proposing to modify the case law of the Court.
Procedural guarantees	Article 9: National administrative procedures and decisions to be justified, necessary, and proportionate. Member state to set time limits to consider requests for cross-border healthcare, taking into account: (a) specific medical condition, (b) patient's degree of pain, (c) nature of patient's disability, and (d) patient's ability to carry out a professional activity. Proposing to codify the case law of the Court.
Incoming patients	Article 5.1.g: Patients from other member states to enjoy equal treatment.
Scope	Only applies to healthcare that is part of healthcare package in member state of affiliation. Maintains political override of Pierik case law.
Providers	Non-contracted providers also within scope of directive.
Reimbursement level	Up to level of costs in member state of affiliation.
Payment	Up front payment by the patient.
Rare diseases	No recitals or articles address this issue.

Negotiating the Proposal for a Patients' Rights Directive

Despite the Commission's willingness this time to address some of the political concerns concerning the case law of the Court, subsequent negotiations became tense and rife with conflict. Political positions came to diverge within and between the two co-legislators. Political actors disagreed on both the *more versus less integration* dimension, where Community competences within the healthcare sector were greatly disputed throughout negotiations, and the *left–right* dimension, where the equality dimension of cross-border healthcare became a controversial theme. Would and should this directive benefit the larger majority of EU citizens or only the few better-off citizens able to pay up front and exercise their rights?

The Commission took an active part in negotiations, far beyond its agenda-setting role (Schmidt [2000]). As the analysis below demonstrates, it allied itself with the European Parliament, expecting the EP to be more in favour of integration and more willing to strengthen patients' rights than the Council. DG SANCO had now acquired the main responsibility for the directive, intending to improve the relationship with the member states after their fierce reactions against the proposal for a service directive (Ruijter [2015]). However, internally the Commission was split. SANCO had its difficulties with DG MARKT, which was not willing to fully let go of the dossier. Alongside negotiations, DG MARKT started infringement procedures against several member states, including Spain, France, and Luxembourg, letting them know that they would be taken to Court if they did not comply with the CJEU rulings (Kostera [2014: 250]).[24] By continuing with the infringement procedures during negotiations, DG MARKT reminded the member states of their obligation to comply with the case law of the Court—political agreement or not. Its strategy was thus to 'coax the member states into action', presenting a political agreement as a 'lesser evil' than legal integration beyond political control (Schmidt [2000]). However, DG SANCO did not agree with this strategy. From the outset, internal friction in the Commission was high (Ruijter [2015: 241]).

[24] These infringement procedures were taken to Court as C–512/08 European *Commission v* French Republic [*France*] [2010] ECR I–8833; C–211/08 European *Commission v* Kingdom of *Spain* [2010] ECR I–5267; and C–490/09 European *Commission v* Grand Duchy of *Luxemburg* [2011] ECR I–249.

Political Positions in the European Parliament

Throughout negotiations, the European Parliament had difficulty with the dossier. The Parliament faced disagreements both within and between the political groups.

The EPP and the Liberals (ALDE) supported the Commission's proposal from the outset. The EPP held the rapporteurship on the dossier, which had been granted to the British MEP, John Bowis. Bowis already had experience on the topic, having held rapporteurship on the EP motion from 2005. From the outset of negotiations, the case law of the Court constituted both a strong argument why political action was needed and a reference point for which political options were feasible (interviews, European Parliament, 17 February 2009, 10 June 2009, 16 November 2009). In the draft report, the rapporteur noted to his fellow colleagues that the dossier was not to be written on a blank sheet. According to Bowis, the case law of the Court had already dictated a large portion, foreclosing certain options (see the quotation at the head of this chapter).

The political negotiations in the European Parliament were thus launched against this background. The rapporteur reminded his fellow EP members of the 'shadow of the law' and urged them not to 'leave policy-making to the lawyers' (draft report PE 415.355, (Rapporteur: John Bowis), 30, 20 November 2008). Both ALDE and EPP made active use of judicial decisions to justify their positions:

> To be honest, from my point of view, we used the position of the Court as an argument, but it wasn't our motivation. Even if the Court had never done this, we would still have wanted to have this kind of legislation. But the fact that the Court had done it made it a lot easier. And it also meant that you could argue to the opponents, who would say, "Look, you can oppose it, but the Court has already said it. Isn't it better that we say it than that the Court says it? And that we can shape it the way we want to shape it?" (interviews, European Parliament, 10 June 2009)

ALDE favoured the greatest possible extent of free movement of healthcare. It thus supported the Commission's proposal but would have preferred a freer circulation of healthcare (interview, EP, 10 June 2009). ALDE worked to abolish prior authorization as far as possible. It also worked to strengthen patients' de facto ability to access cross-border healthcare. Cross-border patients should have access to interpreters when necessary and be reimbursed for transport costs. Furthermore, the ALDE group proposed a European patient ombudsman to investigate complaints concerning cross-border care (interviews, EP, 18 February 2009, 10 June 2009). In sum, ALDE worked for more integration but also to improve equal access to cross-border care by strengthening patients' rights.

While both ALDE and EPP worked for a codification of the case law of the Court, the S&D group faced serious difficulties with the proposal. The group was divided internally on various issues, especially on the question of the correct legal basis for the directive and the issue of prior authorization. The proposal had high priority in the group and was addressed in the S&D bureau among the leadership team (interview, European Parliament, 17 February 2009). The group saw it as necessary to be able to respond to the case-law of the Court.

> Because the worst that could happen—and that goes for all policy areas—would be just to leave it to the European Court to decide. You don't find many politicians who think that would be great. (Interview, European Parliament, 17 February 2009)

The powerful and experienced vice-president of the European Parliament and member of the S&D group, Dagmar Roth-Behrendt, was appointed shadow rapporteur on the proposal and took an active role in negotiations (interviews, European Parliament, 17 February 2009, 10 June 2009). The shadow rapporteur herself largely supported the Commission's proposal, working for a first reading agreement (interviews, European Parliament, 17 February 2009, 10 June 2009). During the EP's first reading, the group was internally divided on the overall principles and consequences of the proposal. The group was also divided on how to respond to the case law of the Court. Not all the members agreed that a political decision would be the right response to what the Court had initiated because it would extend Community competence to what was regarded as a national prerogative:

> We have had the discussion in my committee these days ... And many members are saying 'No, I would rather have a political decision within this area instead of a Court ruling.' This means that [the] EU has to start getting involved with some new topics and problem areas to reach this decision. And people are afraid of that. They prefer letting the Court decide rather than deciding on something that should be left to the nation states. And that, of course, is the dilemma in a way. (interview, European Parliament, 17 February 2009)

The S&D members most supportive of the Commission's proposal viewed it as a European initiative strengthening patients' rights, whereas the more sceptical S&D members were concerned about the Directive's impact on the national healthcare systems and subsidiarity, seeing it mainly as an internal market initiative (interviews, European Parliament, 17 February 2009, 18 February 2009, 10 June 2009). The appointment of Roth-Behrendt as shadow rapporteur was important in this regard. She was generally more in favour of the Commission's initiative than the majority of her political group and thus not regarded as representing the more sceptical portion of the S&D group (interviews, European Parliament, 17 February 2009, 10 June 2009, 15 November 2011). Thus she largely shared a position with rapporteur Bowis from EPP and the shadow rapporteur Jules Maaten from ALDE (interview, European Parliament, 10 June 2009). The relationship within the rapporteur team was described as one of trust and mutual understanding. However, it proved more difficult for the shadow rapporteur to convince her own S&D group to support the Commission's proposal.

The Greens and the united left (GUE/NGL) were generally against the proposal and against the proposed legal basis of the directive being the internal market article 114 TFEU (*EurActiv*, 'Parliament backs EU cross-border healthcare plans', 24 April 2009). The initiative was regarded as too market-biased, aiming to regulate healthcare as commercial goods (interview, European Parliament, 6 December 2010). Accordingly, the Greens and the united left opposed the proposal.

Political Interactions in the European Parliament

The first reading of the proposal took place six months before the 2009 European Parliament election. The election campaign influenced the negotiations in various ways. In the heat of the elections, MEPs appeared less willing to compromise and positions became more divided. Furthermore, several MEPs were not campaigning for the next EP, including rapporteur Bowis and shadow rapporteur Jules Maaten from ALDE. There was therefore an attempt to conclude the first reading before the new parliament and establish an agreement with the Council. At the end of the sixth European Parliament, a first reading agreement was in fact established; however, it was too late to also conclude an agreement with the Council. EP negotiations dragged out owing to the many amendments tabled by the EP committees, and the Council had its own difficulties. The momentum that might have enabled a first reading agreement between the two legislatures did not develop in time (interview, European Parliament, 10 June 2009).

During the first reading, the rapporteur had to establish an internal compromise between the many amendments proposed by the EP committees and individual MEPs. The Committee on Environment, Public Health, and Food Safety (ENVI) was responsible for the dossier. However, the internal procedure in the European Parliament was 'enhanced cooperation', meaning that the rapporteur had to take the amendments of the Committee on Employment and Social Affairs (EMPL) and the Committee on the Internal Market and Consumer Protection (IMCO) into account. More than 700 amendments were tabled in the ENVI Committee alone (interview, European Parliament, 18 February 2009; ALDE Group briefing, 8 February 2009). By the deadline to submit amendments—15 January 2009—a total of more than 1,600 amendments had been proposed (interview, European Parliament, 18 February 2009; interview, Commission, 17 February 2009). The Bowis report managed to merge the many amendments into just over 100. In its first reading, the European Parliament adopted 115 amendments to the Commission's proposal.[25]

During the negotiations, the rapporteur emphasized the need to take action in response to the Court, and the amendments were explained as 'the lesser evil strategy' (Schmidt [2000]), as Bowis asserted in the explanatory statement of his final report:

> "'Jamais poète n'a interpreté la nature aussi librement qu'un juriste la realité." Jean Giraudoux
>
> *(No poet ever interpreted nature as freely as a lawyer interprets the truth.)* Lawyers and politicians: For the past ten years, since the 1998 Kohll and Decker judgment at the European Court of Justice (ECJ), the lawyers of Europe have been deciding policy on patient mobility, because the politicians of Europe have failed to do so. If we do nothing, the Court will continue to interpret the Treaties, where patient mobility rights are concerned. They will provide the clarity that we politicians have failed to provide. If we are content to leave policymaking to lawyers, then we need do nothing—except of course pay the resulting unpredictable bills. (Report A6-0233/2009, 77)

However, Bowis also made clear that judicial decisions precluded certain policy options, particularly regarding authorization rules. In this way, Bowis used the 'voice of law' as a push factor to make fellow MEPs accept strengthened internal market principles in the healthcare sector (Martinsen [2009]; Martinsen and Falkner [2011]). Bowis held that '... tighter authorisation rules

[25] See EP Report on the Proposal, A6-0233/2009 (Rapporteur: John Bowis), 3 April 2009.

would be inconsistent with the rulings of the European Court of Justice (ECJ) which originally put the question on the agenda' (*European Voice*, 'MEPs back cross-border healthcare plan', 31 March 2009). The Bowis report was debated in Strasbourg on 23 April 2009, upon which the first reading vote was held. The debate was fierce and reflected the fact that the three largest political groups had not yet fully reached a compromise. During the debate, the Court and its decisions were a recurrent reference point. Health Commissioner Androulla Vassiliou opened the debate by emphasizing the Court of Justice as the '*origin of the proposal*':

> Allow me to recall briefly the rationale behind this proposed directive, as well as its main objectives and principles. The origin of the proposal lies in a decade of jurisprudence of the European Court of Justice, which ruled that patients have the right to be reimbursed for health care received abroad, even if they could have received that health care at home. This is important. This is a right that the Treaty directly grants to EU citizens. However, if the rulings were clear for the individuals concerned, the question of how they apply to all other cases was obscure. (Vassiliou, EP debate, 23 April 2009)

Indeed, there was no common position in the European Parliament in support of the Bowis report and its amendments. EPP and ALDE supported the report, arguing that their position was 'about rejecting the idea that the Court of Justice makes European law instead of the politicians' (Grossetête, EPP, EP debate, 23 April 2009). However, the S&D group remained internally divided on the dossier. Dagmar Roth-Behrendt, the shadow rapporteur, made clear that, to vote in favour of an amended proposal, the S&D group demanded a double legal basis for articles 95 and 152 EC (articles 114 and 168 TFEU), emphasizing subsidiarity for the healthcare sector. Furthermore, the maintenance of prior authorization for specialized care was vital to the S&D group. The S&D thus took the position that it was necessary to modify the impact of judicial decisions. The S&D shadow rapporteur stated that their vote depended on whether they could obtain concessions on these matters:

> For the vast majority of my group, this involves two items that are critical for us and for our voting behaviour today. The first of these is that we want a dual legal basis. We need to use the health article, Article 152, in order to ensure that the message we are sending out to the world is that this is an issue of health policy as well as freedom of movement. We need this, and it is a condition for our support. Furthermore, we are convinced that prior authorisation, as set out in Article 8(3), is inadequately defined. If we are unable to obtain an improvement in this through the amendments that have been tabled, my group will not, unfortunately, be able to bring itself to vote through this report, which is something that I personally regret, although perhaps

this will act as a spur to do better at second reading if we do not make enough ground today. (Roth-Behrendt, S&D, EP debate, 23 April 2009)

The importance of the dual legal basis and prior authorization was restated by other S&D members during the debate. The debate was closed by Commissioner Vassiliou, who made clear that the proposed provision on prior authorization, article 8.3, codified the case law of the Court and that it would not 'be appropriate to go beyond such provisions with a looser—or indeed unconditional—system of prior authorisation' (Vassiliou, EP debate, 23 April 2009). The Commission thereby stated that it had come some way to meet political concerns since the Service Directive but that further concessions would be 'inappropriate', i.e. contradict the case law of the Court.

The disagreements within the parliament, inside the S&D group, and with the Commission were thus alive and kicking despite almost a year of first reading. These disagreements meant that the first reading of the proposal was approved by only a narrow, simple majority: 297 MEPs voted in favour, 120 voted against, and 152 abstained from voting. Most S&D members abstained, and some voted against. Members of GUE/NGL also voted against.

The EP majority adopted various amendments to the Commission's text. The amendments modified the course of legal integration more substantially than those proposed by the Commission would have done. The EP reacted most strongly against the Commission's proposal to distinguish between non-hospital and hospital care, specifying when prior authorization could be justified. First, the EP modified the proposed definition of hospital care. Instead of a Community definition, the EP adopted a definition 'established by the Member State of affiliation', which would re-introduce a considerable degree of national control (amending article 8.1). Second, the EP modified the Commission's proposal regarding non-hospital care where authorization rules could be justified. Where the proposal allowed for authorization for 'healthcare that requires use of highly specialized and cost-intensive medical infrastructure or medical equipment', the EP modified this provision to 'healthcare which is highly specialized *and/or* requires use of cost-intensive medical infrastructure or medical equipment' (amending article 8.1.b). It also deleted the requirement that this type of healthcare be included on a specific list. In this way, the EP broadened the scope of national discretion over what could qualify within this additional category situated between 'hospital' and 'non-hospital' care. Third, the EP deleted the specific article 8.2, under which this additional type of healthcare would be put on a list controlled by the Commission. In sum, the majority position of the European Parliament during the first reading was to rein in the Court by enhancing national control, i.e. to reduce integration.

In addition to these modifications of the case law of the Court, the EP's first reading introduced a number of other important amendments to the Commission's text. The European legislature inserted a number of requests regarding the rules for application for and refusal of authorization (articles 8.5–8.7). It furthermore added a new article according to which patients with rare diseases would not be subject to prior authorization (article 8.9). Additionally, the EP added a provision under which patients could receive a voucher from their member state of affiliation authorizing cross-border care without having to pay themselves (article 10). This new provision aimed to enhance equality:

> When we say the policy should be about patients with needs, not patients with means, we should make it clear we do not wish to see patients having to travel, clutching cash or credit card to pay upfront for often expensive in-hospital treatment. We should put in place a system of reimbursement direct from home funder to receiving hospital, either through a Central Clearing House to manage the cross-border, cross-currency, cross-system (Beveridge/Bismarck) complications, or by a bi-lateral voucher system for the patient to take to the hospital and guaranteeing the latter payment by the Member State of Affiliation. (draft report PE 415.355 (Rapporteur: John Bowis), 20 November 2008, 31)

The final amendment to note here was the EP's insertion of a new article 11 requiring the Commission to establish a European patient ombudsman to mediate patients' complaints on prior authorization, reimbursement, or harm. These additional amendments adopted by the EP aimed to enhance patients' rights and strengthen equality, so that EU citizens in general would benefit from the Directive independent of their socio-economic resources.

Ultimately, the first reading of the EP meant tightened authorization rules—a result that rapporteur Bowis had previously held to be inconsistent with the case law of the Court. However, in this first reading, the EP majority accepted article 95 as the sole legal basis of the directive. Nevertheless, 272 MEPs either abstained from voting or voted against the proposal as amended. The small majority in favour did not send a strong signal to the Council (interview, European Parliament, 10 June 2009). Rather than acting in consensus, the EP was split over the proposal. The rapporteur team had to initiate negotiations with the Council representing a split parliament, with a considerable portion wanting more national control and expressing serious concern about free movement principles being imposed on national healthcare systems.

Political Positions in the Council of Ministers

The Council negotiations on the dossier were difficult from the beginning. As noted by the then Health Commissioner Androulla Vassillou, only two or three member states were in favour when the proposal was first presented by the Commission (2980th meeting, press conference, 1 December 2009). During the first year of negotiations, member states were divided into three groups: Sweden and Belgium, which supported the Commission's proposal; a set of member states that did not support the proposal but were willing to negotiate, counting, among others, the UK, the Netherlands, France, Germany, and Denmark; and a large group of Southern and Eastern European member states that opposed the proposal and EU intervention in healthcare as such (interviews, Council, 18 February 2009, 20 June 2011).

The different national positions were clearly informed by the extent to which member states had implemented the case law of the Court. Sweden had a case before its domestic supreme administrative court in 2004 and subsequently brought its administrative practice into compliance with CJEU jurisprudence (interview, Council, 14 December 2014). Belgium had implemented the case law from 1998 onwards, and the Belgian system 'fit' the judicial decisions well from the outset (Baeten [2012: 30]). For the second group of member states, politicians and bureaucracies had for a considerable time resisted the impact of litigation (Greer and Jarman [2012]). However, at different paces, they had come to comply with at least some of the relevant rulings. The Netherlands and the UK had had their own preliminary references to the CJEU and had thus had time to accustom themselves to its legal reasoning (interviews, European Commission, 17 February 2009; Council, 8 December 2009). In 2006, the Dutch healthcare reform more thoroughly implemented the case law of the Court (Martinsen [2007: 37]; interview, Council, 8 December 2009). The UK had long resisted, initially claiming that the rulings did not apply to the NHS system; however, in 2010, it adapted its national regulation to the case law of the Court (Baeten [2012: 39]; Davies [2007: 158]; Greer and Rauscher [2011: 230–1]; Obermaier [2009: 121–39]). Denmark and France had undertaken limited and delayed implementations of the case law of the Court (Greer and Martín de Almagro

Iniesta [2014: 373–5]; Martinsen [2014: 196–9]; Obermaier [2009: 87–101]). Germany had adjusted its national health insurance law to the CJEU decisions in 2003 but also in a minimalist way (Greer and Rauscher [2011: 227]).

> ... If you have a tax based system, it might be difficult to get your head around what this must mean for your system.. It might seem very threatening. And I think that this was the main problem for Spain and Portugal and other member states. Of course, I mean also for the UK, and Sweden. They were in a similar situation a couple of years ago. Where we were like 'Well, what do they mean?' But we have ... It's been a process also for our member states to accept this. And I think that the UK came around with such a clear message from the Court about the UK system—I mean the Watts case. And I mean the case law wasn't applied in Sweden until 2004 after some gentlemen in the supreme administrative court in Sweden ... (interview, Council, 14 December 2009)

As legal integration developed from Kohll and Decker on to the Watts case, and as the legal doctrines were fine-tuned, this group of member states had applied cross-border healthcare for a defined scope of non-hospital care while maintaining national control by means of prior authorization for hospital care and parts of non-hospital care. These member states had thus undergone limited national change, with judicial decisions proving to have less impact in terms of internal destructuring and financial destabilization than initially feared (Obermaier [2009]). Although not supporting the Commission's proposal in full, their positions were more pragmatic.

The third group of member states, led by Spain and Poland, were against the proposal from the outset and opposed any codification of the case law, arguing that legal integration had taken a wrong turn into domestic healthcare policies. Poland had not implemented the CJEU rulings, holding that the rulings did not apply to its system (Baeten [2012: 33]). Spain also continued to ignore the cross-border case law throughout the decade over which it unfolded (Greer and Martín de Almagro Iniesta [2014: 376–9]).

> Then you have other member states who are in denial. I mean that they deny that the Court was right. [Member states] which are simply saying that the Court is wrong. But legally, it is a question whether you accept the rule of law, even though it is not in line with your political preference. (interview, European Commission, 17 February 2009)

Most importantly, the political disagreements over how to respond to the case law of the Court concerned the justifiable use of prior authorization. The majority of member states opposed the Commission's proposal of Community definitions of 'hospital care' and 'highly specialized and cost-intensive care' as set out in article 8.1, instead calling for national definitions thereof. Additionally, most member states opposed the proposed article 8.2, according to which a Community list of 'highly specialized and cost-intensive care' would be assembled and regularly updated by the Commission (interviews, European Commission, 17 February 2009; Council, 18 February 2009, 14 December 2014). The member states argued that the formulation of articles 8.1 and 8.2 would not allow them sufficient control, thus endangering the sustainability and steering capacities of national healthcare systems. A large number of member states also raised concerns about inflow of foreign patients and how to maintain sufficient healthcare capacity for national patients (interview, Council, 18 February 2009). However, the potential negative implications of patient inflow were not addressed in the Commission's proposal, which simply stated that 'patients from other Member States shall enjoy equal treatment with the nationals of the Member State of treatment' (article 5.1.g of the proposal).

Political Interactions in the Council of Ministers

The first year of Council negotiations focused on a number of other key issues for the member states. The *legal basis* of the proposal was opposed by many member states, which saw article 95 EC (now article 114 TFEU) as insufficient. At the June 2009 Council meeting, Commissioner Vassiliou agreed to also include article 152 EC (now article 168 TFEU) in the legal basis (see Council press release, 2947th Council meeting, 8–9 June 2009). Thus, the Council controversy over the legal basis was resolved during the first year of negotiations.

However, other disagreements remained. One was whether the role of the *general practitioner* as *gatekeeper* for further treatment could be maintained in an internal market of healthcare. During the Czech presidency, a compromise was formulated allowing member states of affiliation to maintain the same criteria for eligibility and regulatory and administrative formalities for seeking healthcare in another member state, while accepting cross-border access to general practitioners. However, this compromise was still insufficient for some member states, which maintained that patients should be referred to further treatment only by the general practitioners in their member state of affiliation (see Czech presidency progress report, 3 June 2009, 2008/0142(COD), 10).

Additionally, setting *tariffs* and *clear pricing* for cross-border treatment was regarded as problematic. Furthermore, more than half of the member states were against the idea that *non-contracted providers* should be part of the scope of the directive (interviews, Council, 18 February 2009, 30 June 2009). These member states wanted healthcare providers limited to those contracted by the competent national healthcare authority (Czech presidency progress report, 3 June 2009, 2008/0142(COD), 3). The member state position was that the directive should be similar to Regulation 883/2004, under which the patient had access to only providers with which the member state of treatment had a contract.

Indeed, the first year of negotiations was marked by intense political disagreements among the member states and institutional disagreements between the member states and the Commission (interview, Council, 8 December 2009). No clear solution was foreseeable. The Commission was particularly critical of the extended use of prior authorization favoured by the Council negotiations, finding that this extension would conflict with the case law of the Court:

> The Commission has a general reserve on the entire Presidency compromise text. In particular it has major concerns with regard to the approach on quality and safety as provided for in Article 5; *the approach on prior authorisation which in the Commission's view does not reflect the case law*, including the definition of care that can be subject to prior authorisation, which has been significantly broadened. (Czech presidency progress report, 3 June 2009, 2008/0142(COD), 5, emphasis added)

Towards a Common Council Position

Until December 2009, the presidential troika of France, the Czech Republic, and Sweden formulated various compromise texts, and at the end of the Swedish presidency a compromise for a common position was on the table. Among other aspects, the compromise text proposed an extended use of prior authorization, abolishing article 8.2 so that the Commission would no longer control which types of healthcare could be defined as 'highly specialized and cost-intensive'. The compromise text furthermore suggested a dual legal basis.

The Swedish proposal for a common position was vetoed, however, by a blocking minority of Spain, Poland, Romania, Portugal, Greece, Ireland, Hungary, Slovakia, Slovenia, and Lithuania. Spain led the blocking minority (interviews,

Council, 8 December 2009, 14 December 2009). In general, the blocking member states were concerned about cost containment, fearing that despite its declared cost-neutrality, the directive would increase healthcare expenditures. Furthermore, member states maintained their opposition to a court-driven process and how the Commission justified the proposal on the basis of jurisprudence:

> Our reference is not the court law. Our reference has to be what we want for Europe and the European citizens ... And many other things. And we have to be respectful of the court law, but our job is not to answer to the court. Our job must be and should be to answer to the needs of the citizens of Europe. (interview, Council, 9 December 2009)

The presidencies argued that, instead of ignoring the case law of the Court, the legislators should respond to it and regain decision-making power:

> And of course every presidency pointed out that it is not up to Court to set law—or to develop laws—but that it is up to the legislators—to the Council and the European Parliament to set laws. And if they don't do it, the ECJ continues to give judgements in this field. (interview, European Commission, 8 December 2009)

Non-contracted providers were the other major issue during the Swedish presidency. In particular, Spain and Poland maintained their opposition to including non-contracted providers in the Directive (interviews, Council, 9 December 2009). A coalition of member states wanted to exclude providers that had not been contracted by the national healthcare insurer or by the member state of treatment (Kloka and Schmidt [2015]; Nys [2014: 12]). Their position was that including these providers would imply reverse discrimination, where patients could go abroad for non-contracted providers but could not access these providers if they stayed home. In essence, this issue concerned accessibility to private healthcare providers.

> ... for some member states this was an issue of reverse discrimination. Poland said that 'Oh, so a Polish patient that goes to Germany can go to [a] non-contracted provider and then get paid by the Polish social security system, but if the same patient goes to a non-contracted provider in Poland, they will of course not get reimbursed.' (interview, Council, 14 December 2009)

The Commission was inflexible on this point, however. While it had not made any further justifications in its proposal as to why non-contracted providers should also be part of the directive, it now explained its position with reference to the Watts case (interviews, Council, 7 July 2010; Commission, 7 July 2010). In Watts, the cross-border treatment had been carried out by a private provider not contracted by the member state of treatment, i.e. France.

The UK as the member state of affiliation did not entitle NHS patients to obtain hospital treatment in the private sector at the expense of the NHS. The CJEU, however, had not found adequate justification for denying patients access to non-contracted providers in cross-border healthcare.

Additionally, Spain had specific reservations in relation to pensioners from other member states residing in Spain. As specified in Regulation 883/2004, the member state of residence becomes the member state of affiliation for residing pensioners. The member state of origin then pays a lump sum to the new member state of residence. Spain feared that the directive would make it easier for pensioners to return to their member state of origin for treatment and that Spain would then be obliged to cover the cost.[26] During negotiations, the Swedish presidency proposed that the lump sums had to be reviewed in light of the Directive, arguing that the existing lump sums were insufficient. The Commission proposed that the member states of origin should bear the costs for pensioners. However, the majority of sending member states opposed this compromise (interview, European Commission, 8 December 2009).

Apparently, the Spanish regions put significant pressure on their government to veto the Swedish compromise text—as Spain did (interview, Council, 8 December 2009). Poland also voted against the text. The Polish position took the other member states by surprise. Apparently, Poland had not been very active during negotiations; however, the country nevertheless joined the blocking minority against the Swedish compromise text:

> Greece was inflexible. Latvia went ... They went in favour. But what happened then, is absolutely not understandable, because Poland was against, and Romania. That was a surprise. They had never participated in a discussion. Never—seriously—and all of a sudden they were against. Everybody was furious at them. Poland was a big surprise because they were looking ... they looked very constructive, but at the very end, it was a very bloody no. Very determined. Very non- ... (interview, Council, 8 December 2009)

After the failure to reach a political agreement, the Swedish presidency stressed that the member states had now left it for the Court to continue (G. Hägglund, 2980th meeting, Press Conference, 1 December, 2009).

In 2010, Spain assumed the presidency. The leader of the blocking minority was now to chair negotiations, and the member states that had supported the

[26] The new member state of affiliation gets a lump sum from the member state of origin for taking over the healthcare responsibility. The Spanish argument was that this lump sum did not adequately cover the costs of healthcare.

Swedish compromise proposal were sceptical, expecting Spain to halt negotiations (interviews, Council, 8 December 2009, 21 June 2010). Up to March 2010, the Spanish presidency was silent; however, it then presented a specific amendment to the Swedish text intended to address the Southern issue of residing pensioners from other member states (interview, Commission, 7 July 2010; Kloka and Schmidt [2015]). The Spanish text introduced a compromise in an article under which costs for pensioners were shared to a greater extent between the member state of origin and the new member state of residence (interview, Council, 7 July 2010). If a treatment required prior authorization, the new member state of residence would pay the costs. This process would be less costly—and less risky—because the new member state of residence would maintain control by means of authorization. If treatment did not require prior authorization and was carried out in the member state of origin, the member state of origin would resume the costs of care (see article 7.2.b of directive 2011/24). A similar amendment had already been proposed by the Commission during the Swedish presidency but been rejected by the majority of sending member states (see above). What seemed a minor amendment to the Swedish compromise text made it possible for the Council to reach a common position in June 2010. Spain left the blocking minority.

The Council did not act in consensus, however. Poland, Portugal, and Romania voted no to the compromise text, maintaining their opposition to the inclusion of non-contracted providers in the directive (interviews, Commission, 7 July 2010; Council, 21 June 2010). Austria also voted no to the common position owing to considerable opposition from its *Länder*. The Austrian *Länder* were very critical of the Directive, fearing that it could lead to a significant inflow of foreign patients (Kostera [2014: 243–69]). Finally, Slovakia abstained from voting. However, a common council position had been reached.

Inter-institutional Interactions

For the Commission, the Council compromise was difficult to accept because of the increased use of prior authorization. In the Commission's view, the compromise had created an open list of criteria upon which to refuse authorization:

> ...for the Commission, a very difficult part was preauthorization, because the whole list for refusing to grant preauthorization is not a closed one, I would say. No, it's

an open list. It says in article 9(4),[27] that the member state of affiliation may *refuse to grant preauthorization* for reasons *including but not limited to*. And that was for us not a step forward for the citizens, so we have reserved the right to support the European Parliament amendments in the second reading. Because they are much more favourable to the patients. (interview, Commission, 7 July 2010, emphasis added)

To make its position clear, the Commission first issued a declaration after the Council meeting in June 2010 and later a communication to the European Parliament in September 2010 (*COM (2010) 503* as of 20 September 2010). The Commission's declaration took the Council by surprise because issuing a declaration was not common practice (interview, Council, 21 June 2010). Inter-institutional conflicts were thus considerable. In the declaration, the Commission declared that it would not oppose the presidency text but found that it was not sufficiently clear. Thus the Commission reserved the right to support the European Parliament on the issue of prior authorization because the Parliament's position was more in line with the Commission's proposal, especially concerning the Commission's reading of the case law of the Court:

As the position of the European Parliament on prior authorisation and eHealth is more favourable to the patients, closer to the Commission's proposal and to its reading of the existing case-law, the Commission reserves the right to support the European Parliament's amendments on these issues during the second reading and will continue to collaborate closely with both institutions with the aim of further improving the text. (Commission declaration, June 2010)[28]

In the communication, the Commission further detailed why it found the Council's common position problematic. The Commission could not support the extended, non-exhaustive, and nationally controlled possibility of using prior authorization, which it found to conflict with the case law of the Court:

The position of the Council at first reading introduces the possibility for the Member State of affiliation to make the reimbursement of costs of certain types of crossborder healthcare (hospital, specialised care and healthcare which could raise serious and concrete concerns related to the quality or safety of the care) subject to prior authorisation without any explicit request to demonstrate an outflow of patients resulting from the freedom of mobility or any risk to the system. The text simply foresees that the system of prior authorisation shall be limited to what is necessary and proportionate and shall not constitute a means of arbitrary discrimination. *The introduction of*

[27] Article 8(6) of the final directive.

[28] The Commission's declaration was annexed to the Commission's communication to the European Parliament *COM (2010) 503*.

a system of prior authorisation as proposed by the Presidency text is based on a very restrictive interpretation of the jurisprudence. (*COM (2010) 503*, 7, emphasis added)

In the view of the Commission, these Council changes would create legal uncertainty for patients.

In June 2009, a new European Parliament had been elected. Although they had all lost seats during the elections, the three largest political groups were still EPP, S&D, and ALDE, which together had to construct a compromise with the Council. The former rapporteur John Bowis had not run for the new parliament, and therefore the EPP member Françoise Grossetête took over the rapporteurship. Dagmar Roth-Behrendt continued as shadow rapporteur for the S&D group, while Antonyia Parvanova took over as shadow rapporteur for ALDE. The rapporteur team was generally regarded as composed of powerful and experienced MEPs (interview, European Parliament, 15 November 2011).

In the corridors of the European Parliament, some MEPs expressed the feeling that the negotiations had taken a wrong turn:

> And now, behind closed doors, actually, there is a debate going on in the Parliament. 'Do we rather want a bad directive or no directive at all?' And then I say: 'I do not want a directive at all, because I do not want to have a bad directive.' But you can understand the large political groups, they pushed so much for this directive, that when they end up, without a directive there will be ... They will lose face. (interview, European Parliament, 6 December 2010)

During the second reading before the European Parliament, the scope of prior authorization was still the main issue (interview, European Parliament, 21 January 2011). In particular, ALDE and EPP members were critical of how the Council had expanded the scope of prior authorization (interview, European Parliament, 6 December 2010). However, members from the S&D group supported the Council's position on extended national control (interviews, European Parliament, 17 December 2010, 15 November 2011). While most S&D members had abstained from voting during the first reading of the Directive, most were now ready to vote in favour.

Because it had been so difficult to establish a common position in the Council, the Council had not considered the European Parliament's amendments to the Commission's proposal during its own negotiations. The negotiations had proceeded separately. Belgium took over the Council presidency after Spain and now had to initiate negotiations with the European Parliament:

> But one big problem at that moment was that we were having that much difficulty in Council to have an agreement that we didn't care about all the positions in the Parliament. It had no effect at all. Normally it matters. Normally the Parliament

does its amendments and with those amendments we start doing the negotiations in Council. (interview, Council, 20 June 2011)

From October to December 2010, four trialogues and a set of informal meetings were held between the EP rapporteur and shadow rapporteurs, the Belgian Council presidency, and the European Commission (interviews, European Parliament, 21 January 2011; Commission, 23 June 2011). The major issue in the inter-institutional negotiations was the scope of prior authorization (interviews, European Parliament, 21 January 2011; Council, 20 June 2011).

The Commission had entered negotiations with its declaration to the European Parliament to join forces against the Council's common position. However, on 5 October 2010 the CJEU ruled against France on the infringement procedure.[29] Surprising the Commission, the Court did not support its views but instead specified that prior authorization was justified for non-hospital care using major medical equipment. The Court decision came out at an important moment in the inter-institutional negotiations. With the more 'tempered approach' of the Court (Hatzopoulos and Hervey [2013]), the Commission was in a weaker position when arguing that the extended use of prior authorization as adopted by the Council's common position was against jurisprudence. The majority of member states found the judicial turn very fortunate and 'wanted to be closest possible to the new development' (interview, Commission, 23 June 2011). A 'golden moment' had occurred for maintaining extensive national control with regard to cross-border care had occurred:

And the Court ruling—and that was a golden moment—said that OK, in order to ensure continuity of care, in order to ensure proper use of equipment, governments have the competence to do some kind of reassuring and intervening and controlling equal access etc. So that was... It came at a very significant moment. The Commission lost the case. (interview, Council, 20 June 2011)

Establishing the Final Compromise

The Belgian presidency took on the task of mediating positions, acting on the basis of a fragile mandate from the Council (interviews, European Parliament, 21 January 2011; Council, 20 June 2011):

Mrs Grossetête thanks the Belgian Presidency in her speech in plenary. Because they did very, very good work to conciliate member state positions, for some member

[29] See note 24 above.

states [were] very, as I said before, were very against this directive at the beginning. And the Belgian Presidency managed to negotiated and conciliate member state positions. (interview, European Parliament, 21 January 2011)

The EP rapporteur and the shadow rapporteurs were also on fragile ground, acting on behalf of a split Parliament. The results of the final plenary voting were not given (interview, Council, 20 June 2011). The European Parliament had dropped the idea of a patient ombudsman. At the same time, the EP maintained the position that patients with rare diseases should be entitled to cross-border care without prior authorization, even when treatments were not part of the healthcare package back home (Recommendation for a second reading PE 433.081 (Rapporteur: Françoise Grossetête), 5 November 2010, amendment no. 54). The EP majority also insisted on having an exhaustive list defining when prior authorization could be refused (interviews, Council, 22 June 2011; Commission, 23 June 2011). Furthermore, parts of the S&D group pushed hard for adoption of the voucher system so that patients would not have to pay up front but could instead show a 'voucher' or certificate from back home assuring providers that the treatment would be paid for. The MEPs suggesting this amendment argued that it was extremely important to ensure equal rights for all patients, especially those who could not afford to pay up front (interview, European Parliament, 27 September 2010).

The EP position on rare diseases was not acceptable to the Council, however (interview, Council, 22 June 2011). The trialogue found a compromise under which rare diseases were written into the recitals and article 13 but without granting binding rights. Also, patients' rights were not strengthened by means of a voucher system in any binding sense; rather, article 9.5 of the final Directive simply states that member states can apply a voluntary system of advance notification. Despite these concessions to the Council, the European Parliament voted in favour of the compromise on 9 January 2011. On 9 March 2011, the directive was finally adopted by both the Council and the European Parliament. An EU directive on patients' rights in cross-border healthcare had been established.

The Final Directive

The adopted text differed from the original Commission proposal in several aspects. A dual legal basis had been reached. The internal market, under article 114 TFEU, constitutes the main legal basis, with article 168 TFEU on healthcare having been added.

The most significant compromise—and modification of judicial influence—became the extended use of prior authorization, accepted as a means of national control for

(1) hospital care, involving overnight hospital accommodation for at least one night (article 8.2.a.i).
(2) healthcare requiring highly specialized and cost-intensive medical infrastructure or medical equipment (article 8.2.a.ii).

Article 8.2 of the Commission's proposal had been abolished, meaning that the Commission's central role in controlling what was defined as specialized and cost-intensive had been eliminated. Thus, this definition was left up to each member state, allowing it a considerable degree of national control and discretion.

Additionally, the Directive relaxed the burden of proof when prior authorization was justifiable (Hancher and Sauter [2012: 207]). Whereas the proposal required member states to provide evidence that outflow of patients would 'seriously undermine or [was] likely to seriously undermine' the financial balance, planning, or rationalization of the hospital sector, the final directive simply states that prior authorization shall be restricted to what is necessary and proportionate (article 8.1).

Furthermore, whereas the Commission's proposal allowed the member state of affiliation a free movement derogation by means of prior authorization, it included none for the member states of treatment (Hancher and Sauter [2012: 210]). This derogation, however, was adopted by the legislators. A political modification to the principle of non-discrimination was adopted regarding incoming patients from other member states. The directive allows member states to adopt measures that may prevent inflow of foreign patients when 'aimed at fulfilling its fundamental responsibility to ensure sufficient and permanent access to healthcare within its territory' (article 4.3). The safeguard measure inserted by means of article 4.3 is remarkable because it introduces a derogation from the principle of non-discrimination. The article provides member states with greater ability 'to fence off their healthcare markets' (Hancher and Sauter [2012: 208]). In particular, comparing the initial Commission proposal with the final adopted version of the directive, the changes to articles 4 and 8 clearly increased the steering capacities of the member states (Baeten and Palm [2013: 410]).

Table 5.2 Key Provisions in the Adopted Patients' Rights Directive

	Directive 2011/24/EU—Patients' Rights Directive in Cross-border Healthcare
Legal basis	Articles 114 TFEU and 168 TFEU of the Treaty. Modifying how Commission proposed to codify case law of Court.
Prior authorization	Article 7: No longer addresses non-hospital care but rather tariffs and prices. Article 8: Prior authorization (PA) is justified for 'highly specialized and cost-intensive' healthcare and hospital care. Member states define what constitutes 'highly specialized and cost-intensive care'. PA must be limited to what is necessary and proportionate. Modifies case law of Court beyond what was proposed by Commission.
Procedural guarantees	Article 9: National administrative procedures to be based on objective, non-discriminatory criteria that are necessary and proportionate. Member state to specify reasonable periods of time to consider requests for cross-border healthcare, taking into account: (a) specific medical condition and (b) urgency and individual circumstances. More limited set of criteria than originally proposed by Commission.
Incoming patients	Article 4.3: Member state of treatment may depart from principle of non-discrimination and adopt measures for foreign patients' access to treatment to 'ensure sufficient and permanent access to healthcare within its territory'. Modifies principle of non-discrimination.
Scope	Article 7.3: Only applies to healthcare that is part of healthcare package in member state of affiliation. Article 1.3 specifies that directive does not apply to long-term care or access to organs. Article 7.3 maintains override of early Pierik decisions.
Providers	Non-contracted providers also within scope of directive. Codifies case law of Court.
Reimbursement level	Article 7.4: Up to level of costs in member state of affiliation.
Payment	Up front payment of patient.
Rare diseases	No binding measures.

Concerning scope, the Directive limits what it covers. In article 1.3 the final version explicitly excludes long-term care and access to organs. Access to non-contracted providers, however, is maintained in the Directive and as such constitutes a codification of the case law of the Court as established in the Watts and Stamatelaki cases. Thus, when compared with regulation 883/2004, the Directive extends access to include private providers, whether contracted by the member state of affiliation or the member state of treatment.

The final policy output was a result of a lengthy and conflict-ridden decision-making process, aimed at finding the right response to what the Court had initiated (Baeten [2012: 5]). As a result of political contestation, the final document provided less integration and more national control than originally proposed by the Commission (Hervey and McHale [2015: 88]). Furthermore, it contained less equality in access to care than envisaged by sections of the European Parliament. Key parts of the Directive are summarized in table 5.2 above.

Judicial Influence on the EU Patients' Rights Directive

As the analysis has demonstrated, the adopted text SQ_{reg}^2 came to differ from the Commission's proposal in several aspects. In its final version, the patients' rights directive contains at least five derogations from or modifications to free movement. These modifications imply important disincentives for patients to seek cross-border healthcare:

(1) The patient can access only treatment to which s/he is already entitled at home. The override of the early Pierik case law has thus been continued in the Directive.

(2) The patient will be reimbursed only up to the tariff for a similar treatment at home. In particular, patients from member states with low reimbursement levels will be disincentivized to go abroad.

(3) The patient will have to pay up front. Member states are not obliged to adopt an advance notification or voucher system. Patients with small means will be prevented from using the Directive.

(4) The system of prior authorization is maintained for hospital care and highly specialized and cost-intensive care. National control has been extended for the most important public treatments.

(5) Treatment of foreign patients can be refused for capacity, planning, and financial reasons. The principle of non-discrimination does not apply in full.

Responses to the case law of the Court formed the core of political negotiations. CJEU jurisprudence had instigated the political process. As a response to the early jurisprudence, some member states demanded an override of the case law of the Court by means of a Treaty revision. However, an initiative was never taken to override the Court constitutionally. Instead, the Commission proposed a codification of the rulings in its original proposal for a Service Directive. This initiative was rejected by the European Parliament and the member states. These first political responses confirm the expectation that EU decision-making rules make both override and codification of judicial decisions less likely to occur. Despite its defeat on the Service Directive, the Commission continued to refer to the case law as the main reason why a directive was needed. In particular, on the basis of judicial decisions it reasoned that prior authorization should be the exception rather than the general rule. By bringing in the voice of the judiciary, it tried to capitalize on the legitimacy of the Court in a rule-of-law system (Alter and Meunier-Aitsahalia [1994: 542]). However, this strategy proved unsuccessful. The Council and the European Parliament extended the modification of the case law considerably beyond what was suggested by the Commission. Both concerning patient in- and outflows, national control was significantly assured. Thus, the expectation that judicial decisions would be adopted into policy outputs as the Commission proposed was not confirmed.

Attitudes towards the case law shaped political behaviour (Kloka and Schmidt [2015]) but not as a move towards judicialization. Political positions formed for or against the case law of the Court. Most actors agreed on a need to regain political control; however, positions differed regarding how freely healthcare should be offered across borders and how much national control should be maintained. After two rejections, the Commission proposed some modification of the case law of the Court, allowing by means of prior authorization for more national control than originally suggested. However, the political actors in the Council and the EP were still not satisfied. Member state positions differed considerably during negotiations; however, a qualified majority in the Council was finally established. Additionally, the EP managed to form a compromise among S&D, EPP, and ALDE members and finalize negotiations with the Council.

The Commission took a critical position against the legislative compromise, finding it a restrictive reading of the case law of the Court. Nevertheless, it could not call the legislators to order and decided to accept the final compromise on prior authorization. This result demonstrates that the Commission is willing to compromise on its own reading of the case law when necessary. However, it maintained its position on non-contracted providers, and here the opposing member states had to concede and accept codifying jurisprudence. However, with prior authorization extended to highly specialized and cost-intensive healthcare, the inclusion of non-contracted providers was less important from a political point of view.

The final compromise extended the modification of the case law of the Court beyond what had been proposed by the Commission, allowing for more national control of cross-border care. Furthermore, the Directive contains an important element of institutional memory, maintaining the political override of the early Pierik case law. The final text is a significant modification of judicial influence, and had the Commission insisted on its own reading of the case law, no agreement would have been possible. The changed position of the Commission thus became key to facilitating a compromise. The concessions won by the S&D group in the European Parliament and the blocking minority of member states, allowing for more national control, finally resulted in a policy output in which judicial influence was modified. Thus, as implied in the expectation, dynamic positions within and between institutions were conducive to modifying judicial influence on policy outputs.

Political contestation occurred along two dimensions. On one dimension, positions diverged in terms of *left–right* (*left* = equality in patients' access to cross-border care; *right* = patients as consumers benefiting from liberalized national healthcare systems). On the other dimension, the two sides diverged over *more versus less integration* (*more integration* = free movement, i.e. limited use of prior authorization; *less integration* = maintaining prior authorization and subsidiarity). Figure 5.2 places the different positions formed in response to the case law of the Court and the proposal of the Commission on two dimensions between T_1 and T_2. Some member states maintained their position against a directive and in favour of $SQ_{reg}{}^1$, as expressed by regulation 883/2004. However, in T_2, they constituted an insufficient minority.

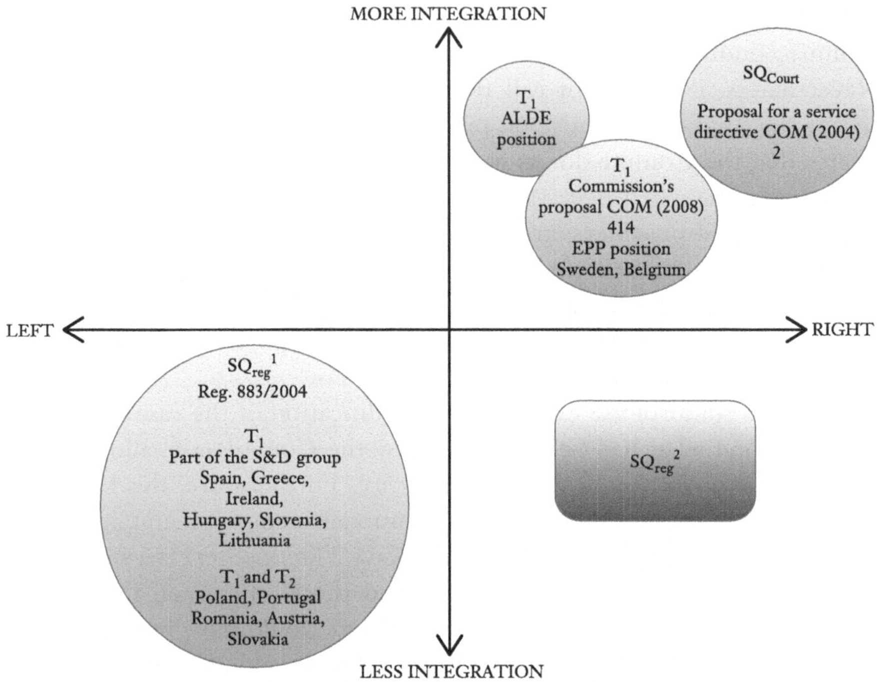

Fig. 5.2 Political Positions in EU Patients' Rights Regulation

Politics Influencing the Judiciary

The law–politics dynamics on patients' rights in cross-border healthcare show not only how politics respond to jurisprudence but also how the Court pays attention to politics. Adaptive behaviour is a reciprocal process. The Court is not immune to political responses. Where the 'judicialisation of politics' theoretical approach assumes politics to be the receptive part of judicial dialogues, we find that politics also influences the judiciary.

In the late phase of the legal-politics game, CJEU interpretations adjusted in accordance with the position of the political majority. Even during the decision-making process, the CJEU adapted its reasoning along the lines of an extended use of prior authorization (Baeten and Palm [2013: 394]). As early as the Hartlauer case,[30] the Advocate-General referred explicitly to

[30] Case C–169/07 *Hartlauer* Handelsgesellschaft mbH v Wiener Landesregierung and Oberösterreichische Landesregierung [2009] ECR I–1721. Opinion of the Advocate-General of 9 September 2008, see footnote 44 of the opinion.

the extended possibility of using prior authorization for highly specialized and cost-intensive healthcare. The adaptive behaviour is most notable in the Commission v France case.[31] Here, the Commission questioned French law requiring prior authorization for non-hospital treatments involving major medical equipment. During the infringement process, the French government had first indicated that it was ready to change the law in question. However, as a result of the development of the decision-making process, France decided to maintain the legislation in question, and the case was taken to Court (Baeten and Palm [2013: 394]). The Court's ruling refused the Commission's position and instead supported the French one, thus accepting that treatments involving major medical equipment can be subject to prior authorization. In other, more recent cases,[32] the Court has repeated a 'tempered' approach, giving member states considerable discretion in defining their health policies and exerting national control over what can be obtained abroad (Hatzopoulos and Hervey [2013]). From not knowing much about the politically difficult terrain it entered (Greer and Jarman [2012: 267]), the Court came to learn. The CJEU had not needed to adapt its position because its previous rulings were based on primary law, thus *in stricto sensu* were amendable only by means of a Treaty amendment. Therefore, the adaptive behaviour of the Court is even more noteworthy. As observed by Hervey and McHale, '[t]he CJEU is not, of course,, obliged to follow the legislature where it interprets Treaty provisions such as Article 56 TFEU, but in practice it usually does so' (Hervey and McHale [2015: 91]). This finding points out that the Court is responsive to policy making and the legislatures and may even ask for 'political guidance' on how to apply more open Treaty provisions (Baeten and Palm [2013: 394]). Not only is Court behaviour responsive to legislative override as identified by Larsson and Naurin (Larsson and Naurin [2016]) but legislative modifications also constitute important political corrections that affect the judiciary.

References

Alter, K.J. and Meunier-Aitsahalia, S. (1994) 'Judicial politics in the European Community: European integration and the pathbreaking Cassis de Dijon decision', *Comparative Political Studies* 26(4): 535–61.

[31] See note 24 above.

[32] See, for example, Commission v Spain, Commission v Luxemburg (both in note 24 above).

Baeten, R. (2012) 'Europeanization of national health systems. National impact and codification of the patient mobility case law', *OSE Paper Series*: 1–44.

Baeten, R. and Palm, W. (2013) 'The compatibility of health care capacity planning policies with EU internal market rules', in J.W. van de Gronden, E. Szyszczak, U. Neergaard, and M. Krajewski (eds), *Health Care and EU Law*, The Hague: T.M.C. Asser Press, pp. 389–413.

Cornelissen, R. (1996) 'The principle of territoriality and the Community Regulations on social security (Regulations 1408/71 and 574/72)', *Common Market Law Review* 33(3): 439–71.

Davies, G. (2007) 'The effect of Mrs Watts' trip to France on the National Health Service', *King's Law Journal* 18(1): 158–67.

Eichenhofer, E. (1999) 'Das Europäische koordinierende Krankenversicherungsrecht nach den EuGH-Urteilen Kohll und Decker', *Vierteljahresschrift für Sozialrecht* 2: 101–22.

Ferrera, M. (2003) 'European integration and national social citizenship changing boundaries, new structuring?', *Comparative Political Studies* 36(6): 611–52.

Ferrera, M. (2005) *The Boundaries of Welfare*, Oxford: Oxford University Press.

Glinos, I.A., Baeten, R., and Maarse, H. (2010) 'Purchasing health services abroad: practices of cross-border contracting and patient mobility in six European countries', *Health Policy* 95(2): 103–12.

Greer, S.L. (2009) *The Politics of European Union Health Policies*, Maidenhead, Berkshire: McGraw-Hill/Open University Press.

Greer, S.L. and Jarman, H. (2012) 'Managing risks in EU health services policy: spot markets, legal certainty and bureaucratic resistance', *Journal of European Social Policy* 22(3): 259–72.

Greer, S.L. and Martín de Almagro Iniesta, M. (2014) 'How bureaucracies listen to courts: bureaucratized calculations and European law', *Law & Social Inquiry* 39(2): 361–86.

Greer, S.L. and Rauscher, S. (2011) 'Destabilization rights and restabilization politics: policy and political reactions to European Union healthcare services law', *Journal of European Public Policy* 18(2): 220–40.

Hancher, L. and Sauter, W. (2012) *EU Competition and Internal Market Law in the Health Care Sector*, Oxford: Oxford University Press.

Hatzopoulos, V. and Hervey, T. (2013) 'Coming into line: the EU's Court softens on cross-border health care', *Health Economics, Policy and Law* 8(01): 1–5.

Hervey, T.K. and McHale, J.V. (2004) *Health Law and the European Union*, Cambridge: Cambridge University Press.

Hervey, T.K. and McHale, J.V. (2015) *European Union Health Law: Themes and Implications*, Cambridge: Cambridge University Press.

Jensen, M.D. and Nedergaard, P. (2011) 'From 'Frankenstein' to 'Toothless Vampire'? Explaining the watering down of the Services Directive', *Journal of European Public Policy* 19(6): 844–62.

Kloka, M. and Schmidt, S.K. (2015) 'Legislative and judicial politics in the post-Maastricht era. The intergovernmentalist paradox in the Council', in C. Bickerton, D. Hodson, and U. Putter (eds), *European Politics in the Post-Maastricht Era. States, Supranational Actors and the New Intergovernmentalism*, Oxford: Oxford University Press, pp. 227–45.

Kostera, T. (2014) 'When Europa meets Bismarck. Cross-border healthcare and usages of Europe in the Austrian healthcare system', Brussels: Université Libre de Bruxelles. Doctoral Thesis.

Lamping, W. (2005) 'European integration and health policy: a peculiar relationship', in M. Steffen (ed.), *Health Governance in Europe. Issues, Challenges and Theories*, London: Routledge, pp. 18–49.

Langer, R. (1999) 'Der Beitrag des Europäischen Gerichtshofs zu den gemeinschaftsrechtlichen Gestaltungsvorgaben für das Sozialrecht', in I. Ebsen (ed.), *Europarechtliche Gestaltungsvorgaben für das deutsche Sozialrecht—Freizügigkeit, wirtschaftliche Grundfreiheiten und europäisches Wettbewerbsrecht als Grenzen sozialstaatlicher Souveränität*, Baden-Baden: Nomos, pp. 3–56.

Larsson, O. and Naurin, D. (2016) 'Judicial independence and political uncertainty: How the risk of override impacts on the Court of Justice of the EU', *International Organization*, 70(2).

Leibfried, S. (2005) 'Social policy—left to judges and the markets?', in H. Wallace, W. Wallace and M.A. Pollack (eds), *Policy-making in the European Union*, Oxford: Oxford University Press, pp. 243–78.

Martinsen, D.S. (2007) 'EU for the patients: developments, impacts, challenges', report prepared for Stockholm: Swedish Institute for European Policy Studies.

Martinsen, D.S. (2009) 'Conflict and conflict management in the cross-border provision of healthcare services', *West European Politics* 32(4): 792–809.

Martinsen, D.S. (2014) 'Public administration, civil servants and implementation', in L. Miles and A. Wivel (eds), *Denmark and the European Union*, London: Routledge, pp. 189–203.

Martinsen, D.S. and Falkner, G. (2011) 'Social policy: problem-solving gaps, partial exits, and court-decision traps', in G. Falkner (ed.), *The EU's Decision Traps. Comparing Policies*, Oxford: Oxford University Press, pp. 128–45.

Mossialos, E., McKee, M., and Palm, W. (2002) *EU Law and the Social Character of Health Care*, Brussels: Peter Lang.

Mossialos, E., McKee, M., Palm, W., Beatrix, K. and Marhold, F. (2001) 'The influence of EU law on the social character of health care systems in the European Union', report prepared for Brussels: The Belgian Presidency of the European Union.

Nys, H. (2014) 'The transposition of the Directive on patients' rights in cross-care healthcare in national law by the member states: still a lot of effort to be made and questions to be answered', *European Journal of Health Law* 21(1): 1–14.

Obermaier, A. (2009) *The End of Territoriality? The Impact of ECJ Rulings on British, German and French Social Policy*, Farnham, Surrey: Ashgate.

Palm, W. and Glinos, I.A. (2010) 'Enabling patient mobility in the EU: between free movement and coordination', in E. Mossialos, G. Permanand, R. Baeten, and T. Hervey (eds), *Health Systems Governance in Europe. The role of European Union Law and Policy*, Cambridge: Cambridge University Press, pp. 509–61.

Palm, W., Nickless, J., Lewalle, H., and Coheur, A. (2000) 'Implications of recent jurisprudence on the co-ordination of health care protection systems', report for Brussels: AIM: Association Internationale de la Mutualite.

Peeters, M. (2012) 'Free movement of patients: Directive 2011/24 on the application of patients' rights in cross-border healthcare', *European Journal of Health Law* 19(1): 29–60.

Pollack, M.A. (2003) *The Engines of European Integration, Delegation, Agency, and Agenda Setting in the EU*, Oxford: Oxford University Press.

Rosa, S.D.L. (2012) 'The Directive on Cross-border Healthcare or the art of codifying complex case law', *Common Market Law Review* 49(1): 15–46.

Ruijter, A.d. (2015) 'A silent revolution: the expansion of EU Power in the field of human health. A rights-based analysis of EU health law and policy', Doctoral thesis, University of Amsterdam.

Sauter, W. (2011) 'Harmonisation in healthcare: the EU Patients' Rights Directive', Tilburg University Discussion Paper DP 2011–030.

Schmidt, S.K. (2000) 'Only an agenda setter?: The European Commission's power over the Council of Ministers', *European Union Politics* 1(1): 37–61.

Szyszczak, E. (2011) 'Patients' rights: a lost cause or missed opportunity?', in J.W.v.d. Gronden, E. Szyszczak, U. Neergaard, and M. Krajewski (eds), *Health Care and EU Law*, The Hague: T.M.C. Asser Press, pp. 103–31.

Van der Mei, A.P. (2003) *Free Movement of Persons Within the European Community. Cross-Border Access to Public Benefits*, Oxford, Portland, OR: Hart Publishing.

Weiler, J. (1991) 'The transformation of Europe', *Yale Law Journal* 100: 2403–83.

6

Regulating the Posting of Workers: Rejecting and Modifying Court Influence

> We oppose everything that goes beyond codifying what the European Court of Justice has done, because we believe in the importance of single market, and it's clear from the case law of the ECJ that member states have been using such national control measures to place disproportionate burdens in the path of national businesses that are conducting businesses in foreign countries.
>
> (Interview, Council, 25 July 2012)

> Viking and Laval, for example, they use a lot. You see it very, very particularly coming back in article 9, which we think is a good thing since—as far as we see it—article 9 is a good reflection of the case law, but it's also very difficult to... It's a matter of interpretation, of course. How do you see the case law of the Court? We've not been asking the Court to interpret article 9 for us. It's a number of cases, a variety of cases from which the Commission has picked certain elements, and well, you see that the positions differ or that the interpretations differ....
>
> (Interview, Council, 25 July 2012)

> We hope to send the positive signal that Social Europe is back on track in recognising that the fundamental difficulties created by these EC judgments and trying to restore a balance where we think the balance has been destroyed. It's difficult;

> because we have German elections coming up in September, we have the elections next year. Thus, on the one hand, one wants to solve the question, but on the other hand, people begin to posture for the elections and to play electoral politics, so it's not the easiest time to try and solve difficult problems like this.
>
> (Interview, European Parliament, 29 May 2013)

The EU's regulation of posted workers is a regulatory field at the intersection of the internal market and social policy. The DG on Employment, Social Affairs, and Equal Opportunities (EMPL) is the part of the Commission that is responsible for the regulation of posted workers, but it is closely shadowed by the DG on the Internal Market and Services (MARKT). The Posting of Workers Directive (PWD) can be regarded as a social policy with internal market content and implications that intend to balance social rights with free movement provisions.[1] The PWD is a classic illustration of the dilemmas between cross-border movement and national social institutions. Specifically, the PWD regulates what national legislation should apply to firms that post workers to another member state where they perform temporary work. The directive attempts to balance two objectives with embedded contradictions. On one hand, firms in the European Union should be able to compete freely to realize the full benefits of the single market. For some firms, the main competitive advantage is lower wage costs. On the other hand, member states intend to ensure certain living standards for their workers by regulating minimum wages and social rights. The directive has been considered a way to avoid social dumping, where workers compete by means of lower wages or social standards. Because of the socio-economic heterogeneity of the European Community, it has been difficult for European and national political actors to agree on the main goal of the legislation: to facilitate competition or to ensure social rights and combat social dumping. The dispute has unfolded between law and politics. The timeline of the process is traced in the analysis below and summarized in figure 6.1.

This chapter traces the process of regulating the posting of workers in the European Union over time. It details some of the fundamental regulatory dilemmas contained in the directive and how the process has unfolded

[1] Directive 96/71/EC of the European Parliament and the Council of 16 December 1996 concerning the posting of workers in the framework of the provision of services.

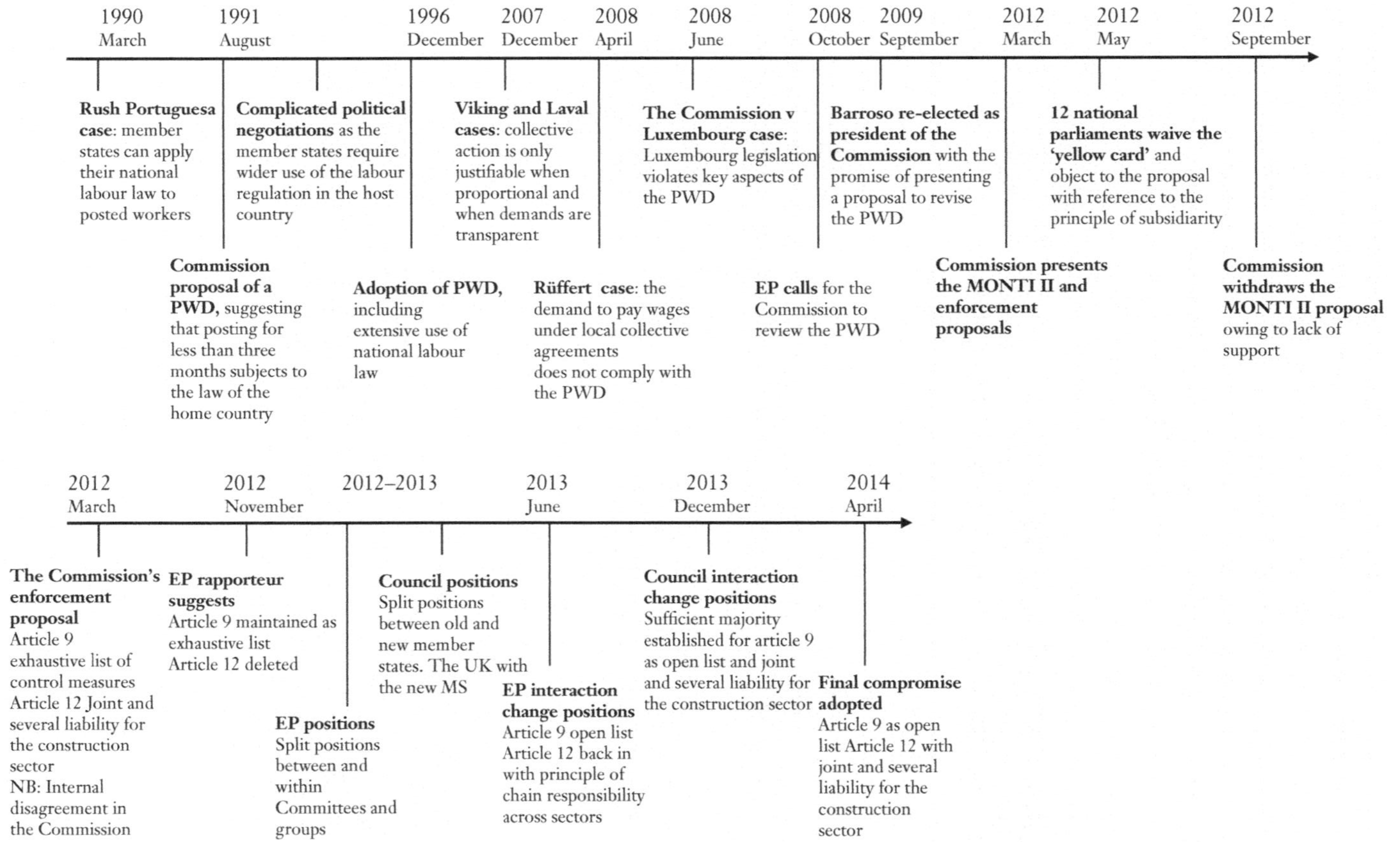

Fig. 6.1 Timeline of EU Posting of Workers' Regulation

between SQ_{reg}^1, SQ_{Court}, and SQ_{reg}^2. Below, I examine the process in which the Directive was first adopted, which established the regulatory status quo, SQ_{reg}^1. Then, the Court generated a new status quo, SQ_{Court}, which severely disrupted SQ_{reg}^1. The subsequent sections examine how political bodies have responded to SQ_{Court} by first rejecting the Monti II proposal and subsequently modifying judicial influence with the enforcement directive, which established a new regulatory status quo, SQ_{reg}^2.

Creating a Regulatory Status Quo: Adopting the Posting of Workers Directive

The Posting of Workers Directive was adopted in 1996 by the European Parliament and the Council of Ministers. The Directive had a long preparation phase, originating in the late 1980s when the relationship between public procurement regulations and the single market was debated (Cremers et al. [2007: 526]). At that time, the trade unions in the construction sector requested the implementation of a social clause in the public procurement regulations that was consistent with the ILO Convention 94,[2] to ensure that member states complied with the working conditions and collective agreements of hosting countries. However, the Council of Ministers did not support the idea of an obligatory clause and instead adopted a voluntary clause (Cremers et al. [2007]). Against this background, in the 1991 social action programme the European Commission announced that it would propose a separate directive on the posting of workers based on the Charter of Fundamental Social Rights for Workers (Kolehmainen [1998: 75]). In the same programme, the Commission also announced that it would establish a principle of chain liability in cases of subcontracting. The Commission later dropped the initiative on chain liability, whereas the proposal for the posting of workers directive was advanced.[3] It took European legislators five years to adopt the Commission's proposal.

[2] Convention by the International Labour Organization (ILO) concerning Labour Clauses in Public Contracts, effective 20 September 1952.

[3] *COM (91) 230 final*, Proposal for a Council Directive concerning the posting of workers in the framework of the provision of services, 1 August 1991.

The European Parliament was originally involved in the process through the cooperation procedure but became a co-legislator because of the Maastricht Treaty. The adoption of the PWD was considered a decisive result for social Europe. The negotiations on and adoption of the Directive strengthened the social dimension of the Community. However, the process also emphasized the dividing lines within the Community, with fierce battles between deregulation and social protection, between posting and hosting member states, and between EU regulation and national law and practices, as well as more ideological conflicts between left and right. When the Directive was adopted in 1996, the posting member states were primarily Southern European countries with the status of 'low-cost countries'. With the 2004 enlargement of the EU, posting increasingly concerns movement from Central and Eastern Europe to the older member states. This flow of service providers from East to West is often portrayed as the Polish plumber taking up temporary work in older, high-cost member states (Hemerijck [2013]). The conflicts of interest have only intensified after the two recent EU enlargements (Cremers et al. [2007]).

The Directive can be considered an instrument to address the tensions of a single market. On one hand, the free movement of services is a fundamental principle, and on the other hand, the social protection of workers is a fundamental interest of trade unions and many member states. The Directive accentuates the inherent conflicts between the rationales of economic integration and the social dimension of Europe. The posting of workers is a regulatory field of high political salience, which evokes strong ideological controversies (Klüver and Sagarzazu [2013]). How should the social protection of posted workers and the risk of social dumping be weighed against the free provision of services? Is the free provision of services more fundamental than the protection of posted workers? Which laws apply to the employment contracts of posted workers? Between member states, interests have diverged depending on whether member states are primarily posting or hosting posted workers. According to ideological controversies, interests have also diverged regarding the extent to which labour markets should be regulated and social rights should be protected. In political negotiations, the posting member state may attempt to maximize the competitive advantage of potentially lower national standards back home. However, the host member state may try to extend its own domestic standards to posted workers to avoid the competitive disadvantages related to national activities and workers (Kolehmainen [1998: 72]).

Commission Proposing to Modify the Case Law of the Court

The dynamics between law and politics have played an important role in the development of posted worker regulations. As the regulatory field has developed, the case law has frequently been both supported and opposed. The case law has been a decisive point of orientation in the legislative process and a 'focal point' for considering regulatory scope. The negotiations between 1991 and 1996 on the original Directive were characterized by a recurrent reference to jurisprudence, especially case C–113/89 Rush Portuguesa.[4] Rush Portuguesa became a landmark ruling for interpreting the relationship between the freedom to provide services and national labour law. In the case, the European Court interpreted the constitutional principles of articles 59 EEC (now article 56 TFEU) and 60 EEC (now article 57 TFEU) of the Treaty:

> Community law does not preclude Member States from extending their legislation, or collective labour agreements entered into by both sides of industry, to any person who is employed, even temporarily, within their territory, no matter in which country the employer is established; nor does Community law prohibit Member States from enforcing those rules by appropriate means. (paragraph 18 of the judgment, case C–113/89 Rush Portuguesa)

Primarily, Rush Portuguesa became an important reference for hosting member states. Member states used the case as a justification for enacting or strengthening national labour law on posted workers (Davies [2002: 300]). The Commission, however, took a different stance and found that this interpretation impeded the free movement of services (Davies [2002]).

On 1 August 1991, the Commission presented its proposal. Originally, the Commission proposal clarified the balance between the freedom to provide services and national social regulation. It also modified the implications of the Rush Portuguesa case, which the Commission found had led to a disproportionate application of national labour standards at the expense of the free movement of posting firms. The Commission stated that legal uncertainty existed concerning which national legislation should apply to posted workers. In its view, this uncertainty could distort competition.

[4] Case C–113/89, *Rush Portuguesa* Ld[a] v Office national d'immigration [1990] ECR I–01417.

Article 3 of the proposal became the most disputed provision during the negotiations. This article was fundamentally changed as a result of inter-institutional interactions. The Commission, the European Parliament, and the Council took different positions over article 3 and interpreted and used the case law differently during their discussions.

In its original proposal, the Commission referred to the Rush Portuguesa case but proposed modifications to the case's implications in article 3.2 (*COM (91) 230*, 10–11).[5] In that article, it suggested that, when workers were posted for less than three months, they should be subject to the home member state's labour laws.[6]

For postings extending longer than three months, the Commission noted that 'several general principles can be deduced from the case law of the Court' (*COM (91) 230*, 10). The freedom to provide services was emphasized as a fundamental principle of the Treaty, but the Commission repeated the Court's reasoning that national restrictions to the free provision of services could be legitimate if they protect the 'general interest', such as the protection of workers. Thus, the Commission's interpretation of the case law was selective and strategic. In the original proposal for the regulation of posted workers, the Commission creatively distinguished between posting in the first three months, where the free movement of services should not be restricted, and longer postings, where the reasoning of the Court should apply. Because posting is often short-term, three months would indeed be a considerable period of time for posted workers to work under the labour law of their home member state.

Political Responses to the Commission's Proposal

However, this temporal distinction was not accepted by the European legislators. In the first phase of negotiations between 1991 and 1993, the European Parliament was only involved through the cooperation procedure. However, this limited involvement did not prevent the EP from influencing the process. The Parliament took the position that the application of home state

[5] In its original proposal, the Commission referred to case 279/80 Criminal proceedings against Alfred John *Webb* [1981] ECR 03305 and Rush Portuguesa (see note 4 above). See also annex 1.

[6] See article 3.2 of the original proposal *COM (91) 230*, 22.

regulation during the first three months was unacceptable. It suggested that this period be reduced to one month. The EP intervention was accepted by the Commission. The Commission adapted its position and presented a new proposal on 15 June 1993. In this new proposal, the period during which the home member state's legislation should apply was changed from three months to one month in article 3.2.[7] By this time, the EP had acquired a position as co-legislator through the co-decision procedure.

Despite its responsiveness, the Commission's new proposal was not accepted by the Council. In the subsequent political negotiations, the member states worked to ensure their autonomy to regulate their national labour markets to the greatest possible extent. First, the proposed article 3.2 was amended by the member states. The period during which the home member state's legislation was applicable was reduced from one month to only eight days. Thus, the Commission's goal to modify the line of reasoning in Rush Portuguesa was unsuccessful.

Furthermore, in the final negotiations, Finland, Germany, Austria, Luxembourg, and France successfully pushed to allow more room for the host country's national labour laws or collective agreements in the directive (Kolehmainen [1998: 79, note 26]). Article 3 was thus fundamentally changed from what the Commission had proposed. Article 3(1) established which laws of the host member state should be applied to posted workers, particularly those regarding minimum wages, working time, and paid annual leave. The original article 3 that was proposed by the Commission only contained the two parts mentioned above. However, the member states expanded this provision to ten subparagraphs and thus extended the ability of host member states to apply national standards to posted workers. Article 3(1) provided the basic level of protection. Here, host state legislation applied to posted workers. Three other particular articles extended the ability of hosting states to apply national legislation to posted workers. Article 3(7) established that the minimum level in article 3(1) 'shall not prevent application of terms and conditions of employment which are more favourable to workers'. Furthermore, article 3(8) added that minimum laws could also derive from certain types of collective agreement, not solely from legislation. Thus, article 3(8) stipulated that other broadly applicable collective agreements could define the host state standards that could be applied to posted workers. Finally, article 3(10) allowed for the application of additional host state standards as laid down in

[7] *COM (93) 225*, 15 June 1993.

collective agreements or other than those referred to in article 3(1). Articles 3(7) and 3(10) in particular are considered important political achievements in this regard. Article 3(7) stated that member states were not restricted from applying national standards that were more favourable to posted workers. Article 3(10) added that member states were allowed to take further measures concerning the terms and conditions of employment for posted workers, which made the terms and conditions of employment established in article 3(1) de facto non-exhaustive (Kolehmainen [1998: 86]).

Codifying or Extending Early Case Law

The political battle over article 3 demonstrates that politics extended the protection of national labour markets beyond a strict interpretation of CJEU case law. While the Commission proposed to modify the implications of the judicial decision, political negotiations far extended other actors' strict interpretation of the case law. It has been argued that the majority of member states and the European Parliament reinforced the Rush Portuguesa decision and used it as 'blanket permission' to extend the application of host state labour law (Davies [2002: 301]). The political actors used the Rush Portuguesa case as a strategic reference point.

It has also been argued that the member states were only willing to adopt the PWD because it largely preserved the nationalization of labour law, and it protected national labour markets (Kolehmainen [1998]). The regulatory status quo $SQ_{reg}{}^{1}$ that was created by the original PWD codified the political interpretation of CJEU case law. This interpretation granted extensive permission to apply national labour standards to posting firms. The political negotiations allowed considerable protection of national labour markets beyond a minimum understanding of them, which was particularly expressed in the much amended and extended version of article 3. The initial strategic behaviour of the Commission was unsuccessful. Its attempt to balance the free movement of services with the protection of social rights was counteracted by the two legislators. A policy output was only produced because the Commission was willing to adapt and conform to the legislators' positions. According to Davies, the Commission's strategy was unsuccessful because of timing. Instead of rushing in and basing its proposal on the Rush Portuguesa case, had it waited for the line of case law to adjust and mature, the Commission might have had a stronger position to strengthen the free movement of services (Davies [2002: 306]). However, later political responses demonstrate that waiting for the Court to clarify its position probably would not have made the Commission more successful. It has always been difficult to mobilize a sufficient majority to extend the free movement of services in posting situations, despite the rather dramatic change of legal precedent that occurred after the Rush decision.

A New Court-generated Status Quo: From the Rush Dictum to the Laval Quartet

Soon after the adoption of the PWD, the Court had to consider the next line of cases.[8] These subsequent cases have been interpreted as the Court beginning to 'qualify the apparently blanket permission handed out in Rush' and placing more emphasis on the freedom to provide services (Davies [2002: 301]). In these cases, the Court seemed to depart from its early reasoning in the Rush Portuguesa case—or the way the case had been interpreted by legislators. The judicial decisions gradually began limiting host states' ability to freely apply national labour market standards (Davies [2002: 306]). In the subsequent line of cases, the Court developed its position more fully.

These cases were an early warning that the 'Rush dictum' was not a rock-solid basis for promoting national labour law over the free movement provisions in the EU. However, the cases did not change the position of the member states, which continued to regard the regulatory status quo as the one established in the extensive article 3 of the PWD.

However, with the 'Laval Quartet', member states could no longer disregard the Court's change in precedent. Political responses became necessary. The famous cases Viking, Laval, Rüffert, and Commission v Luxembourg

[8] See, for example, joined cases C-369/96 and C-376/96, Criminal proceedings against Jean-Claude *Arblade* and Arblade & Fils SARL, Bernard Leloup, Serge *Leloup* and Sofrage SARL [1999] ECR I-8453, Case C-165/98 Criminal proceedings against André *Mazzoleni* and Inter Surveillance Assistance SARL, as the party civilly liable, third parties: Eric Guillaume and Others [2001] ECR I-2189, Joined cases C-49/98, 50/98, 52-54/98, 68-71/98 *Finalarte* Sociedade de Construção Civil Ld^a^, Portugaia Construções Ld^a^ and Engil Sociedade de Construção Civil SA v Urlaubs- und Lohnausgleichskasse der Bauwirtschaft and Urlaubs- und Lohnausgleichskasse der Bauwirtschaft v Amilcar Oliveira Rocha, Tudor Stone Ltd, Tecnamb-Tecnologia do Ambiante Ld^a^, Turiprata Construções Civil Ld^a^, Duarte dos Santos Sousa and Santos & Kewitz Construções Ld^a^ [2001] ECR I-7831.

completely disrupted the balance established by the PWD.[9] The four cases were decided in a short period between late 2007 and the summer of 2008 and sent shockwaves through the European political landscape and among the social partners in the EU. Together, these cases have become known as the 'Laval Quartet'; they connected the Court's interpretations of how the free movement of services should be weighed against national labour regulation (Malmberg [2010]). With these cases, a wide distance was created between $SQ_{reg}{}^{1}$ and SQ_{Court}.

The *Viking* case concerned the right to strike in relation to the right of establishment in article 42 of the Treaty. Viking was a ferry operator that ran between Finland and Estonia. It reflagged a vessel from Finland to Estonia. The company was thus able to lower its wage costs to the Estonian wages. The Finnish Seamen Union planned to take collective action against Viking. The justifiability of this collective action against a firm's right to free movement was brought to the CJEU as a preliminary reference. In the case, the European Court stated that, on one hand:

> the right to take collective action for the protection of workers is a legitimate interest which, in principle, justifies a restriction of one of the fundamental freedoms guaranteed by the Treaty. (case C–438/05, paragraph 77)

On the other hand, the European Court noted that the right to strike can only be exercised within certain limits, which may be rather narrow (Davies [2008: 127]). The CJEU asked the national court to consider whether the Finnish Seamen Union did not

> have other means at its disposal which were less restrictive of freedom of establishment in order to bring to a successful conclusion the collective negotiations entered into with Viking, and, on the other, whether that trade union had exhausted those means before initiating such action. (case C–438/05, paragraph 87)

The *Laval* case also concerned a foreign firm's right to free movement—here, the freedom to provide services in relation to the right to strike. Laval was a Latvian firm that posted workers for construction companies in Sweden. The Swedish trade unions took collective action against Laval to induce it to enter

[9] Case C–438/05 The International Transport Workers' Federation and the Finnish Seamen's Union v *Viking* Line ABP and OÜ Viking Line Eesti [2007] ECR I–10779. Case C–341/05 *Laval* un Partneri Ltd v Svenska Byggnadsarbetareförbundet, Svenska Byggnadsarbetareförbundets avdelning 1, Byggettan and Svenska Elektrikerförbundet [2007] ECR I–11767. Case C–346/06 Dirk *Rüffert* v Land Niedersachsen [2008] ECR I–1989. Case C–319/06 *Commission* of the European Communities v Grand Duchy of *Luxembourg* [2008] ECR I–4323.

negotiations with them concerning the level of pay for the posted workers. The Swedish trade unions requested that Laval sign a collective agreement that provided more favourable conditions than the minimum conditions established by the PWD and that were stipulated in the national provisions for minimum protection (Malmberg [2010: 5]). The European Court ruled against the collective action taken in Sweden. It concluded that article 49 of the Treaty (now article 56 TFEU) and article 3 of the PWD precluded a trade union from forcing a provider from another member state to enter negotiations and sign a collective agreement on rates of pay that are more favourable than the minimum conditions legislated in the PWD. The CJEU also considered articles 3(7) and 3(10) of the PWD but found that these articles could not justify the additional standards with which the Swedish trade unions wanted Laval to comply (see case C–341/05, paragraphs 79–85 of the judgment). Thus, in the Laval case, the Court disregarded one of the primary political results of the PWD negotiations. The balance of free movement principles with national labour law established by the political bodies was unimportant to the Court. In a subsequent judgment, the Swedish labour court required the trade unions to pay punitive damages (Malmberg [2010]).

The Rüffert case followed. It challenged the public procurement act of Lower Saxony in Germany (Blauberger [2012: 115]). This act stated that a construction firm could only win a tender if it complied with the relevant collective agreement and paid the wages agreed on. In the Rüffert case, the company that had won the tender had subcontracted work to a Polish service provider, which paid its Polish workers lower wages than those established by the relevant collective agreement (Seikel [2015]). Against this background, Lower Saxony annulled the contract with the German company and imposed financial penalties. In the case, the CJEU ruled that to demand wages according to the local collective agreement was inconsistent with the PWD. The public procurement act of Lower Saxony was found to be an unjustified barrier to the free movement of services, especially because it protected only workers in the public sector (Blauberger [2012]). In addition, the Court ruled that article 3(8) of the PWD, which allowed collective agreements to be applicable, could not be used because the relevant collective agreement had not been declared universally applicable (case C–346/06, paragraph 39). Thus, in the Rüffert case, the Court again disregarded the legislative intentions established in the PWD.

In the last case of the 'Laval Quartet', Commission v Luxembourg, the Commission found that Luxembourg had not implemented the PWD correctly. In particular, the case concerned Luxembourg's transposition of the Directive's articles 3(1) and 3(10). The Commission took the view that the idea of public policy in article 3(10) could not be defined unilaterally by a member state, which would give the member state extensive discretion to impose national standards on posting companies (case C–319/06, paragraph 16). In the case, the Court considered the rather complex relation between the exhaustive list of article 3(1) in the PWD and the open character of article 3(10). On this matter, the Court ruled that article 3(10) constituted a derogation of the fundamental principle of freedom to provide services (case C–319/06, paragraph 31). As a derogation, the article must be interpreted strictly (case C–319/06, paragraph 31). In this way, the Court limited the leeway that the member states had created for their own discretion during political negotiations. 'That provision in the first indention of article 3(10) of Directive 96/71 constitutes an exception to the system put in place by that directive and a derogation from the fundamental principle of freedom to provide services on which the directive is based and must be interpreted strictly' (case C–319/06, paragraph 49).

As the final case of the 'Laval Quartet', this case constituted another judicial step to unsettle what the Council and the EP had established in the Directive. This case also conveyed the Court's view regarding what should be the balance between Treaty-based economic freedoms and national social standards. The Commission v Luxembourg case emphasized the exhaustive character of article 3(1) and severely challenged what the member states had agreed on. In the case, the Court declared that economic freedoms are the fundamental concern and that national derogations are only justifiable under certain conditions.

The 'Laval Quartet' tipped the balance towards the internal market. It departed from the political rationale established in the PWD. With this line of cases, the Court departed from the 'Rush dictum' and substantiated the supremacy of economic freedoms over national social regulation—and the autonomy to exercise these freedoms according to national regulatory traditions. The judicial decisions established a 'new approach' under which article 3(1) was regarded as an exhaustive list (Kilpatrick [2009: 849]). Prior to the 'Laval Quartet' it had been generally held that member states could apply higher standards than those referred to in article 3(1) or other standards, primarily because of article 3(7) (Kilpatrick [2009]). The Court had changed the regulatory status quo and established a new SQ_{Court}. The new approach left little room for member states to apply standards beyond the minimum level of the host state standards established in article 3(1). This departure from the Rush dictum on one hand limited hosting member states' autonomy but, on the other hand, clarified which social standards were applicable to the posting firm.

Thus, this case law created a potential socio-economic divide between old and new member states, with old member states that demanded their right to fight against social dumping and new member states that requested more open labour markets. The judicial decisions were generally interpreted as establishing that European economic freedoms had trumped the labour and social constitutions of the member states (Joerges and Rödl [2009: 18]). This judicial message caused great concern, especially in the old member states and among their social partners. A political response was necessary.

Initial Political Responses: Requesting a Legislative Override

The shock caused by the Laval Quartet was deep.[10] The judicial decisions were widely discussed by political actors, and they sparked a fundamental debate in the EU regarding whether economic freedoms trump social rights (*EU Observer*, 'Policy-makers grapple with EU's controversial workers law', 3 June 2010). Subsequent to the Viking and Laval decisions, the German government was formally asked for its opinion, and some members of the German Parliament proposed that Germany should not ratify the Treaty of Lisbon in response to the legal decisions (Bücker [2010: 30–31]; Bundestags-Drucks (BT-Drs.) 16/8879). The Confederation of German Trade Unions demanded a reform of the PWD to revise article 3, and to clarify that the article only referred to minimum conditions and allowed member states to establish more favourable working conditions (Walter [2010: 49]). Moreover, the ETUC was alarmed by the judgments and argued that the CJEU 'had confirmed a hierarchy of norms, with market freedoms highest in the hierarchy and the fundamental rights of collective bargaining and action in second place' (European Social Partners [2010: 10]). The European social partners requested that European legislators 'clarify in non-ambiguous terms at the level of the Treaties that the exercise of the economic freedoms must respect fundamental social rights' (European Social Partners [2010: 14]). The ETUC argued that the PWD must be revised to confirm the minimum conditions for posted workers to avoid social dumping (*EU Observer*,

[10] The social partners in the construction sector subsequently termed their state as in 'Laval shock' (interview, social partners, March 2012).

'Policy-makers grapple with EU's controversial workers law', 3 June 2010). The European trade unions regarded the Court's decisions as contrary to social justice and required that the legislation be amended to override the Court. They advanced two key demands (*COM (2012) 130*, 5):

- a revision of the Posting of Workers Directive to include a reference to 'equal pay for equal work' and to allow hosting member states to apply more favourable conditions than those established in article 3(1) of the Directive; and
- the introduction of a 'social progress protocol' to the Treaty to establish the priority of fundamental social rights over economic freedoms.

The European employer organization Business Europe assumed the opposite position and welcomed the legal decisions. Business Europe did not believe that the PWD or the Treaty needed revision (Walter [2010: 49]; *EU Observer*, 'Policy-makers grapple with EU's controversial workers law', 3 June 2010).

The European Parliament became a leading force in requesting a response to the litigation. In October 2008, the Parliament provided a report that urged the Commission to revise the PWD to definitively confirm that (1) economic freedoms are not superior to fundamental social rights and (2) trade unions have a right to take action (S&D position paper, 'Defending workers when businesses cross borders', October 2008). The topic became a highly contentious political issue affecting José Manuel Barroso's re-election as president of the European Commission. To support the re-election of the presidential candidate, the left wing of the Parliament demanded that the Commission promise to prioritize revision of the Directive. Thus, Barroso's re-election depended on his promising to present a solution to the problem created by the Court (interviews, European Parliament, 16 and 29 May 2013). Standing before the EP in September 2009, Barroso committed to deliver on this issue and to propose legislation in his new term that presented a solution to the 'case law problem' (European Commission, Hearing in the European Parliament, 2 June 2010).

Commission Proposals on How to Respond to the Case Law

Despite the apparent commitment from the president, the Commission took another two-and-a-half years to present its proposal. The Commission was first expected to present its initiative in December 2011, then in February 2012, and then in March 2012. Forming an internal position in the Commission between DG EMPL and DG MARKT was difficult. Furthermore, because of the political importance in the proposal, other commissioners became involved and took considerable interest in it (interview, Commission, 30 March 2012). In addition, having committed himself before the Parliament, Barroso had a personal stake in the matter. The proposals were requested for a long time and were extremely important but required internal coordination and agreement in the Commission, which proved difficult to achieve (interviews, Council, 22 February 2012; social partners, 20 March 2012; Commission, 30 March 2012). The salience of the issue was high:

> [T]his is an area where a lot of DGs are involved, so we have worked very closely together with DG MARKT, DG Enterprise, DG MOVE, DG Home, DG Justice, Fundamental rights, [and] the legal service ... So a lot of the commissioners themselves also have strong interests in this proposal, particularly the President due to his commitments made to the European Parliament. (interview, Commission, 30 March 2012)

Drafts of the proposals were leaked to stakeholders, who criticized them for not striking an appropriate balance between economic freedom and social provisions. The social partners were divided. Business Europe strongly opposed some of the leaked drafts of an enforcement directive because it proposed a general principle of chain liability (interview, social partners, 20 March 2012). In contrast, the European trade unions were highly critical of the draft leaked on how to regulate collective action in relation to free movement principles. The reactions from the political actors 'in town' made the Commission cautious and delayed the presentation of its proposals (interview, Council, 22 February 2012).

On 21 March 2012, the Commission finally presented two documents: (1) a proposal for a regulation on the right to take collective action in the context of free movement provisions called the Monti II regulation;[11] and (2) a proposal for an enforcement directive on the posting of workers.[12] The proposal on the Monti II regulation primarily responded to the Viking and Laval cases

[11] *COM (2012) 130*, Proposal for a Council Regulation on the exercise of the right to take collective action within the context of the freedom of establishment and the freedom to provide services. The proposal was named after the former Commissioner and former Italian Prime Minister Mario Monti, who had drafted a similar clause while he served as commissioner for the single market.

[12] *COM (2012) 131*, Proposal for a Directive of the European Parliament and of the Council on the enforcement of Directive 96/71/EC concerning the posting of workers in the framework of the provision of services.

and addressed the right to take collective action in relation to free movement provisions. The proposal for an enforcement directive did not fully reform article 3 of the PWD, as requested by the social partners and the EP. However, key provisions of the proposal responded to the case law, concerning the national control measures that a host member state could take to ensure that it complied with the directive. The proposal referred not only to the Rüffert and Commission v Luxembourg cases but also the cases of Rush Portuguesa, case C–445/03 Commission v Luxembourg, and the Finalarte cases, among others.[13] Thus, both initiatives addressed the Court's change in the status quo to SQ_{Court}, i.e. the line of case law that broke with the Rush dictum (see Annex 1).

Therefore the European executive brought the case law into the political process and proposed to codify jurisprudence. The Commission's proposals on the appropriate response to the case law initiated significant political disagreements. Political positions were formed along two poles: one pole largely agreed with and used the Court's new approach, and another pole considered that 'the Laval Quartet' had created immense problems and requested that the judicial decisions be overturned. The decision-making processes involved in the two proposals are examined in two separate sections below. This analysis begins with the responses to the Monti II proposal and then examines the decision-making process on the proposal for an enforcement directive.

The Monti II Proposal

The Monti II proposal presented the Commission's interpretation of the case law and advanced what it considered to be the appropriate response to the Court's precedent. According to the Commission, the proposal attempted to balance economic freedoms in relation to collective action. In its proposal, the Commission emphasized that the Court for the first time had recognized that

> … the right to take collective action, including the right to strike, as a fundamental right forms an integral part of the general principles of EU law the observance of which the Court ensures. It also explicitly stated that since the European Union has not only an economic but also a social purpose, the rights under the provisions of

[13] See note 4 above for Rush Portuguesa and notes 8 and 9 above for Rüffert, Commission v Luxembourg, and Finalarte. Case C–445/03 *Commission* of the European Communities v Grand Duchy of *Luxembourg* [2004] ECR I–10207.

the Treaty on the free movement of goods, persons, services and capital must be balanced against the objectives pursued by social policy ... (*COM (2012) 130*, 2)

The explanatory memorandum in the proposal primarily addressed the case law. The proposal provided a lengthy analysis of the jurisprudence and the Commission's view on how to address it. In fact, the main justification and reasoning for the proposal related to the case law and refers to it forty-one times (see Annex 1). The Commission here attempted to rely on a form of judicial legitimacy (Alter and Meunier-Aitsahalia [1994]) to dismiss political opposition.

Despite the Commission's attempts to assure its own and the Court's commitment to social Europe, the proposal was ill received. The Commission's strategic efforts to downplay the tensions between free movement principles and social rights were unsuccessful. On one hand, the Commission stated that the right to take collective action was not endangered (interview, Commission, 30 March 2012). On the other hand, the Commission stated that the right to strike was not 'an absolute', and the exercise of this right must be 'subject to certain restrictions' (*COM (2012) 130*, 4).

The national parliaments, the left-wing political groups in the European Parliament, and the European and national trade unions heavily criticized the proposal shortly after it was presented. The primary criticism held that economic freedoms were prioritized over the right to collective action. Critics argued that the Commission had not learned the lesson but had presented a proposal that essentially attempted to codify the case law of Viking and Laval (interviews, social partners, 27 March 2012; national parliament, 2 December 2013). As a result, the proposal was very short-lived.

Rejecting Monti II: National Parliaments as Veto Actors

The national parliaments were the first to respond against codifying the case law. The Lisbon Treaty had empowered national parliaments through the Early Warning Mechanism (EWM). This mechanism allows parliaments to issue reasoned opinions up to eight weeks after the presentation of a Commission proposal and to raise reasoned objections based on the principle of subsidiarity.[14] The EWM gives two votes to the national parliaments of each member state: one per chamber to bicameral parliaments and two to unicameral parliaments. To show the yellow card, reasoned opinions

[14] For the Early Warning Mechanism, see article 12 of the Lisbon Treaty and the Protocol (No 2) on the application of the principles of subsidiarity and proportionality, articles 6 and 7.

must carry a minimum of eighteen votes, which amounted to one-third of the fifty-four votes in EU27. Although the national parliaments had often issued reasoned opinions against Commission proposals, they had never before been able to act in coordination and mobilize the eighteen votes needed to show the yellow card. The capacity of the national legislators to intervene in EU decision making surprised the other EU legislators (interview, European Parliament, 3 December 2012).

The Danish parliament was the first to submit an opinion, and it subsequently initiated coordinated action among the parliaments (Cooper [2013]). In April 2012, the Danish parliament hosted a COSAC meeting among the European Affairs Committees.[15] At this meeting, the Monti II proposal was substantially discussed, and opinions were exchanged. The meeting was important for spreading a counter-mobilization among the national parliaments. After the meeting, more parliaments submitted opinions. The Dutch Tweede Kamer was the last to submit its reasoned opinion. In the final hours before the eight-week deadline expired, the national parliaments showed their very first yellow card. Collectively, twelve national parliaments took action. Seven unicameral parliaments (the Danish, Finnish, Swedish, Latvian, Portuguese, Luxembourgeois, and Maltese parliaments) and the chambers of the Polish Sejm, the French Sénat, the Belgian House of Representatives, the British House of Commons, and the Dutch Tweede Kamer submitted reasoned opinions to the Commission. The twelve parliaments opposed Monti II for breaching the principle of subsidiarity. Several parliaments in particular emphasized that the EU treaty protected the right to strike (*EU Observer*, 'National parliaments show "yellow card" to EU law on strikes', 29 May 2012; interview, national parliament, 2 December 2013). By showing the yellow card, the national parliaments added political weight to the subsidiarity principle and expressed the issue as coming within the purview of the national parliaments and for national legislators to regulate (interview, national parliament, 2 December 2013).

The national parliaments mobilized opposition to the Commission's proposal. Moreover, they acquired a sufficient number of votes to show the yellow card, which has been interpreted as an act through which the national parliaments constituted themselves as a 'virtual third chamber' in EU politics and a new forum for democratic politics (Cooper [2012, 2013]). The national

[15] The Conference of Parliamentary Committees for Union Affairs (COSAC) brings together the EU affairs committees of the national Parliaments and the Members of the European Parliament. Plenary meetings occur twice a year.

parliaments' ability to act was unexpected. When the Lisbon Treaty extended the powers of the national parliaments through the EWM, the mechanism was not expected to be an effective tool in EU decision making (Bellamy and Kröger [2012], interview, national parliament, 2 December 2013). However, since this mechanism was implemented, the national parliaments have submitted many reasoned opinions, which have forced the Commission to respond to the demands of national legislators. Showing the yellow card against Monti II undoubtedly enhanced the political self-understanding of the national parliaments (interview, national parliament, 2 December 2013) and made them potential veto players in the EU 'legal-politics' game. Thus, the national parliaments should be considered when assessing the EU system of divided powers.

The EWM allows the Commission to maintain, amend, or withdraw a proposal. On 12 September 2012, the Commission informed the European legislators that it would withdraw the Monti II proposal because of a general lack of support: '[c]ontrary to what the different reasoned opinions say, the regulation does not create any problems of subsidiarity. Nonetheless, we have decided to implement the withdrawal procedure, in the light of the lack of support expressed for this proposal' (European Commission, quoted in *EuroPolitics*, 'Commission withdraws Monti II proposal', 13 September 2012).[16] The Commission's withdrawal was welcomed by the national parliaments that had submitted reasoned opinions, the MEPs from a large majority of political groups, and the trade unions (*EurActiv*, 'Brussels drops plans for EU law limiting right to strike', 14 September 2012). The Commission's first position on the appropriate response to the case law had thus been rejected by a group of national parliaments, which acted as a new set of veto players. Nevertheless, the case law still required a political response, as emphasized by the British S&D MEP Stephen Hughes:

> The Commission's proposal—known as Monti II—has been opposed by our Group right from the beginning ... However, the Commission's announcement on the withdrawal of the text leaves a vacuum. There are still huge legal uncertainties left by the European Court of Justice rulings (in the Laval case) regarding the rights of workers. The problem remains, and the Commission has the responsibility to act. (EurActiv, 'Brussels drops plans for EU law limiting right to strike', 14 September 2012)

[16] See also letters sent from the Commission to the national parliaments: http://ec.europa.eu/dgs/secretariat_general/relations/relations_other/npo/letter_to_nal_parl_en.htm.

The Proposal for an Enforcement Directive

After the national parliaments rejected the Monti II proposal, negotiations proceeded on the proposal for a directive concerning the enforcement of the Posting of Workers Directive. Despite requests from the European trade unions, the Commission had decided not to completely amend the PWD but to concentrate on improving enforcement with its proposal. The Commission's strategy was to attempt to meet different concerns: to address social dumping while avoiding disproportionate restrictions on the free movement of services and the freedom of establishment. In this way, the appropriate balance resembled the balance proposed in the negotiations during the original PWD. However, as with the original PWD, negotiations on the enforcement directive involved vital political issues, not merely enforcement technicalities.

The Commission was expected to present its proposal in December 2011 but refrained on several occasions. In the agenda-setting stage, the Commission renewed the idea of liability between contractors and subcontractors, which had been on hold since the early Social Action Program in 1991. The proposal, as formulated in January and February 2012 but never presented,[17] suggested a principle of joint and several liability for all sectors (interviews, social partners, 20 March 2012; Commission, 30 March 2012). However, it did not propose the principle of chain responsibility that was envisaged by the Commission in 1991.[18] Despite this modification, drafting a principle of joint and several liability for all sectors was not well received, particularly by Business Europe (interview, social partners, 20 March 2012). The original draft was then modified to suggest that the principle should apply to the construction sector only (*COM (2012) 131*). With this amendment, the Commission was ready to present its proposal on 21 March 2012.

The Content of the Enforcement Proposal

Whereas the PWD is a short document that contains five pages, twenty-five recitals, and nine articles, the proposal on the enforcement of the directive

[17] The unpresented proposal was shared with the author by key respondents interviewed.

[18] There exist two primary types of liability: joint and several liability, where the main contractor can be held responsible for the first subcontractor (i.e. the principle applies at one level of the employment relationship); and chain responsibility, where the principle of liability applies to the entire chain of subcontractors (Houwerzijl and Peters [2008]).

spanned sixty pages, thirty-four recitals, and twenty-three articles. The explanatory memorandum described the political context since the adoption of the PWD and provided reasoned support for the initiative on the basis of the developments in the case law. In its proposal, the Commission referred to the Court thirty-six times. According to the Commission, the 'Laval Quartet' required clarification regarding the interpretation of key provisions of the Directive, such as 'the concept of public policy, the material scope of the terms and conditions of employment by the Directive and the nature of mandatory rules, in particular the minimum wage' (*COM (2012) 131*, 4–5). The Commission stated that the objective of the proposal was not to reopen the original directive but to improve its implementation, application, and practical enforcement (*COM (2012) 131*, 11).

Two articles of the proposal particularly divided actors and institutions (interviews, Council, 25 July 2012; European Parliament, 3 December 2012). Table 6.1 sets out how one provision was a direct response to the case law. Another provision became a significant issue in political negotiations, in part because some Council members considered it an important preventative mechanism against future Court cases.

The Commission developed the scope and limits of article 9 by reference to the case law (*COM (2012) 131*, 15).[19] Its formal interpretation of the rulings was that they would only justify an exhaustive list of control measures: 'Member states may *only* impose the following administrative requirements and control measures' (article 9.1, emphasis added).[20] However, internally, the Commission's position was not unified. Apparently, DG EMPL preferred an open list, but DG MARKT argued for an exhaustive list (interview, Council. 7 February 2014). This issue became significant in subsequent negotiations.

Viewed along the conflict lines of the two-dimensional matrix *more integration versus less integration* and *left–right*, both an exhaustive list and an obligatory principle of joint and several liability would be a move towards more European integration, i.e. less national autonomy. Looking at the enforcement directive, the left–right dimension involved the actions and control

[19] The Commission here referred to the Finalarte cases; the Arblade cases (in both instances, see note 8 above); case C–490/04 *Commission* of the European Communities v Federal Republic of *Germany* [2007] ECR I–6122; C–445/03 Commission v Luxembourg (see note 13 above); and case C–515/08 Criminal proceedings against Vítor Manuel dos *Santos Palhota* and Others [2010] ECR I–09133.

[20] See pp. 15–17 of *COM (2012) 131*, which referred to, among other cases, Rush Portuguesa (see note 4 above), Commission v Germany (see note 20 above) and Finalarte (see note 8 above).

Table 6.1 Key Provisions in the Commission Proposal on an Enforcement Directive

	Commission proposal *COM (2012) 131* as of 21 March 2012
List of national control measures	Article 9: Proposing an exhaustive list of permitted control measures. According to the Commission, only the following would be justified in light of the case law: • 9.1.a: Service provider obliged to declare to competent national authority identity of service provider, number of posted workers, and duration and location of work to be performed; • 9.1.b: Obligation to make relevant documents available, including employment contracts, payslips, timesheets, and proof of payment of wages; • 9.1.c: Translation of these documents, provided that they are not excessively long; and • 9.1.d: Obligation for contact person at posting firm to be designated to negotiate with social partners in hosting member state. Proposing to codify the case law of the Court.
Joint and several liability	Article 12: Proposing joint and several liability for contractors to direct subcontractors regarding their minimum wages, social security contributions, and taxes. Proposed to apply to construction sector only, not as general principle of chain responsibility, but limited to first subcontractor.

measures that could be used against social dumping, which would assure the social and labour market rights of the worker. An exhaustive list of control measures would weaken social rights because it would be increasingly difficult for hosting member states to apply additional national standards. In contrast, an obligatory principle of joint and several liability would strengthen social rights because the contractor would be held responsible if the subcontractor violated the social rights of posted workers. Thus, the Commission's proposal intended to increase integration on both dimensions. Consistent with the case law, the Commission proposed a move to the right by proposing an exhaustive list of control measures; meanwhile, it introduced liability to protect the posted workers' rights in a subcontracting relationship, i.e. a step to the left. However, because the Commission proposed neither a full principle of chain liability for all sectors nor an open list of control measures, its general position still leaned to the right. The position of the Commission in relation to SQ_{Court} is summarized with the other political positions in this chapter's concluding figure 6.3.

Political Positions in the European Parliament

The European Parliament had difficulty finding common ground during the negotiations, especially regarding the proposed articles 9 and 12. The positions on the matter were split among political groups and between the EP committees on employment (EMPL) and the internal market (IMCO). The EMPL committee was responsible for the proposal, but it soon faced significant disagreements on the dossier. The conservative EPP group had gained rapporteurship and had appointed Danuta Jazlowiecka from Poland as rapporteur. Jazlowiecka submitted her report in November 2012. According to the respondents, the report primarily mirrored the rapporteur's own position rather than communicating a position shared among EMPL members or a common EPP position (interviews, European Parliament, 3 December 2012, 16 and 29 May 2013; Council, 17 December 2012). Some respondents even contended that the position in the report was similar to the position of the Polish government (interviews, Council, 4 and 17 December 2012; European Parliament, 29 May 2013). Considerable dissatisfaction with the work of the rapporteur was expressed. In her draft report, the rapporteur suggested that the exhaustive list of control measures was maintained largely as proposed by the Commission, but article 12 should be deleted (draft report PE 498.030 (Rapporteur: Danuta Jazlowiecka), 8 November 2012). Thus, the initial position of the rapporteur was to remove the already modified principle of joint and several liability. She found joint and several liability to be 'highly disproportionate'. Regarding article 9, an exhaustive list was considered to be necessary to establish legal certainty: 'The rapporteur firmly opts for clarity in the context of controls, what can only be guaranteed by a closed list of possible control measures. The legal certainty is obtained by a clear communication of what is to be controlled' (EMPL Draft report PE 498.030 (Rapporteur: Danuta Jazlowiecka), 41).

The IMCO committee shadowed the negotiations in the EMPL. Emilie Turunen from the Green Group was appointed as rapporteur. In her draft opinion, she took a different position from that of the EMPL rapporteur. The IMCO draft opinion proposed that article 9 be amended to an open list but one over which hosting member states were mandated to take certain control measures. The draft opinion thus formulated article 9 as what member states 'shall ... but are not limited to' apply as control measures. This position on article 9 involving member state obligations and a non-exhaustive list was consistent with the position of the ETUC regarding the best approach to address social dumping (interview, European Parliament, 16 May 2013). In addition, the draft opinion proposed a general principle of joint and several liability (IMCO draft opinion PE 496.470v01-00 (Rapporteur: Emilie Turunen), 24 September 2012).

The draft opinion was not supported by the majority on IMCO, however. The final IMCO opinion thus maintained the exhaustive list of article 9 as proposed by the Commission and deleted article 12 in the same manner as the main EMPL rapporteur had proposed in her draft report (IMCO opinion PE 496.470v03-00 (Rapporteur: Malcolm Harbour[21]), 12 March 2012, 3).

Political Interaction in the European Parliament

Difficult negotiations concerning the draft report followed in the EMPL committee. In particular, the S&D group was against the rapporteur's approach. British MEP Stephen Hughes acted as the S&D shadow rapporteur to the document. The position of the S&D group was that article 9 should be an open list, where wording such as 'shall' rather than 'may' should make the listed control measures obligatory. The joint and several liability stipulated in article 12 should be general, not limited to the construction sector. The positions between the EPP rapporteur and the S&D group were diverse and made negotiations difficult from the beginning. In addition, the S&D position was supported by other groups on the left in the EP. Moreover, several

[21] Given the changes in the final IMCO opinion, Turunen refused to remain as rapporteur on the final text for which reason Harbour signed as IMCO rapporteur.

members of the EPP group and ALDE would have accepted some openness in the list of control measures and a voluntary principle of liability.

Rapporteur Jazlowiecka was thus under pressure and isolated during the EMPL negotiations. In May 2013, the rapporteur took a more pragmatic turn. She presented a compromise, suggesting that article 9 be an open list, but maintained that article 12 should be removed (interview, European Parliament, 29 May 2013). However, this compromise was insufficient for the S&D group, and their position found support from the majority of EMPL members during the Committee vote on the tabled amendments.[22] On 20 June 2013, the EMPL committee adopted sixty-one amendments to the Commission's proposal. The list of control measures in article 9 became a non-exhaustive one and emphasized that member states may impose 'any administrative requirements and control measures that they deem necessary for effective enforcement' (see amendment 51 of the final EMPL report A7-0249/2013 (Rapporteur: Danuta Jazlowiecka)). In addition, the amendment of article 9 indicated that certain control measures 'shall' be taken. These measures required the posting firm to (a) inform the competent authorities regarding the character of the work performed, (b) appoint a contact person, and (c) make central documents available, such as the proof of identity of the posted workers, employment contracts, payslips, timesheets, and social security documentation. Furthermore, the principle of joint and several liability was amended to a principle of chain responsibility that applied across sectors and to all possible subcontractors (amendment no. 54 in the final report A7-0249/2013 (Rapporteur: Danuta Jazlowiecka)). The final EMPL position had changed significantly from what the rapporteur had originally proposed. The majority of EMPL members had found a common position that considerably strengthened social rights and actively responded to the case law.

> We hope to send the positive signal that Social Europe is back on track in recognising the fundamental difficulties created by these EC judgments and trying to restore a balance where we think the balance has been destroyed. It's difficult; because we have German elections coming up in September, we have the elections next year. Thus, on the one hand, one wants to solve the question, but on the other hand, people begin to posture for the elections and to play electoral politics, so it's not the easiest time to try and solve difficult problems like this. (interview, European Parliament, 29 May 2013)

[22] A total of 833 amendments were tabled in the EMPL Committee.

Political Positions in the Council of Ministers

The member states were also substantially divided regarding the enforcement proposal. The divisions were largely between hosting and posting states. The majority of old member states assumed the position of hosting member states and defended their right to control posting companies. The Eastern European member states and the UK adopted the position of defenders of the internal market; they favoured article 9 as proposed by the Commission but were opposed to article 12 on joint and several liability regardless of the sector (interviews, Council, 25 July 2012, 4 and 17 December 2012, 11 June 2013). The UK and Poland took the lead on this position. With their allied member states, they argued that an exhaustive list of national control measures was a codification of the case law, which would ensure transparency for the posting firms and establish legal certainty (interviews, Council, 25 July 2012).[23] Meanwhile, an exhaustive list would depart from $SQ_{reg}{}^{1}$, as adopted by the PWD, by constraining the use of national labour law.

Judicial decisions were thus an important reference in Council negotiations, but the member states disagreed on how the Court's decisions should be interpreted and which control measures were actually consistent with the judicial decisions. As one government representative stated:

> We oppose everything that goes beyond codifying what the European Court of Justice has done, because we believe in the importance of single market and it's clear from the case law from the ECJ that member states have been using such national control measures to place disproportionate burdens in the path of legislative businesses that are conducting businesses in foreign countries. (interview, Council, 25 July 2012)

Other member states, which advocated a non-exhaustive list of control measures, found that the exhaustive list proposed by the Commission reflected an interpretation of the case law that was too strict:

> When we look at article 9, we don't really have a problem with it. For we think with the Commission that this is a good translation of the jurisprudence of the Court of Justice. What we do see is that many countries disagree with us on that. And that they either think that the Commission has been too strict in their interpretation

[23] On 25 July 2012, three research interviews were conducted with three Council representatives.

of the case law or for other reasons want to have a more open list, which we don't prefer. (interview, Council, 25 July 2012)

Thus, the member states disagreed on what constituted legal certainty and how the case law should be interpreted. When asked whether the case law had been used as a reference in Council negotiations, another government representative stated:

Absolutely. Especially from the Commission's side for example. Viking and Laval, for example, they use a lot. You see it very, very particularly coming back in article 9, which we think is a good thing since—as far as we see it—article 9 is a good reflection of the case law, but it's also very difficult to ... It's a matter of interpretation, of course. How do you see the case law of the Court? We've not been asking the Court to interpret article 9 for us. It's a number of cases, a variety of cases of which the Commission has picked certain elements and well, you see, that the positions differ or the interpretations differ ... (interview, Council, 25 July 2012)

Council representatives determined that the case law constituted an important reference but disagreed on whether it should support a non-exhaustive or an exhaustive list of control measures. Thus, the political interpretation of what constituted legal certainty was subject to interpretation. It is also clear that these interpretations were used selectively and informed by political preferences.

The negotiations in the Council were marked by clear conflicts over national control measures and joint and several liability—as well as the appropriate interpretation of the case law. The conflicts concerning article 9 were the most intense. In particular, Germany, France, Sweden, and Denmark insisted on a non-exhaustive list and argued against the Commission's proposal on how to codify the case law (interviews, Council, 17 December 2012, 11 June 2013): 'It may be that this is a codification (of the case law), but it is too narrow. You don't reach broad[ly] enough' (interview, Council, 17 December 2012). The Netherlands had originally taken a position between the two Council coalitions and favoured joint and several liability and an exhaustive list of control measures. The Netherlands thus supported the Commission's proposal on both articles. The Dutch determined that if the jurisprudence of the Court was to be respected, an exhaustive list was necessary. During the negotiations, the Dutch position became more pragmatic: the Dutch became open to a non-exhaustive list with the condition that member states would be required to inform the Commission regarding which control measures they would take (interview, Council, 11 June 2013).

Political Interactions in the Council of Ministers

Negotiations during the first part of 2013 focused on turning article 12 into a voluntary instrument. The UK and Poland had strong reservations against mandatory joint and several liability. Their positions were that, because joint and several liability would only apply in cross-border situations, mandatory joint and several liability would be discriminatory and contrary to the free movement of services. The UK and Poland also maintained that mandatory joint and several liability was against the principle of subsidiarity (interview, Council, 4 December 2012). The UK Minister of Employment Relations Jo Swinson stated the British position on article 12 as follows:

> On this point, the Government will not agree to anything that would change UK law by mandating joint and several liability in subcontracting chains. I believe that this is an issue on which Member States should be able to decide for themselves the most appropriate way to ensure that workers in subcontracting chains have their rights upheld. A mandatory system of joint and several liability will also undermine the EU's aim to facilitate the posting of workers. In Member States which already use joint and several liability, these provisions apply to all workers in covered sectors. The Commission's proposal relates only to posted workers—these provisions would lead to different treatment when the main contractor uses a company with posted workers to when they contract with a company not using posted workers. This will create an uneven playing field. (as stated in the Seventeenth Report of Session 2013–14, UK House of Commons, European Scrutiny Committee)

By contrast, the member states that already had some form of joint liability in their national regulation could not accept the removal of the principle from the text of the directive.[24] The CJEU had already ruled against the Belgian system of joint liability and had found it incompatible with the freedom to provide services.[25] Therefore, it was important for these member states to have a provision in the directive that stated that this type of joint and several liability did not conflict with EU law. In this way, a provision that stated

[24] Over the years, eight member states have introduced different forms of joint liability in the subcontracting chain (for the different forms, see Houwerzijl and Peters [2008]). The member states that had some form of joint liability during the negotiations were Austria, Belgium, Finland, France, Germany, Italy, the Netherlands, and Spain.

[25] Case C–433/04 *Commission* of the European Communities v Kingdom of *Belgium* [2006] I–10653. However, in another case, C–60/03 *Wolff & Müller* GmbH & Co. KG v José Filipe Pereira Félix [2004] I–09553, the Court found the German liability system for minimum wage payment to be a justified measure in relation to free movement principles.

that member states *may* take such actions could shield the national systems against future rulings from the Court (interviews, Council, 17 December 2012, 7 February 2014). Even a voluntary principle was considered an important anticipatory shield against future Court cases. A weakened principle was better than nothing and a safeguard and anticipatory protective measure against future jurisprudence. 'If anybody asks "shall we have a directive if it's only voluntary?" then, you can say that this is a significant, important signal, and it gives a certain juridical guarantee towards the CJEU' (interview, Council, 7 February 2014). At the meeting of the Employment, Social Policy, Health and Consumer Affairs Council (EPSCO) on 15 October 2013, the member states' views were too far apart, particularly on article 12. No common position was established. Specifically, France insisted on a mandatory principle of joint and several liability for all sectors (interview, Council, 7 February 2014). A majority established support for a non-exhaustive list of control measures and some type of joint liability, but the majority was still insufficient. The alliance led by the UK and Poland opposed any form of joint and several liability and argued that it would create internal market barriers. Almost two-thirds of the member states, including Germany and France, favoured a non-exhaustive list of control measures to be stipulated in article 9. The Netherlands changed its position to support a non-exhaustive list. Moreover, the Commission changed its position to support an open list. The Commission had previously held that only an exhaustive list was consistent with judicial decisions, but was now willing to modify its interpretation. Thus, DG MARKT's interpretation of the case law had to yield to DG EMPL's position because DG EMPL's position was also the position of the EP and the Council majority.

Until the EPSCO meeting in October 2013, the likely compromise was envisioned as a non-exhaustive list combined with either a voluntary principle or no principle of joint liability. However, this compromise no longer seemed possible. The balance had tipped towards strengthened social rights. Combating social dumping became more central in the negotiations. France in particular had led the social alliance and insisted that there was no possibility for a package deal in which a non-exhaustive list could be present if joint and several liability were abandoned (interview, Council, 7 February 2014). Thus, at the EPSCO meeting in autumn 2013, no common position could be established in the Council.

The December 2013 EPSCO meeting was the last opportunity to establish a common position if a first-reading agreement with the European Parliament could be reached before the Parliament's election in May 2014. Confronted with time pressures, the Council agreed on a compromise on 9 December 2013. The compromise substantially extended social regulation beyond the lowest common denominators of an exhaustive list of control measures and a voluntary principle of joint and several liability. The Council agreed on a non-exhaustive list of control measures and administrative requirements in article 9, provided that these requirements were justified and proportionate according to Union law. In addition, a monitoring role was assigned to the Commission, which required the member states to inform the Commission and service providers regarding the control measures they would use. The applied control measures should also be made publicly available for service providers on a website to ensure transparency. An important compromise was established over article 12. The Lithuanian president proposed a voluntary principle of subcontracting liability. The member states could adopt these national provisions (see the presidency compromise text, inter-institutional file 2012/0061, 17072/13 of 4 December 2013). However, during Council negotiations, article 12 was made partly mandatory. In the Council's common position, article 12 finally stated that member states *may* hold contractors liable for the entire chain of subcontractors in all sectors (article 12.1) but *shall* hold the first contractor liable in the construction sector (article 12.2).[26] The Council's common position added that member states may decide not to hold a contractor liable if the main contractor showed due diligence in avoiding abuse by its subcontractor(s) (article 12.3). It was also added that member states may take enforcement measures other than subcontracting liability in the construction sector 'to tackle fraud and abuse in situations when workers have difficulties in obtaining their rights' (article 12.3a). An important compromise had been established among the member states that strengthened social protection to a greater extent than the UK and Poland, among others, had previously been willing to accept.

However, between the EPSCO meetings in October and December, the close relationship between Poland and the UK had been harmed. Throughout the negotiations, Poland had been the member state that was most against the adoption of an open list of control measures and the principle of joint and several liability (interview, Council, 7 February 2014). However, Cameron's feature article in the *Financial Times*, 'Free movement within Europe needs to be less free', was considered by Poland to be inappropriate (*Financial Times*,

[26] See the Council's common position, inter-institutional file 2012/0061, 17611/13 of 10 December 2013.

26 November 2013). The UK's statements were not directly related to the posting of workers but addressed social security for migrant workers. In the article, Cameron declared that access to EU cross-border welfare should be limited. These statements provoked fierce Polish reactions. Former President Lech Walesa responded that the UK had acted in an 'irrational and short-sighted way' (*Financial Times*, 'Poland attacks Cameron view on migrants', 23 December 2013). Cameron's statements influenced Council decision making on the enforcement directive, and Poland moved closer to France and away from the UK. France was able to convince Poland of the importance to signal unity for a social Europe. As noted by a Council representative:

> [y]ou could see that France and Poland suddenly became closer at the Council meeting. France was very committed to achieve a result—in part due to domestic politics, aiming to contain Le Pen somehow before the EP elections ... So France tried to convince Poland that it's better to be with us than with the UK. (interview, Council, 7 February 2014)

Thus, at the EPSCO meeting in December, Poland and Ireland changed positions and voted in favour of a compromise. The change in Poland's position was considered a breakthrough in the Council (interview, Council, 7 February 2014). A mandate was assigned to the Council's president to initiate negotiations in trialogue with the European Parliament and the Commission.

Inter-institutional Interactions: Establishing the Final Compromise

Against this background, the negotiations with the European Parliament began in January 2014. The European Parliament, on one hand, welcomed that the Council had reached a common position. On the other hand, it was noted that the Council's position was less ambitious than the mandate EMPL had been granted (*EurActiv*, 'Posted workers directive is "not a done deal yet"', 11 December 2013). Nevertheless, the EP rapporteur announced that there would be a real opportunity to reach an agreement between the two legislators before the last EP plenary session in April 2014. The S&D group was more reluctant; it noted that the matter was extremely sensitive and that it and the ETUC wanted a significant solution, not a 'lukewarm compromise with the Council ahead of the EU elections' (*EurActiv*, 11 December 2013). The S&D group required a general binding principle of chain responsibility and a list of mandatory control measures called the 'shall' list. However, behind the official statements, the S&D group was divided between a more pragmatic faction and a more 'confrontational' faction that was closely linked to the ETUC and led by the shadow rapporteur Stephen Hughes (interview, European Parliament, 17 April 2014). The more 'confrontational' faction insisted on the 'shall' list and a principle of chain responsibility applicable across all sectors.

Negotiations between the Council and the EP were detailed and difficult. To the end, it was difficult to determine whether a compromise could be established. For the Council, a blocking minority could easily have arisen again if Poland reverted to its original position. For the EP, internal disagreements in the S&D group and between the rapporteur and the shadow rapporteurs increased the sensitivity of the situation. However, with the leadership of France in the Council and the pragmatic position of the EP, a compromise was established between the two legislators by February 2014. The outcome largely mirrored the final Council compromise. Key parts of the directive are summarized in table 6.2.

Table 6.2 Key Provisions of the Adopted Enforcement Directive

	Directive 2014/67—Enforcement directive on the posting of workers
List of national control measures	Article 9: Adopted as a non-exhaustive list of control measures; Commission to be notified which control measures will be applied. Notification procedure, however, not *ex ante* authorization of Commission to control national measures but functions as a means of transparency. Modifying the case law of the Court.
Joint and several liability	Article 12: Establishes obligatory principle of liability for construction sector, affecting first subcontractor. Chain responsibility may be adopted for all other sectors. If contractor has shown due diligence as defined by national law, member state may decide not to hold contractor liable. Protective measure against future Court cases.

On 5 March 2014, twenty-five member states voted in favour of the EP-Council compromise. Hungary, Latvia, and Estonia voted against it (interview, Council, 11 April 2014). Remarkably, the former leaders of the blocking minority, the UK and Poland, also voted for the compromise. The reversal of these two member states is especially notable because the distance between the position accepted in the compromise and their original position is considerable. On 18 March 2014, the EP Employment and Social Affairs Committee adopted the compromise from the trialogue. Overall, thirty committee members voted in favour, and eleven voted against (press release, EPP group, 18 March 2014). The EP plenary vote occurred on 16 April 2014, at which a solid majority voted in favour of the compromise. Overall, 474 MEPs voted in favour, and 158 voted against, with 39 abstentions (European Parliament, *Legislative Observatory*, 2012/0061(COD)—16/04/2014, Text adopted by Parliament, 1st reading/single reading, summary). The votes against included some of the MEPs from the S&D group, including the shadow rapporteur Stephen Hughes, who maintained that the output did not sufficiently strengthen social rights. In addition, the ETUC expressed its dissatisfaction with the output (ETUC press release, 16 April 2014).

On 13 May 2014, the Council held their final vote. Only Hungary and Latvia voted against the compromise, while Estonia abstained from voting (Council of the European Union, voting results, 9818/14). After much opposition, the UK joined the majority. It thus avoided the isolated position of a no-voter.

> 'Currently, the UK wants to distance itself from the EU, but otherwise, it is normally that you want to avoid … being noted as having voted against. That you want to avoid, if you can' (interview, Council, 11 April 2014).

Directive 2014/67 on the enforcement of the posting of workers was adopted just before the eighth EP election.[27]

Judicial Influence on EU Regulation of the Posting of Workers

From the beginning, the interplay between law and politics affected the development of EU regulation of the posting of workers. The negotiations on the

[27] Directive 2014/67/EU of the European Parliament and of the Council of 15 May 2014 on the enforcement of Directive 96/71/EC concerning the posting of workers in the framework of the provision of services and amending Regulation (EU) No 1024/2012 on administrative cooperation through the Internal Market Information System ('the IMI Regulation').

original directive reflected different interpretations and different uses of the case law, which generated different positions. The European Commission found that member states' use of the Rush case to justify the application of national labour law to posted workers impeded the free movement of services. It proposed that the impact of the judicial decisions should be modified. However, the member states of the EU15 and the European Parliament continued to use the Rush dictum to argue that national labour-law standards in the host state should be fully applicable to posted workers. Thus, the judicial decision was codified or even reinforced in the original PWD adopted in 1996. A regulatory status quo SQ_{reg}^{1} was created but differed from the position of the Commission. The Commission acted strategically and downplayed the importance of the Rush dictum, but its strategic efforts were unsuccessful. The two legislators developed their own position, which used the 'voice of law' to justify and extend the application of national labour law. In this regulatory point of departure, the Commission had to accept and adapt to the position of the two legislators.

The analysis above emphasizes the CJEU as a dynamic institution. The Court later departed from the Rush dictum and created a new judicial status quo that substantially differed from the earlier one. A new SQ_{Court} was created that promoted free movement principles. The discrepancy between the politically created status quo SQ_{reg}^{1} and the judicially created status quo SQ_{Court} required a political response. The European Parliament demanded that the Commission act. In its proposals, the Commission argued for the need to establish new legal certainty and proposed to codify the judicial decisions. In both proposals, the Commission capitalized on 'the voice of law' and justified its initiatives with significant reference to the Court. However, the Commission's introduction of the judicial decisions into EU decision making was considered a setback for social rights by the majority of political actors.

The Commission's Monti II proposal on the appropriate balance between free movement principles and the right to take collective action was rejected by the national parliaments, which showed their strength as the 'new actors on the block'. The national parliaments as new veto players showed the yellow card and rejected the Commission's proposal on how to respond to the case law. The Commission's proposal on Monti II suggested codifying the case law and departed from the SQ_{reg}^{1} of the original Posted Workers' Directive. On political dimensions, the codification would be a considerable move to the right that would weaken workers' rights to take collective action, and it would strengthen European integration by limiting the national autonomy to take collective action. Consistent with the reasoned opinion procedure, the national parliaments showed the yellow card primarily to protect subsidiarity, i.e. choosing less integration over a position on the right–left dimension. The positions on this sensitive matter are shown in figure 6.2 below.

However, we should expect future conflicts over how to establish the appropriate balance and how to solve the discrepancy created between SQ_{reg}^{1} and SQ_{Court}. Ultimately, non-adoption is an insufficient political response, which leaves a regulatory vacuum and a high degree of legal uncertainty. The Commission is thus expected to identify a solution to the 'case law problem' that former president Barroso once promised to deliver. In analysing patients' rights in cross-border healthcare in chapter 5, we found that political non-adoption can push the Commission to adapt its position and to present a proposal that modifies the course of legal integration. This is a likely future scenario for the relationship between free movement and the right to take collective action.

The positions on the enforcement proposal proved to be dynamic. Through the interaction that unfolded between T_1 and T_2 in and among institutions, the discrepancy among positions was reduced. In T_1, the Commission presented an exhaustive list of control measures that codified

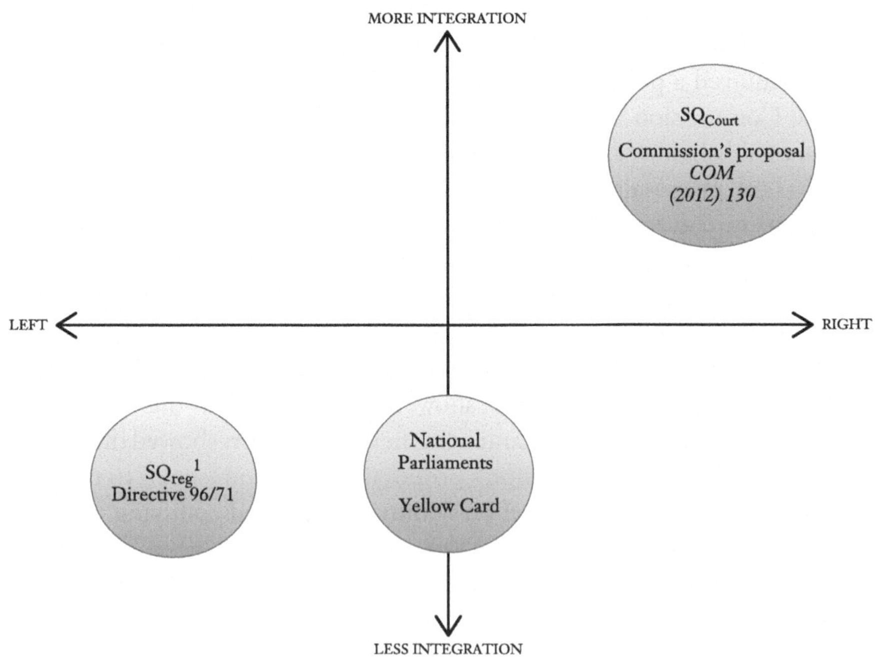

Fig. 6.2 Rejecting Judicial Influence on the Right to Collective Action

the Court's judicial decisions, but it was internally divided on the issue. DG MARKT insisted on an exhaustive list, whereas DG EMPL envisaged a more open approach. Thus, internally, the Commission also interpreted and used the case law differently. From the outset the Commission's official position regarding control measures was supported by the EPP rapporteur, the new member states, the Netherlands, and the UK. On the conflict-line of integration, the same alliance, except for the Netherlands, was firmly against the adoption of the proposed article on joint and several liability and considered it to be against the principle of subsidiarity and a distortion of competition. On the other side, members of the S&D group and most old member states under the leadership of France insisted on an open list of control measures and different degrees of joint liability. Other members of the S&D group shared the position of the ETUC in demanding chain responsibility and an open list that obligated member states to take certain control measures.

Between T_1 and T_2, intra- and inter-institutional interaction unfolded along these conflict lines. During the negotiations, the positions changed considerably. First, the Netherlands changed its position to favour a non-exhaustive list. The EPP group and the EMPL committee pushed the EPP rapporteur to change position. France pushed Poland to join the majority of member states in favouring strengthened social rights and more European integration. Finally, the UK changed its position to avoid isolation. Gradually, a compromise in and among the institutions was established and the judicial influence on EU regulations was modified. The different positions of the institutions and the changes in position between T_1 and T_2 are presented in figure 6.3 below.

The analysis confirmed the expectation that the decision-making rules make both overrides and codification unlikely in an EU setting of significant thresholds. New decisive actors with a specific interest in defending the principle of subsidiarity were identified. The Monti II proposal was rejected because of the swift action by the national parliaments. The post-Lisbon institutional setting includes new decisive actors, which further raises the thresholds for codification or overrides.

The case studies did not support the expectation that judicial decisions will be adopted in policy outputs as the Commission proposes. The Commission disagreed internally but took a formal position on how jurisprudence should influence political integration. However, it was unsuccessful in its attempts to strategically bring jurisprudence into EU decision making. Furthermore, the analysis showed that both the Commission and the political actors

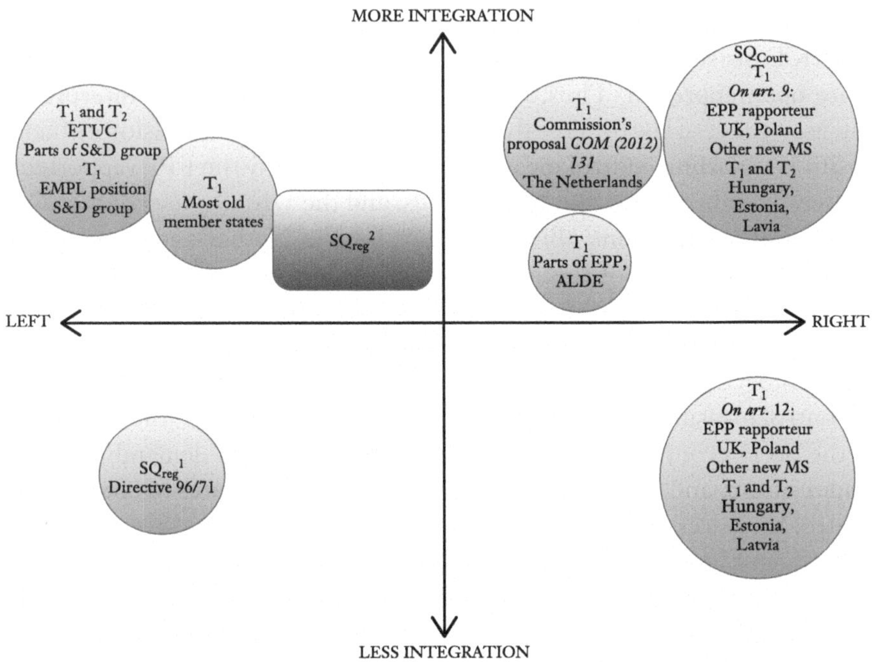

Fig. 6.3 Modifying Judicial Influence on Regulating the Posting of Workers

interpreted the legal decisions differently, depending on how they perceived the law or how the law served their interests. The interpretation and use of case law proved to be both plural and political.

Consistent with the final expectation, the analysis indicates the importance of interaction. If positions are divergent but dynamic, a compromise can be established that modifies the judicial influence on the final policy output. As the Commission and political actors interacted with one another, their positions changed considerably. What was unlikely at the outset became the policy output. Concerning the enforcement directive, a sizeable blocking minority changed their positions from right to left and from less to more integration. The adoption of a non-exhaustive list of control measures modified the judicial influence on EU regulation and extended the member states' autonomy within the scope of EU law. The adopted principle of joint and several liability also became a response to the Court's decisions because it constitutes an *anticipatory protective measure* to avoid future jurisprudence against specific measures.

Despite its fragmented character, EU politics modified the judicial influence on the enforcement directive. In the future, EU legislative politics must address the discrepancy created between $SQ_{reg}{}^{1}$ and SQ_{Court} when Monti II was rejected. This action requires the Commission to advance a new proposal that will probably present a more modified response to the case law.

References

Alter, K.J. and Meunier-Aitsahalia, S. (1994) 'Judicial politics in the European Community: European integration and the pathbreaking Cassis de Dijon decision', *Comparative Political Studies* 26(4): 535–61.

Bellamy, R. and Kröger, S. (2014) 'Domesticating the democratic deficit? The role of national parliaments and parties in the EU's system of governance', *Parliamentary Affairs* 67(2): 437–57.

Blauberger, M. (2012) 'With Luxembourg in mind .... the remaking of national policies in the face of ECJ jurisprudence', *Journal of European Public Policy* 19(1): 109–26.

Bücker, A. (2010) 'The decisions of the European Court of Justice in the Viking, Laval and Rüffert cases from a German legal perspective', in A. Bücker and W. Warneck (eds), 'Report 111: Viking—Laval—Rüffert: Consequences and policy perspectives', European Trade Union Institute, 29–49.

Cameron, D (2013) 'Free movement within Europe needs to be less free', *Financial Times*, 26 November.

Cooper, I. (2012) 'A 'virtual third chamber' for the European Union? National parliaments after the Treaty of Lisbon', *West European Politics* 35(3): 441–65.

Cooper, I. (2013) 'A yellow card for the striker: how national parliaments defeated EU strikes regulation', EUSA Conference Paper. Baltimore: European Union Studies Association.

Cremers, J., Dølvik, J.E., and Bosch, G. (2007) 'Posting of workers in the single market: attempts to prevent social dumping and regime competition in the EU', *Industrial Relations Journal* 38(6): 524–41.

Davies, A.C.L. (2008) 'One step forward, two steps back? The Viking and Laval cases in the ECJ', *Industrial Law Journal* 37(2): 126–48.

Davies, P. (2002) 'The Posted Workers Directive and the EC Treaty', *Industrial Law Journal* 31(3): 98–306.

Hemerijck, A. (2013) *Changing Welfare States*, Oxford: Oxford University Press.

Houwerzijl, M. and Peters, S. (2008) 'Liability in subcontracting processes in the European construction sector', a report for Dublin: European Foundation for the Improvement of Living and Working Conditions.

Joerges, C. and Rödl, F. (2009) 'Informal politics, formalised law and the 'Social Deficit' of European integration: reflections after the judgments of the ECJ in Viking and Laval', *European Law Journal* 15(1): 1–19.

Kilpatrick, C. (2009) 'Laval's regulatory conundrum: collective standard-setting and the Court's new approach to posted workers', *European Law Review* 34(6): 844–65.

Klüver, H. and Sagarzazu, I. (2013) 'Ideological congruency and decision-making speed: the effect of partisanship across European Union institutions', *European Union Politics* 14(3): 388–407.

Kolehmainen, E. (1998) 'The Directive concerning the posting of workers: synchronization of the functions of national legal systems', *Comparative Labour Law and Policy Journal* 20: 71–104.

Malmberg, J. (2010) 'The impact of the ECJ judgements on Viking, Laval, Rüffert and Luxembourg on the practice of collective bargaining and the effectiveness of social action', Briefing Note, Brussels: Directorate General for Internal Policies.

Marks, G. and Steenbergen, M. (2002) 'Understanding political contestation in the European Union', *Comparative Political Studies* 35(8): 879–92.

Seikel, D. (2015) 'Class struggle in the shadow of Luxembourg. The domestic impact of the European Court of Justice's case law on the regulation of working conditions', *Journal of European Public Policy* 22(8): 1166–85.

Social Partners, European (2010) 'Report on the Joint Work of the European Social Partners on the ECJ Rulings in the Viking, Laval, Rüffert and Luxembourg cases', Brussels: Business Europe, ETUC, CEEP, UEAPME.

Walter, T. (2010) 'Germany. The practical consequences of the Rüffert decision', in A. Bücker and W. Warneck (eds), 'Report 111: Viking—Laval—Rüffert: Consequences and policy perspectives', European Trade Union Institute, 43–51.

7

Conclusion

We have come to learn that we live in judicialized times, where legislative politics become increasingly restrained by courts. In the European Union, this judicialization of politics is regarded as profound and expanding. The relationship between law and politics in this process builds up an 'image of politics under law' (Armstrong [1998]). Legislative politics is generally held not to be able to respond to law for at least two reasons: (1) EU legislative politics is too fragmented to be able to rein in the Court (Kelemen [2008: 35]), and (2) politicians have short-term horizons (Alter [1998: 130–3]; Pierson [1996: 135–6]). They care about re-election rather than the long-term, complex implications of jurisprudence. In the absence of a constitutional override of jurisprudence, the European Court is renowned as perhaps the most autonomous EU institution. In addition, the Court has been considered the most legitimate supranational institution, able to strengthen social rights where politics cannot (Caporaso and Tarrow [2009: 615]).

However, the progressive narrative of judicial impact has not gone unchallenged (Conant [2002]; Davies [2012a]; Rasmussen [2013]; Wincott [2001]). Although legal integration has been studied in depth, systematic and comparative analyses of the actual impact of those Court decisions have been limited. What are the national and supranational impacts of the continuous flow of CJEU case law? What is the effective reach of judicial decisions? The domestic impact of legal integration has been found to vary across member states, and is sometimes contained or not complied with (Conant [2002]). In regard to the supranational legislative impact, the dynamic court view posits a self-sustaining causal dynamic between legal and political integration. Although a causal link between litigation and legislation is plausible, so far it has not been proven empirically. To examine such a causal link and the associated mechanisms is, however, of major importance to the general impact of court decisions and to whether legislative politics retain the de facto capacity to steer the process of integration.

This book has examined the extent to which and the conditions under which CJEU judicial decisions influence EU social policy outputs. The overall finding is that judicial influence on EU social policy outputs varies over time and that EU legislative politics has the capacity to condition the general impact of legal integration. Rather than confirming the 'judicialisation of politics' in which parliamentary sovereignty 'has lost its grip' (Stone Sweet [2000: 196]), this overall finding demonstrates how the broader reach of jurisprudence results from continuous interplay between law and politics, but through which the interpretations, perceptions, and interests of political actors and governing majorities matter for judicial influence on politics. Despite fragmentation, majoritarian rule has not withered away.

The Extent of Judicial Influence on Policy Output

To what extent are Court-generated rules, principles, and interpretations attained in EU legislative acts? When the SQ_{Court} challenges the established SQ_{reg}^{1}, does SQ_{reg}^{2} confirm what the Court established?

The 'law attainment' analysis demonstrates that judicial influence varies over time between full and no impact, depending on how the Commission, the Council, and the European Parliament respond to jurisprudence. *Codification* does take place, but it tends to do so when Court interpretations are less politically important or occurred at an earlier time. Judicial decisions differ considerably in their socio-economic and political implications. Between 1961 and 2014, the CJEU concluded 7,547 preliminary references and infringement procedures (see figure 1.1 in chapter 1). The large majority of these cases are likely not to produce political responses because they primarily address very specific, technical or apolitical issues. Certainly, political actors are unable to foresee the full implications of a case when a ruling is first issued. As are other actors, political actors are limited by bounded rationality and reduced attention spans (Jones [1999]; Simon [1985]). They may underplay or misperceive the political implications of a case. They may also ignore or deny that litigation challenges their domestic institutions or the established regulatory status quo, focusing their political attention elsewhere. However, while the interplay between law and politics is dynamic, it does not necessarily move quickly. As legal certainty grows, political actors have time to respond collectively. The analysis presented in this book has demonstrated that responses tend to occur slowly and are somewhat delayed, but this should not be understood as the inability to act. As in most political systems, the pace of EU daily decision-making offers no quick repairs.

The analysis and the case studies identify the *overriding* of legal integration in two instances. Both took place before the 2004 enlargement and did not involve the European Parliament as co-legislator. In 1980, the Council adopted an amending regulation that overturned the legal interpretations of the Pierik judgment, which had diminished national control over cross-border healthcare. Through legislative correction, domestic control was re-established (see chapter 5). This early incident of override has had recent legislative implications because it was re-confirmed and written into the patients' rights directive. In 1992, the member states again overturned the Court's interpretation, which had extended the exportability of social benefits across borders. The Court could have ruled against the legislative correction but decided to accept it (see chapter 3). This demonstrates the Court's preparedness to adapt to politics.[1] Furthermore, the politically adopted special rule on non-exportability, which overturned jurisprudence, has acquired a life of its own through its own expansive logic. Over time, the special rule has been applied increasingly to benefits over which national control has been ensured. As demonstrated in the analysis of the opt-out from the forty-eight-hour work-week (see chapter 4), such special rules, exemptions, or opt-outs can produce their own logic of differentiation, where an increasing number of national laws or benefits are shielded from judicial impact (Martinsen and Wessel [2014]; see also Bonjour and Vink [2013], for migration policies).

Although it occurs, override is not a frequent legislative response. However, the fact that institutional and political hurdles normally prevent override does not prove codification. Instead, political responses are capable of reining in the Court. *Modification* of judicial influence is a more likely political correction. Through modification, political actors limit the impact of judicial decisions. The many expectations and challenges, high hopes or deep concerns first attached to such innovative rulings are reduced and sometimes even hollowed out through the political decision-making process.[2] The European Court's ability to produce broader legislative change depends on EU political majorities. When the Court ruled on cross-border

[1] For similar findings on the adaptive behaviour of the Court, where the Court softens its approach and adapts to political positions, see among others Bonjour and Vink (2013); Genschel (2011); Genschel et al. (2011); and Hervey and McHale (2015).

[2] Cf. Rosenberg (2008).

healthcare mobility, it created both hopes and fears. The final policy was a disappointment to some and a relief to others. Through the process of establishing the final compromise, patients' ability to obtain cross-border healthcare was de facto modified and national control was increased. In addition, in the negotiations for the enforcement directive, judicial influence was modified along important dimensions. The SQ_{Court}, extending free movement for posting firms, was reined in, and additional control measures as well as liability for the first subcontractor were politically adopted. While the originally drafted open list of control measures directly responded to the case law of the Court, subcontracting liability was an important indirect response and protective measure to avoid future jurisprudence, ruling against national chain responsibility. In patients' rights as in the posting of workers, the political responses constitute considerable modifications of the de facto impact of judicialization.

Establishing sufficient political majorities in response to judicial decisions is indeed onerous. Sometimes, such efforts fail, and *non-adoption* results. Non-adoption constitutes legislative gridlock, producing a stalemate among EU legislators in which no legislation is adopted (Binder [1999]). These situations occurred when the Commission proposed to codify jurisprudence on healthcare into the service directive and freedom of services and establishment into the Monti II regulation. In both initiatives, the Commission aimed to coax legislators into adoption, drawing on the perceived legitimacy of the Court (Alter and Meunier-Aitsahalia [1994]). For the working time directive, the Commission again miscalculated political majorities when it proposed to override the new definition of working time laid down by the Court. In all three cases, a considerable discrepancy between SQ_{Court} and SQ_{reg}[1] resulted. Non-adoption thus constitutes political deadlock, which creates legal uncertainty. It can be argued that in the absence of a political response, SQ_{Court} constitutes the state of legal affairs. However, as demonstrated in the working time and cross-border healthcare case studies, member states have considerable leeway to refuse to comply with disputed rulings. If the meaning or appropriateness of judicial decisions is questioned, and political clarification is called for but not produced, national authorities are in a better position to avoid compliance. Rules that few follow become the state of legal affairs. Non-adoption constitutes regulatory limbo, which is harmful to both the legitimacy of the Court and the effectiveness of EU regulation. As guardian of the Treaty, the Commission will face pressure to produce a new proposal that is better suited to the EU's political majorities. Thus, the position of the Commission changed from presenting a codification of jurisprudence to modification in the cross-border healthcare case. The Commission accepted a political result, which was at the very margin of what it considered acceptable in the light of the case law of the Court. After all, a drastic modification of legal integration was a better result than the continued state of legal uncertainty entailed in the political gridlock of non-adoption.

Conditions of Judicial Influence

The overall finding of variable judicial influence on EU policy outputs begs the question what explains such variation. I identified that legislative politics condition judicial influence. My findings contest two general claims in the existing studies of EU law and politics:

(1) EU politics, despite its multitude of actors and their diverse perceptions, interests, and interpretations, is not too fragmented to respond. The EU is indeed a highly fragmented regulatory polity; it is divided vertically between the EU and member states and horizontally among the Commission, the Council, and the Parliament. However, this book's findings show that the EU is sometimes able to overcome institutional hurdles and counteract judicialization. At other times, political gridlock prevents such responses, which has severe consequences for the state of legal affairs in the EU. Such a situation puts pressure on the Commission to generate a new proposal.

(2) The analysis points to EU legislators as rather persistent actors. If the long-term perspective of political actors fails, civil servants in the governments or political assistants in the European Parliament act behind the scenes, providing some institutional memory and continuity. The assumption of short time horizons cannot satisfactorily explain why political positions remain fixed for years or why political battles over case law continue despite changing governments and new MEPs taking over complex political files.

EU politics must be brought into account to explain why judicial influence on EU policy outputs varies. However, in doing this, we should avoid simple causality and consider a set of conditioning factors.

Time as a Conditioning Factor

The findings of this book demonstrate that time matters in the relationship between legal and political integration. After testing the statistical association between different factors and the likelihood of codification, time was found to affect likelihood. In line with Weiler's hypothesis (Weiler [1991, 1994]), EU legislators become less willing to codify jurisprudence into secondary legislation over time. Political voices for or against the case law of the Court appear to grow louder and become increasingly important over time. This pattern suggests that we should consider *learning* when assessing the relationship between law and politics. When political actors realize the hard and binding character of law, the importance of decision making increases (Weiler [1991: 2426]). Accordingly, political actors called for the Commission to provide a legislative response to litigation on cross-border healthcare, and to be re-elected president of the Commission, Barroso was forced to promise a legislative response to the 'Laval Quartet'. Furthermore, jurisprudence reflects a specific socio-economic *context* in time, which might be variably conducive to the Court's ability to produce social change. The gender equality case law of the 1970s and 1980s coincided with greater general political and societal support for improving gender equality (Hantrais [2007: 123]). In comparison, today's EU efforts to improve gender equality face political gridlock. In addition, the political and socio-economic setting of the Community from the late 1970s to the late 1990s differs strikingly from the EU28 of today. Today's EU is characterized by greater socio-economic heterogeneity among the member states. Political positions differ regarding case law and split on ideological lines as well as the degree of integration.

Decision-making Rules as Conditioning Factors

The decision-making rules frame institutional and political interactions. These rules define the major political hurdles to overcome in responding collectively to the Court. My analysis substantiates what has often been noted in discussions of the law–politics interaction; that constitutional override faces the highest possible thresholds in the EU. In the three case studies, the legal interpretations of access to cross-border healthcare were based on the Treaty; therefore, a constitutional override would be the only way to fully overturn jurisprudence. However, despite the constitutional hindrance to responding, EU legislators adopted a strong modification of the judicial approach, rendering it nearly unacceptable to the Commission. Thus, even when judicial decisions concern the Treaty, the Court is not fully shielded from political corrections. This result also proves that both the Commission and the Court may adapt to such corrections despite the fact that the Commission could have pursued an annulment procedure.

The thresholds for political responses are lower for legal innovations based on the EU's regulations and directives, but still exceedingly high. The agenda-setting power of the Commission and the bicameral legislative structure implies three veto points for initiatives. In addition, the voting rules raise the hurdles further. These decision-making rules in part explain why it is extremely difficult to establish sufficient majorities for legislation to override the Court and why political gridlock often results. However, this book also highlights why the same decision-making rules inhibit legislative codification of CJEU rulings—a finding that has so far been overlooked in discussions of the law–politics relationship. In this debate, the dynamic court view has claimed its triumph (Stone Sweet and Brunell [2012]) on the assumption that, because constitutional override does not occur, politics necessarily subjects itself to judicialization.

Decision-making rules complicate both override and codification. However, the political implications of litigation must be taken into account. Certainly, judicial decisions that are technical or very specific do not attract much political attention or produce much ideological tension. If the Commission proposes their codification, EU legislative politics tend to approve. As demonstrated in the analysis over time, more politically contested proposals, which are identified here by how long the decision-making process took, are less likely to be codified because political positions on them are split. The rules of the game as well as the political substance of jurisprudence condition the likelihood of judicialization.

The Role of the Commission as a Conditioning Factor

To set the law–politics dynamic in motion, the Commission plays a key role. Can the position of the Commission therefore explain how judicial influence varies? Both the longitudinal analysis and the three case studies identify inter-institutional disagreements between the Commission and EU legislators on responses to case law. In this case, the Commission is the first mover; it acts as gatekeeper and filters judicial decisions to affect which ones political actors respond to and how. The Commission is thus in a position to select, prioritize, and propose which judicial decisions should have a general legislative impact, and when. The findings show that the Commission has its own position on whether jurisprudence serves the course of integration. If legal integration goes against the Commission position on the way forward, it does not shy away from proposing to override or modify the impact of jurisprudence. Thus, it counteracted legal innovations concerning the exportability of non-contributory social benefits and proposed to overturn litigation by means of the special rule. It proposed to override the new definition of working time, including on-call time, as laid down by the Court. In addition, it proposed to modify the Rush Portuguesa case law, which had allowed rather unrestricted use of national labour law for posted workers. The analysis also demonstrates that when the Commission's proposal departs from SQ_{Court}, it tends to refer to jurisprudence in its explanatory memorandums and recitals more rarely or not at all. To initiate a correction of the Court is a difficult position for the Commission. As the guardian of the Treaty, Court–Commission inter-institutional disagreement does not serve the function or legitimacy of the Commission. When the Commission initiates a statute correcting the Court, it is likely to downplay such a purpose. Therefore, we should assume that there have been more instances in which the Commission has suggested restraining the Court than have been identified here. By means of process tracing, I have attempted to uncover such departures from litigation as exhaustively as possible, but I acknowledge that more overrides or modifications may exist. What is clear is that when the Commission draws on the SQ_{Court} to legitimize its initiatives, it refers considerably to jurisprudence, often making this the main justification for taking legislative action. The 'voice of law' becomes the explanation for why legislative action is necessary (Martinsen [2009]).

When responding to and utilizing the case law of the Court, the Commission is not a unitary actor. Its reading of jurisprudence differs internally. The analysis of cross-border healthcare and posted workers shows that the DG MARKT pushed for a more liberal reading of jurisprudence than the DG EMPL or the DG SANCO. The analysis also shows that the DG MARKT was less in line with political reality and had to yield to more pragmatic readings of the case law than it had first envisioned. In addition, disagreements on how to read the case law were identified between the Commission's legal service and the DG EMPL in the case of the working time directive. Thus, behind the Commission's official position loom internal disagreements. Even for the guardian of the Treaty, readings of the case law are far from given but differ internally. This diversity substantiates the Commission's interpretation and use of case law as both plural and political.

The findings have not supported the expectation that judicial decisions are adopted into policy outputs as the Commission proposes. When the Commission brings jurisprudence into decision making, it does so both for strategic reasons and as guardian of the Treaty. However, its attention span and strategic abilities prove insufficient, as it often miscalculates legislative positions. Furthermore, the Commission appears to disregard the importance of the whole span of legislative politics as it has evolved. The case of the working time directive shows that the Commission had not paid sufficient attention to the fixed and unified position of the European Parliament, and its arena-shifting strategy concerning the social partners did not succeed. The case of posted workers demonstrates that the Commission was taken by surprise when new actors, the national parliaments, rapidly showed the yellow card against the Monti II proposal. Although a first mover with the ability to design proposals carefully and wait for the right moments to present them, the Commission is an actor limited by incomplete information and perspective. Although capitalizing on the perceived legitimacy of the Court, introducing litigation into decision making often instigates an unmanageable process in which the policy output differs remarkably from the policy the Commission initiated.

Political Positions as Conditioning Factors

Legislative responses to judicial decisions include a process of many steps in which the political positions between and within institutions matter. When the SQ_{Court} challenges SQ_{reg}^{1}, it may invoke political conflict lines around which positions split. The case studies disaggregated the political institutions into their different individual and corporate actors. A range of different political positions on how to respond to CJEU decisions surfaced. When judicial decisions invoke key political conflict lines, disagreements on how to respond loom large. The extent to which interaction can diminish political disagreement thus becomes crucial to the ability to compromise. The case studies suggest that when unified positions are established within institutions but inter-institutional frictions remain between institutions, legislative gridlock is likely to result. The output 'non-adoption' could, however, be expected from the fragmented character of the EU polity. In the dynamic court view, non-adoption proves judicialization because politics is unable to override or modify the case law. According to this view, the Court-generated status quo becomes the final word. This book's findings, however, demonstrate that political gridlock does not lead to judicialization. In the case of the working time directive, the majority of member states did not comply with the SQ_{Court}—member states either disobeyed or shirked their European obligations by means of the opt-out. In the case of cross-border healthcare, non-adoption of the service directive's healthcare provision pushed the Commission to shift the dossier from the DG MARKT to the DG SANCO and present a proposal that ultimately modified judicial impact considerably. The legal uncertainty produced by political deadlock and considerable discrepancies between SQ_{Court} and SQ_{reg}[1] is not a viable situation, and it is harmful to the legitimacy of the Court, the Commission, and EU legislators said to govern a rule of law system.

The pressure to re-establish legal certainty in part explains why political positions become dynamic. Through continuous interaction, key political actors provide the ground for compromise. Civil servants in Council working groups, Council presidencies, Commission civil servants, EP rapporteurs, and shadow rapporteurs establish the common denominator for responding to the Court. Modification results from compromise, which is a normal feature of legislative politics. Modification rather than override or codification becomes the more likely output when politics divide actors. Why do political positions change during the course of interaction? The analysis identified different logics and dynamics at play. The logic of appropriateness—where political actors convince one another of the need to retake control—plays out (March and Olsen [2006, 1998]; Miller [1992]). However, strategic considerations are also part of the game, formed by the institutional setting as well as actors' orientation and interactions (Scharpf [1997]). In addition, the external context and domestic adaptation to the case law of the Court affect positions. Poland left the blocking minority on the enforcement directive owing to a more general dispute over free movement and cross-border welfare. In addition, member state positions on patients' rights in cross-border healthcare proved reliant on the extent to which jurisprudence had been implemented by national authorities. Some member states had already adapted to the course of legal integration, while others had simply ignored it, rejecting it as wrong.

Judicial decisions shape political behaviour towards judicialization but not in a predetermined way. While most—but not all—political actors agree on the authority of the Court, they disagree on how to read case law and sometimes treat the law in a rather unorthodox manner. 'Law in the books' is different from 'law as politicized', and law that results from political interaction can move very far from a strict legal reading.

Both how jurisprudence invokes ideological and integrationist conflict lines and how political positions form and interact with judicial decisions condition judicial influence. By tracing the political positions and subsequent interaction between T_1 and T_2, this book has demonstrated that EU legislative politics influence and interact with law. Instead of jurisprudence wiping out politics, political positions and interaction are key to explaining why some legal decisions have more impact than others. Political actors in the Council and the EP, and sometimes national parliaments and social partners, respond and engage with judicial decisions in meaningful ways, despite institutional thresholds and fragmented EU collective politics.

On Law and Politics in European Integration

This book has taken up the call for further examination of the complex interaction between law and politics in European integration (Armstrong [1998]; De Búrca [2005]; Pollack [2013]; Rasmussen [2013]; Wincott [2001]). It has demonstrated that political responses to legal integration condition judicial influence on EU social policy outputs.

The findings support neither a conventional version of intergovernmentalism, nor a new one, in which member states, especially powerful ones, are in the driver's seat. Contemporary EU politics reflect a blend of diverse political actors and institutions, interacting to reach legislative compromises. The European Parliament plays a decisive role. Its rapporteurs, shadow rapporteurs, and Committee members are key actors in the new legal-political game. In the Council, alliances creating majority positions regarding the case law of the Court are decisive. Individual member states are not more powerful than their ability to construct and maintain an alliance. However, the new legal-political game also features national parliaments with formal Treaty mandates to respond to Commission proposals. In addition, social partners can be assigned a formal role to negotiate. This blend of actors reads, interprets, and uses judicial decisions differently—in line with ideology, conviction, and interest. At times, they are able to find common ground in their responses, limiting the impact of jurisprudence.

Modifications cannot reverse legal integration, but they can reduce the impact of judicial decisions considerably. After searching for overrides but finding few, the dynamic court view has concluded that judicialization of politics has taken place. The constrained court view disagrees, turning to the national level to demonstrate non-compliance or little effect of judicial decisions. However, in the daily decision-making process through which secondary legislation is produced, politics responds to law and aims to steer the course of integration. Such responses to judicial decisions are all about politics. If jurisprudence serves the perceptions or interests of political actors, they will use it and advocate for it. When it does not, they will argue against it. This is not to say that law is unimportant or that judicial influence does not occur. It is also not to say that politics has absolute control or gets the final word. Certainly, policy options are framed by jurisprudence and certain options will never be on the table. However, the framing is far less definitive and more negotiable than conventional interpretations of the law–politics relationship posit. Uncovering the political interplay between judicial decisions and policy outputs thus tell us in what way law serves specific political interests and why it is opposed by others. The recurrent interaction between judicial and legislative politics, not one rather than the other, sets the course of integration.

Thus the findings of this book do not reject the notion that judicial decisions can influence EU policy outputs. In comparison, the CJEU is an unusual, powerful, international Court (Alter [2009]). Jurisprudence affects the context, that is, the policy options of legislators. After judicial decisions, non-contracted providers became part of the patients' rights directive. Litigation also affects the conduct of political actors. Politicians must consider litigation when deciding how to behave in the legal-political game. Judicial influence is not a question of whether but a question of degree. In considering this question of degree, this book demonstrates that law is a conditioned instrument of political integration. Social integration is not left to the courts (Leibfried [2010]; Leibfried and Pierson [2000]). Political integration does not occur through law but through concerted action. There is no automatic link between litigation and legislation. Politics has the power to restrain and modify the court. In addition, the Court adapts to such legislative restraints. It is not politically blind and may even look for guidance. Ultimately, a court decoupled from political reality will harm its own legitimacy, as politics will increasingly oppose its rulings. If member states 'defy or ignore the judgments of a supranational court, they undermine the court's status as the authoritative voice of the law and resolver of disputes' (Kelemen

[2001: 624]). This need for reciprocity is important in democratic politics, where some degree of responsiveness and balance between majoritarian and counter-majoritarian institutions is crucial to the legitimacy of the polity. It is also important for democratic accountability (Bovens [2007]; Martinsen and Jørgensen [2010]). EU legislators are also responsible for the broader impact of jurisprudence. Legislators have the capacity to intervene and should thus be held accountable for policy outputs. Political accountability should not shield behind legal integration.

These findings have general implications for the study of judicial politics. The findings show that even in EU politics, where thresholds to constrain judicial activism are higher than in the United States (Conant [2002: 218]; Pollack [2003: 171]), politicians can respond to and condition the extent of judicial influence. The interaction between courts and legislators should attract new scholarly attention. It appears that political voices are raised against jurisprudence in different law–politics contexts, as identified in the interactions between the US Supreme Court and Congress (Bailey and Maltzman [2011]; Miller [2009]) and in the German Federal Constitutional Court and Bundestag (Vanberg [2005]) as well as in responses to international courts (Ginsburg [2014]). In the USA, Miller notes that there are more conflicts between Congress and the courts today than there have been for a very long time (Miller [2009: 5]), and Congress's court-stripping actions are generally conducted by social conservatives and opposed by liberals (Miller [2009: 10, 162–9]). In the EU, both the left and the right attempt to assert legislative power over the Court, depending on the ideological reading of jurisprudence. Furthermore, legislative responses may aim to protect subsidiarity. In conclusion, the findings of this book show that, even during times of fragmented politics and diverse conflict lines, EU politics condition the extent to which litigation affects legislation. It demonstrates that the Court is not an independent source of political change. This invites us to bring political positions and interaction back into the equation when examining the judicial–legislative relationship in the EU and beyond.

References

Alter, K. (1998) 'Who are the 'Masters of the Treaty'? European governments and the European Court of Justice', *International Organization* 52(01): 121–47.

Alter, K. (2009) *The European Court's Political Power: Selected Essays*, Oxford: Oxford University Press.

Alter, K.J. and Meunier-Aitsahalia, S. (1994) 'Judicial politics in the European Community: European integration and the pathbreaking Cassis de Dijon decision', *Comparative Political Studies* 26(4): 535–61.

Armstrong, K.A. (1998) 'Legal integration: theorizing the legal dimension of European integration', *JCMS: Journal of Common Market Studies* 36(2): 155–74.

Bailey, M.A. and Maltzman, F. (2011) *The Constrained Court: Law, Politics, and the Decisions Justices Make*, Princeton, NJ: Princeton University Press.

Binder, S.A. (1999) 'The dynamics of legislative gridlock, 1947–96', *American Political Science Review* 93(03): 519–33.

Bonjour, S. and Vink, M. (2013) 'When Europeanization backfires: the normalization of European migration politics', *Acta Politica* 48(4): 389–407.

Bovens, M. (2007) 'Analysing and assessing accountability: a conceptual framework 1', *European Law Journal* 13(4): 447–68.

Caporaso, J.A. and Tarrow, S. (2009) 'Polanyi in Brussels: supranational institutions and the transnational embedding of markets', *International Organization* 63(04): 593–620.

Conant, L.J. (2002) *Justice Contained, Law and Politics in the European Union*, Ithaca, NY: Cornell University Press.

Davies, B. (2012a) 'Pushing back: what happens when member states resist the European Court of Justice? A multi-modal approach to the history of European law', *Contemporary European History* 21(3): 417–35.

De Búrca, G. (2005) 'Rethinking law in neofunctionalist theory', *Journal of European Public Policy* 12(2): 310–26.

Genschel, P. (2011) 'One trap, many exits, but no free lunch: how the joint-decision trap shapes EU tax policy', in G. Falkner (ed.), *The EU's Decision Traps. Comparing Policies*, Oxford: Oxford University Press, pp. 54–73.

Genschel, P., Kemmerling, A., and Seils, E. (2011) 'Accelerating downhill: how the EU shapes corporate tax competition in the single market', *JCMS: Journal of Common Market Studies* 49(3): 585–606.

Ginsburg, T. (2014) 'Political constraints on international courts', in C. Romano, K.J. Alter and Y. Shany (eds), *The Oxford Handbook of International Adjudication*, Oxford: Oxford University Press, pp. 483–502.

Hantrais, L. (2007) *Social Policy in the European Union*, Basingstoke: Palgrave Macmillan.

Hervey, T. and McHale, J. (2015) *European Union Health Law: Themes and Implications*, Cambridge: Cambridge University Press.

Jones, B.D. (1999) 'Bounded rationality', *Annual Review of Political Science* 2(1): 297–321.

Kelemen, R.D. (2001) 'The limits of judicial power: trade–environment disputes in the GATT/WTO and the EU', *Comparative Political Studies* 34(6): 622–50.

Kelemen, R.D. (2008) 'The Americanisation of European law? Adversarial legalism *à la Européenne*', *European Political Science* 7(1): 32–42.

Leibfried, S. (2010) 'Social policy: left to the judges and the markets?', in H.S. Wallace, W. Wallace, M.A. Pollack, H. Wallace, and A.R. Young (eds), *Policy-Making in the European Union*, Oxford: Oxford University Press, pp. 253–83.

Leibfried, S. and Pierson, P. (2000) 'Social policy. left to courts and markets?', in H.S. Wallace and W. Wallace (eds), *Policy-Making in the European Union*, Volume IV, Oxford: Oxford University Press, pp. 267–92.

March, J.G. and Olsen, J.P. (1998) 'The institutional dynamics of international political orders', *International Organization* 52(4): 943–69.

March, J.G. and Olsen, J.P. (2006) 'The logic of appropriateness', in M. Moran, M. Rein, and R.E. Goodin (eds), *The Oxford Handbook of Public Policy*, Oxford: Oxford University Press, pp. 689–708.

Martinsen, D.S. (2009) 'Conflict and conflict management in the cross-border provision of healthcare services', *West European Politics* 32(4): 792–809.

Martinsen, D.S. and Jørgensen, T.B. (2010) 'Accountability as a differentiated value in supranational governance', *American Review of Public Administration* 40(6): 742–60, doi:10.1177/0275074010366300.

Martinsen, D.S. and Wessel, A.U. (2014) 'On the path to differentiation: upward transfer, logic of variation and sub-optimality in EU social policy', *Journal of European Public Policy* 21(9): 1255–72.

Miller, M.C. (1992) 'Congressional committees and the Federal courts: a neo-institutional perspective', *The Western Political Quarterly* 45(4): 949–70.

Miller, M.C. (2009) *The View of the Courts from the Hill: Interactions between Congress and the Federal Judiciary*, Charlottesville, VA: University of Virginia Press.

Pierson, P. (1996) 'The path to European integration: a historical institutionalist analysis', *Comparative Political Studies* 29(2): 123–63.

Pollack, M.A. (2003) *The Engines of European Integration, Delegation, Agency, and Agenda Setting in the EU*, Oxford: Oxford University Press.

Pollack, M.A. (2013) 'New EU legal history: what's new, what's missing', *American University International Law Review* 28(5): 1257–311.

Rasmussen, M. (2013) 'Rewriting the history of European public law: the new contribution of historians', *American University International Law Review* 28(5): 1187–223.

Rosenberg, G.N. (2008) *The Hollow Hope: Can Courts Bring About Social Change?*, Chicago: University of Chicago Press.

Scharpf, F.W. (1997) *Games Real Actors Play: Actor-centered Institutionalism in Policy Research*, Boulder, CO: Westview Press.

Simon, H.A. (1985) 'Human nature in politics: the dialogue of psychology with political science', *American Political Science Review* 79(02): 293–304.

Stone Sweet, A. (2000) *Governing with Judges: Constitutional Politics in Europe*, Oxford: Oxford University Press.

Stone Sweet, A. and Brunell, T. (2012) 'The European Court of Justice, state noncompliance, and the politics of override', *American Political Science Review* 106(01): 204–13.

Vanberg, G. (2005) *The Politics of Constitutional Review in Germany*, Cambridge: Cambridge University Press.

Weiler, J. (1991) 'The transformation of Europe', *Yale Law Journal* 100: 2403–83.

Weiler, J.H.H. (1994) 'A quiet revolution: the European Court of Justice and its interlocutors', *Comparative Political Studies* 26(4): 510–34.

Wincott, D. (2001) 'The Court of Justice and the European policy process', in J. Richardson (ed.), *European Union, Power and Policy-Making*, London: Routledge, pp. 179–97.

ANNEX 1: JUDICIAL INFLUENCE ON POLICY OUTPUTS OVER TIME

Commission Proposal	Adopted Act	Policy process (days)	Council voting	Decision procedure (EP co-decision=1)	References to judicial decisions	References to specific cases	Which provisions?	Commission response	Political response
COM (2012) 131 proposed 21/3/2012	Council directive 2014/67/EU of 15 May 2014—**Enforcement directive on the posting of workers**	784	QMV	1	36	C–346/06 (Rüffert); C–319/06 (Commission v Luxembourg); C–49/98–71/98 (Finalarte)	Arts 9 and 12	**Codification**	**Modification**
COM (2012) 130 proposed 21/3/2012	Not adopted. Rejected by the national parliaments. Withdrawn by the Commission. 12 September 2012 **Proposal on a regulation on the right to take collective actions (Monti II)**	171	Una	1	41	C–438/05 (Viking); C–341/05 (Laval)	Arts 1, 2, and 3	**Codification**	**Non-adoption**

(continued)

Commission Proposal	Adopted Act	Policy process (days)	Council voting	Decision procedure (EP co-decision=1)	References to judicial decisions	References to specific cases	Which provisions?	Commission response	Political response
COM (2008) 414 proposed 2/7/2008	Directive 2011/24/EU of 9 March 2011—**Patients' rights**	981	QMV	1	37	C–158/96 (Kohll); C–368/98 (Vanbraekel); C–372/04 (Watts); and others	Legal basis, Arts 7 and 8	**Modification**	**Modification**
COM (2009) 410 proposed 30/7/2009	Council Directive 2010/18/EU of 8 March 2010—**Amending parental leave**	222	Una	0	3	C–180/95 (Draehmpaehl); C–271/91 (Marshall)	Art. 2	**Codification**	**Codification**
COM (2004) 830 proposed 23/12/2004	Regulation (EC) No 629/2006 of 5 April 2006—**Amending 1408/71 (coordinating social security)**	469	Una	1	2	C–43/99 (Leclere)	Annex IIa	**Codification**	**Codification**
COM (2004) 607 proposed 22/9/2004	Not adopted. Rejected by the social partners. 8 December 2012 **Proposal to amend the Working Time Directive**	2,996	QMV	1	2	C–303/98 (SiMAP); C–151/02 (Jaeger)	Art. 2a	**Override**	**Non-adoption**

COM (2004) 2 proposed 5/3/2004	Article on healthcare not adopted. Commission proposed an amended **proposal for a service directive** on 4/4/2006, excluding health *COM (2006) 160*	759	QMV	1	28	C–157/99 (Smits and Peerbooms) among others	Art. 23	**Codification**	**Non-adoption**
COM (2003) 468 proposed 31/7/2003	Regulation (EC) No 647/2005 of 13 April 2005—**Amending 1408/71 (later annulled)**	623	Una	1	33	C–215/99 (Jauch); C–43/99 (Leclere); C–160/96 (Molenaar)	Annex IIa	**Codification**	**Codification**
COM (2003) 657 proposed 5/11/2003	Council Directive 2004/113/EC of 13 December 2004—**Implementing equal treatment**	405	QMV	0	3	C–200/91 (Coloroll); C–43/75 (Defrenne II)	Art. 4	**Codification**	**Modification**
COM (2000) 334 proposed 7/6/2000	Directive 2002/73/EC of 23 September 2002—**Amending 76/207 (equal treatment)**	836	QMV	1	34	149/77 (Defrenne); C–450/93 (Kalanke); C–222/84 (Johnston)	Arts 2.2 and 6.1	**Codification**	**Codification**
COM (2000) 832 proposed 15/1/2001	Directive 2002/74/EC of 23 September 2002—**Amending 80/987 (insolvency)**	617	QMV	1	20	C–479/93 (Frankovich); C–117/96 (Mosbaek); C–198/98 (Everson)	Art. 8a	**Codification**	**Codification**

(*continued*)

Commission Proposal	Adopted Act	Policy process (days)	Council voting	Decision procedure (EP co-decision=1)	References to judicial decisions	References to specific cases	Which provisions?	Commission response	Political response
COM (1999) 565 proposed 25/11/1999	Council Directive 2000/78/EC of 27 November 2000—**Framework equal treatment**	404	QMV	0	9	C–109/88 (Danfoss); C–127/92 (Enderby); C–400/93 (Royal Copenhagen); and others	Arts 2b, 6, and 9	**Codification**	**Codification**
COM (1998) 662—98/0318 (SYN) proposed 24/11/1998	Directive 2000/34/EC of 22 June 2000—**Amending 93/104 (working time)**	583	QMV	1	1	Based on C–84/94 UK v Council	Art. 5	**Codification**	**Codification**
COM (97) 486 proposed 8/10/1997	Council Directive 98/49/EC of 29 June 1998—**Supplementary pension rights**	265	Una	0	5	C–279/93 (Finanzamt Köln-Altstadt v Schumacher); C–272/94 (Guiot); and others	Arts 6 and 7	**Codification**	**Modification**
COM (97) 378 proposed 18/7/1997	Council Regulation (EC) No 1223/98 of 4 June 1998—**Amending 1408/71**	322	Una	0	2	C–251/94 (Eduardo Lafuente Nieto)	Annex VI, 4b	**Codification**	**Codification**

COM (96) 340 proposed 17/7/1996	Council Directive 97/80/EC of 15 December 1997—**Burden of proof**	517	Una	0	27	C–109/88 (Danfoss); C–318/86 (Commission v France); C–127/92 (Enderby); C–400/93 (Royal Copenhagen); and others	Art. 4	**Codification**	**Codification**
COM (91) 230 proposed 19/6/1991	Directive 96/71/EC of 16 December 1996—**Posting of workers**	2,008	QMV	1	6	C–113/89 (Rush Portuguesa); and others	Art. 3	**Modification**	**Codification**
COM (91) 247 proposed 12/7/1991	Council Regulation (ECC) No 1249/92 of 30 April 1992—**Amending 1408/71**	294	Una	0	3	20/85 (Roviello)	Annex VI	**Codification**	**Codification**
COM (85) 396 proposed 8/8/1985	Council Regulation (EEC) No 1247/92 of 30 April 1992—**Amending 1408/71**	2,481	Una	0	3	Based on 139/82 (Piscitello); joined cases 379–381/85 and 93/86 (Giletti)	Annex II a, art. 10a	**Override**	**Override**
COM (90) 335 proposed 3/8/1990	Council Regulation (EEC) No 2195/91 of 25 June 1991—**Amending 1408/71**	337	Una	0	2	302/84 (Ten Holder); 58/87 (Rebmann)	Arts 13(2)f and 45	**Codification**	**Codification**
COM (88) 27 proposed 5/2/1988	Council Regulation (EEC) No 3427/89 of 30 October 1989—**Amending 1408/71**	641	Una	0	1	41/84 (Pinna)	Art. 73, annex VI	**Modification**	**Modification**
COM (88) 538 proposed 18/10/1988	Council Regulation (EEC) No 2332/89 of 18 July 1989—**Amending 1408/71**	286	Una	0	1	377/85 (Burchell)	Arts 76 and 79	**Codification**	**Codification**

BIBLIOGRAPHY

EU Legislative Documents Cited

Amended proposal for a Council Directive COM (93) 225 of 15th June 1993 concerning the posting of workers in the framework of the provision.

Communication from the Commission to the Council, the European Parliament, the European Economic and Social Committee and the Committee of the Regions and the social partners at Community level COM (2003) 843) of 15th January 2004 concerning the re-exam of Directive 93/104/EC concerning certain aspects of the organization of working time.

Communication from the Commission to the European Parliament COM (2010) 503 of 20th September 2010 pursuant to Article 294(6) of the Treaty on the Functioning of the European Union concerning the position of the Council at first reading on the adoption of a Directive of the European Parliament and of the Council on the application of patients' rights on cross-border healthcare.

Communication from the Commission services SEC (2006) 1195/4 of 26th September 2006 Consultation regarding Community action on health.

Council Directive 75/117/EEC of 10 February 1975 on the approximation of the laws of the Member States relating to the application of the principle of equal pay for men and women.

Council Directive 76/207/EEC of 9 February 1976, on the implementation of the principle of equal treatment for men and women as regards access to employment, vocational training and promotion, and working conditions.

Council Directive 79/7/EEC of 19 December 1978 on the progressive implementation of the principle of equal treatment for men and women in matters of social security.

Council Directive 86/378/EEC of 24 July 1986 on the implementation of the principle of equal treatment for men and women in occupational pension.

Council Directive 86/613/EEC of 11 December 1986 on the application of the principle of equal treatment between men and women engaged in an activity, including agriculture, in a self-employed capacity, and on the protection of self-employed women during pregnancy and motherhood.

Council Directive 92/85/EEC of 19 October 1992 on the introduction of measures to encourage improvements in the safety and health at work of pregnant workers and workers who have recently given birth or are breastfeeding (tenth individual Directive within the meaning of Article 16 (1) of Directive 89/391/EEC).

Council Directive 93/104/EC of 23 November 1993 concerning certain aspects of the organisation of working time.

Council Directive 96/34/EC of 3 June 1996 on the framework agreement on parental leave concluded by UNICE, CEEP and the ETUC.

Council Directive 97/80/EC of 15 December 1997 on the burden of proof in cases of discrimination based on sex.

Council Directive 97/81/EC of 15 December 1997 concerning the Framework Agreement on part-time work concluded by UNICE, CEEP and the ETUC - Annex: Framework agreement on part-time work.

Council Directive 2003/86/EC of 22 September 2003 on the right to family reunification.

Council Regulation (EEC) No 2793/81 of 17 September 1981 amending Regulation (EEC) No 1408/71 on the application of social security schemes to employed persons and their families moving within the Community and Regulation (EEC) No 574/72 fixing the procedure for implementing Regulation (EEC) No 1408/71.

Council Regulation (EEC) No 1247/92 of 30 April 1992 amending Regulation (EEC) No 1408/71 on the application of social security schemes to employed persons, to self-employed persons and to members of their families moving within the Community.

Directive 96/71/EC of the European Parliament and of the Council of 16 December 1996 concerning the posting of workers in the framework of the provision of services.

Directive 2000/34/EC of the European Parliament and of the Council of 22nd of June 2000, amending Council Directive 93/104/EC concerning certain aspects of the organisation of working time to cover sectors and activities excluded from that directive.

Directive 2003/88/EC of the European Parliament and of the Council of 4th November 2003 concerning certain aspects of the organisation of working time.

Directive 2011/24/EU of the European Parliament and of the Council of 9 March 2011 on the application of patients' rights in cross-border healthcare

Directive 2014/67/EU of the European Parliament and of the Council of 15 May 2014 on the enforcement of Directive 96/71/EC concerning the posting of workers in the framework of the provision of services and amending Regulation (EU) No 1024/2012 on administrative cooperation through the Internal Market Information System ('the IMI Regulation').

European Parliament Report A6-0105/2005 of 25th April 2005 on the proposal for a directive of the European Parliament and of the Council amending Directive 2003/88/EC concerning certain aspects of the organisation of working time.

European Parliament Report A6-0129/2005 of 29th April 2005 on patient mobility and healthcare developments in the European Union".

European Parliament Report A6-0233/2009 of 3rd April 2009 on the proposal for a directive of the European Parliament and of the Council on the application of patients' rights in cross-border healthcare.

European Parliament Resolution A5-0026/2004 of 29th January 2004 on the organisation of working time (Amendment of Directive 93/104/EC).

Proposal for a Council Regulation COM (1980) 580 of 21st October 1980 amending Regulation (EEC) No. 1408/71 on the application of social security schemes to employed persons and their families moving within the Community and Regulation (EEC) No. 574/72 fixing the procedure for implementing Regulation (EEC) No 1408/71.

Proposal for a Council Directive COM (1990) 317 of 20th September 1990 concerning certain aspects of the organisation of working time.

Proposal for a Council Directive COM (91) 230 final of 1st August 1991 concerning the posting of workers in the framework of the provision of services.

Proposal for a Council Directive COM (1998) 662 – SYN 98/0318 of 18th November 1998 amending Directive 93/104/EC of 23 November 1993 concerning certain aspects of the organisation of working time to cover sectors and activities excluded from that directive.

Proposal for a Council Regulation COM (2012) 130 of 21st March 2012 on the exercise of the right to take collective action within the context of the freedom of establishment and the freedom to provide services.

Proposal for a Directive of the European Parliament and the Council COM (2002) 149 of 20th March 2002 on working conditions for temporary workers.

Proposal for a Directive of the European Parliament and of the Council COM (2004) 2 of 3rd March 2004 on services in the internal market.

Proposal for a Directive of the European Parliament and of the Council COM (2004) 607 of 22nd September 2004 amending Directive 2003/88/EC concerning certain aspects of the organisation of working time.

Proposal for a Directive of the European Parliament and of the Council COM (2008) 414 of 2nd July 2008 on the application of patient rights in cross-border healthcare.

Proposal for a Directive of the European Parliament and of the Council COM (2008) 600/4 amending Council Directive 92/85/EEC on the introduction of measures to encourage improvements in the safety and health at work of pregnant workers and workers who have recently given birth or are breastfeeding.

Proposal for a Directive of the European Parliament and of the Council COM (2012) 131 of 21st March 2012 on the enforcement of Directive 96/71/EC concerning the posting of workers in the framework of the provision of services.

Proposal for a Directive of the European Parliament and of the Council COM (2012) 614) of 14th November 2012 on improving the gender balance among non-executive directors of companies listed on stock exchanges and related measures.

Regulation (EC) No 647/2005 of the European Parliament and of the Council of 13 April 2005 amending Council Regulations (EEC) No 1408/71 on the application of social security schemes to employed persons, to self-employed persons and to members of their families moving within the Community and (EEC) No 574/72 laying down the procedure for implementing Regulation (EEC) No 1408/71.

Regulation (EEC) No 1612/68 of the Council of 15 October 1968 on the freedom of movement for workers within the Community.
Regulation (EEC) No 1408/71 of the Council of 14 June 1971 on the application of social security schemes to employed persons and their families moving within the Community.
Regulation (EC) No 883/2004 of the European Parliament and of the Council of 29 April 2004 on the coordination of social security systems.
Report from the Commission COM (2000) 787 final) of 1st December 2000 - State of implementation of Council Directive 93/104/EC of 23 November 1993 concerning certain aspects of the organisation of working time ("Working Time Directive").

Legal Decisions Cited

Arblade and Arblade & Fils SARL, Bernard Leloup, Serge Leloup and Sofrage SARL (Criminal proceedings). ECJ joined cases C-369/96 and C-376/96 [1999] ECR I-8453.
Barber (Douglas Harvey) v Guardian Royal Exchange Assurance Group. ECJ case C-262/88 [1990] ECR I-1889.
BECTU (Broadcasting, Entertainment, Cinematographic and Theatre Union) v Secretary of State for Trade and Industry. ECJ case C-173/99 [2001] ECR I-4881.
Bilka-Kaufhaus GmbH v Karin Weber von Hartz. ECJ 170/84 [1986] ECR 1607.
'Cassis de Dijon' (Rewe-Zentral AG v Bundesmonopolverwaltung für Branntwein). ECJ case 120/78 [1979] ECR 649.
CIG (Confederación Intersindical Galega) v Servicio Galega de Saúde (Sergas). ECJ Case C-241/99 [2001] ECR I-5139.
Commission of the European Communities v Grand Duchy of Luxembourg. ECJ case C-445/03 [2004] ECR I-10207.
Commission of the European Communities v Kingdom of Belgium. ECJ case C-433/04 [2006] I-10653.
Commission of the European Communities v Federal Republic of Germany. ECJ case C-490/04 [2007] ECR I-6122.
Commission of the European Communities v European Parliament and Council of the European Union. ECJ case 299/05 [2007] ECR I-8695.
Commission of the European Communities v Grand Duchy of Luxembourg. ECJ case C-319/06 [2008] ECR I-4323.
Costa v Ente Nazionale per L'Energia Elettrica (E.N.E.L.) ECJ case 6/64 [1964] ECR 585.
Danfoss (Dansk Arbejdsgiverforening) v Handels- og Kontorfunktionærernes Forbund i Danmark. ECJ case 109/88 [1989] ECR 3199.

Dassonville v Procureur du Roi. ECJ case 8/74 [1974] ECR 837.
Defrenne I (*Defrenne*) v. Belgian State. ECJ case C-80/70 [1971] ECR 445.
Defrenne II (*Defrenne*) v. Société anonyme belge de navigation aérienne Sabena. ECJ case C-43/75 [1976] ECR 455.
Decker v Caisse de maladie des employés privés. ECJ case C-120/95 [1998] ECR I-1831.
Dekker v Stichting Vormingscentrum voor Jong Volwassenen (VJV-Centrum) Plus. ECJ case 177/88 [1990] ECR I-3941.
Enderby v Frenchay Health Authority and Secretary of State for Health. ECJ C-127/92 [1993] ECR I-5535.
European Commission v Kingdom of Spain. ECJ case C-211/08 [2010] ECR I-5267.
European Commission v France (French Republic). ECJ case C-512/08 [2010] ECR I-8833.
European Commission v Grand Duchy of Luxemburg. ECJ case C-490/09 [2011] ECR I-249.
Finalarte Sociedade de Construção Civil Ld[a], Portugaia Construções Ld[a] and Engil Sociedade de Construção Civil SA v Urlaubs- und Lohnausgleichskasse der Bauwirtschaft and Urlaubs- und Lohnausgleichskasse der Bauwirtschaft v Amilcar Oliveira Rocha, Tudor Stone Ltd, Tecnamb-Tecnologia do Ambiante Ld[a], Turiprata Construções Civil Ld[a], Duarte dos Santos Sousa and Santos & Kewitz Construções Ld[a]. ECJ case C-49/98, 50/98, 52-54/98, 68-71/98 [2001] ECR I-7831.
Geraets-Smits and Peerbooms (B.S.M. *Geraets-Smits* v Stichting Ziekenfonds VGZ and H.T.M. *Peerbooms* v Stichting CZ Groep Zorgverzekeringen). ECJ case C-157/99 [2001], ECR I-5473.
Giletti v Caisse régionale d'assurance maladie Rhône-Alpes, Directeur régional des affaires sanitaires et sociales de Lorraine v Domenico Giardini, Caisse régionale d'assurance maladie du Nord-Est v Feliciano Tampan and Severino Severini v Caisse primaire centrale d'assurance maladie. ECJ joined Cases 379 to 381/85 and 93/86 [1987] ECR 955.
Hartlauer Handelsgesellschaft mbH v Wiener Landesregierung and Oberösterreichische Landesregierung. ECJ case C-169/07 [2009] ECR I-1721.
Jaeger v Landeshauptstadt Kiel. ECJ case C-151/02 [2003] ECR I-8389.
Jauch v Pensionsversicherungsanstalt der Arbeiter. ECJ case C-215/99 [2001] ECR I-1901.
Jenkins v Kingsgate (Clothing Productions) Ltd. ECJ case 96/80 [1981] ECR 911.
Kohll v Union des caisses de maladie. ECJ case C-158/96 [1998], ECR I-1931.
Laval un Partneri Ltd v Svenska Byggnadsarbetareförbundet, Svenska Byggnadsarbetareförbundets avdelning 1, Byggettan and Svenska Elektrikerförbundet. ECJ case C-341/05 [2007] ECR I-11767.
Leclere and Alina Deaconescu v Caisse nationale des prestations familiales. ECJ case C-43/99 [2001] ECR I-4265.

Luisi and Carbone v Ministero del Tesoro. ECJ joined cases 286/82 and 26/83 [1984] ECR 377.
Mazzoleni and Inter Surveillance Assistance SARL, as the party civilly liable, third parties: Eric Guillaume and Others (Criminal proceedings). ECJ case C-165/98 [2001] ECR I-2189.
Müller-Fauré and van Riet (V.G. *Müller-Fauré* v Onderlinge Waarborgmaatschappij OZ Zorgverzekeringen UA and E.E.M. *van Riet* v Onderlinge Waarborgmaatschappij ZAO Zorgverzekeringen). ECJ C-385/99 [2003], ECR I-4509.
Patridge v Adjudication Officer. ECJ case C-297/96 [1998] ECR I-3467.
Pinna v Caisse d'allocations familiales de la Savoie. ECJ 41/84 [1986] ECR 1.
Pierik v Bestuur van het Algemeen Ziekenfonds Drenthe-Platteland. ECJ case 117/77 [1978] ECR 825.
Pierik v Bestuur van het Algemeen Ziekenfonds Drenthe-Platteland. ECJ case 182/78 [1979] ECR 1977.
Piscitello v Istituto nazionale della previdenza sociale (INPS). ECJ case 139/82 [1983] ECR 1427.
Royal Copenhagen A/S (Dansk Industri, formerly Industriens Arbejdsgivere) v Specialarbejderforbundet i Danmark. ECJ C-400/93 [1995] ECR I-1275.
Rush Portuguesa Ld[a] v Office national d'immigration. ECJ case C-113/89 [1990] ECR I-1417.
Rüffert v Land Niedersachsen. ECJ case C-346/06 [2008] ECR I-1989.
Santos Palhota and Others (Criminal proceedings). ECJ case C-515/08 [2010] ECR I-9133.
SiMAP (Sindicato de Medicos de Asistencia Publica) v v Conselleria de Sanidad y Consumo de la Generalidad Valenciana. ECJ case C-303/98 [2000] ECR 1-7963.
Smith v Maccarthy Ltd. ECJ case 129/79 [1980] ECR 1275.
Snares v Adjudication Officer. ECJ case C-20/96 [1997] ECR I-6057.
Stamatelaki v NPDD Organismos Asfaliseos Eleftheron Epangelmation (OAEE). ECJ case C-444/05 [2007], ECR I-3185.
The International Transport Workers' Federation and the Finnish Seamen's Union v. Viking Line ABP and OÜ Viking Line Eesti. ECJ case C-438/05 [2007] ECR I-10779.
United Kingdom of Great Britain and Northern Ireland v Council of the European Union. ECJ case C-84/94 [1996] ECR I-5755.
Van Gen (NV Algemene Transport- en Expeditie Onderneming & van Gend & Loos) v Netherlands Inland Revenue Administration. ECJ case 26/62 [1963] ECR 1.
Watts (The Queen) v Bedford Primary Care Trust and Secretary of State for Health. ECJ C-372/04 [2006], ECR I-4325.
Wolff & Müller GmbH & Co. KG v José Filipe Pereira Félix. ECJ case C-60/03 [2004] I-09553.

INDEX

The manufacturer's authorised representative in the EU for product safety is Oxford University Press España S.A. of El Parque Empresarial San Fernando de Henares, Avenida de Castilla, 2 - 28830 Madrid (www.oup.es/en or product.safety@oup.com). OUP España S.A. also acts as importer into Spain of products made by the manufacturer.
Printed and bound by CPI Group (UK) Ltd, Croydon, CR0 4YY
14/09/2026
02216305-0004